FIFTY-STATE SURVEY

The Law of Indemnification and Its Interplay with Liability Insurance

INSURANCE COVERAGE LITIGATION COMMITTEE

AMERICAN BAR ASSOCIATION
Litigation Section

Cover by ABA Design

Printed in the United States of America.

24 23 5 4 3 2

CONTENTS

INTRODUCTION

Indemnity is compensation given to make another whole from a loss already sustained. It generally contemplates reimbursement by one person or entity of the entire amount of the loss or damage sustained by another. Indemnity takes two forms: common law and contractual.

This survey is limited to considerations of contractual indemnity, but note that, historically, many states looked to the law relating to common law indemnity in developing their respective jurisprudence on contractual indemnity. Common law indemnity is the shifting of responsibility for damage or injury from one tortfeasor to another tortfeasor.[1] It has been referred to as "an extreme form of contribution,"[2] which reflects that common law indemnity initially arose as a judicial means of avoiding the harsh result of the now substantially abrogated rule prohibiting contribution among joint tortfeasors.[3] The circumstances under which common law indemnity exists vary widely depending upon the applicable state law.[4]

Contractual indemnity, on the other hand, is that which is voluntarily given to a person or entity, as security or protection to prevent his or her suffering damage.[5] As benefiting its name, contractual indemnity is created by express contract and is a promise to safeguard another from existing or future loss or liability, or both.[6] This form of indemnity may arise where one or both of the indemnitor and indemnitee are culpable, but the parties have agreed that the risk of such culpability will be borne entirely by just one of them. In this way, contractual indemnity may result from the agreement of one to answer for a legal obligation that would otherwise rest with another. This contractually created indemnity is the subject of this survey because of its potential implications on another important form of contractual indemnity: the liability insurance policy. The existence and application of an agreement by one to indemnify another where a policy of liability insurance potentially covers a loss implicates many issues, two of which are paramount relative to this survey.

The first issue arises where a person or entity obtains for its benefit a liability insurance policy that will indemnify the insured for its liability for damages, and the insured in turn agrees to indemnify a third party for the third party's liability for damages. What is the effect on the insurer's agreement to indemnify the insured pursuant to the liability insurance policy? Must the insurer indemnify the insured for its indemnification of the third party?

---

1. Galliher v. Holloway, 474 N.E.2d 797, 803 (Ill. App. Ct. 1985). Common law indemnity is also referred to as "equitable" or "implied" indemnity.

2. Slattery v. Marra Bros. Inc., 186 F.2d 134, 138 (2d Cir. 1950). In contrast to indemnification, contribution involves only partial reimbursement of one who has discharged a common liability. Braye v. Acher-Daniel-Midlands Co., 659 N.E.2d 430, 433 (Ill. App. Ct. 1995). While contribution involves partial reimbursement of one which has discharged a common liability, indemnity requires reimbursement of the entire amount of liability. Mullen v. Cogdell, 643 N.E.2d 390, 400 (Ind. Ct. App. 1994). One involves the sharing of a loss; the other the shifting of the entire loss. McClesky v. Noble Corp., 577 P.2d 830, 833 (Kan. Ct. App. 1978). "The distinction between contribution and indemnity is that contribution asks another to share in debt, while indemnity would require another to pay it all." Marshall v. Casey, 532 N.E.2d 1121, 1123 (Ill. App. Ct. 1989).

3. Restatement (Second) of Torts § 886B; Nat'l Serv. Indus., Inc. v. B.W. Norton Mfg. Co., 937 P.2d 551 (Utah Ct. App. 1997).

4. A survey of the differing standards and application of common law indemnity is beyond the scope of this survey.

5. Keesler v. City of Peekskill, 152 N.Y.S.2d 919, 920 (1955); New Jersey v. Connolly, 72 A. 363, 364 (N.J. 1909); Eggers v. Centrifugal & Mech. Indus., Inc., 440 S.W.2d 512, 515 (Mo. Ct. App. 1969).

6. Dresser Indus., Inc. v. Page Petroleum, Inc., 853 S.W.2d 505, 508 (Tex. 1993).

The standard Commercial General Liability Policy[7] contains an exclusion for contractually assumed liability,[8] but coverage is restored by an exception for liability assumed in an "insured contract,"[9] a defined term under the policy.[10] Included within the definition of "insured contract" is "that part of any . . . contract or agreement under which [the insured] assume[s] the tort liability of another."[11] If an insured's agreement to indemnify a third party constitutes the assumption of the third party's tort liability, then loss or damage flowing from this assumed obligation is not excluded from coverage.

Whether the insured's agreement to indemnify is enforceable is critical, no matter the perspective. If the insured's indemnity obligation is unenforceable under applicable law, then the insured has no obligation and the insurer likely has no risk of loss. But even where an insured agrees to an otherwise unenforceable indemnity, if the agreement envisions the purchase of insurance for the loss, then the indemnity may be upheld and the presence of insurance saves the otherwise void indemnity.

Additionally, an insured may agree to indemnify a third party for loss or damage and include the indemnitee as an additional insured under the very liability policy arguably bound to cover the insured for its indemnity obligation. Under these circumstances, because the insurer is obligated directly to the indemnitee/third party (as an additional insured) to the extent of the coverage, whether the "insured contract" exception to the exclusion for contractually assumed liability applies may become secondary. What happens, however, if the insured's indemnity obligation applies only in limited circumstances or only up to a certain dollar limit and the liability policy's coverage is greater? Is the insurer's obligation to the third party/indemnitee/additional insured limited to the amount of the insured's obligation to indemnify, or is the insurer exposed to the full extent of the dollar amount of coverage stated in the policy?

The second important manner in which the presence of an indemnity may implicate an insurer's ultimate risk arises where a person or entity obtains for its own benefit a liability insurance policy and the insured is the beneficiary of an agreement by a third party to indemnify the insured for its liability for damages. The indemnity flowing from a third party to the insured is significant: The insurer could attempt to recoup its payments under

---

7. *See* ISO Forms CG 00 01 11 85; CG 00 02 11 85; CG 00 02 02 86; CG 00 01 11 88; CG 00 02 11 88; CG 00 01 10 93; CG 00 02 10 93; CG 00 01 01 96; CG 00 02 01 96; CG 00 01 07 98; CG 00 02 07 98; CG 00 01 10 01; CG 00 02 10 01; CG 00 01 12 04; CG 00 02 12 04; CG 00 01 12 07; CG 00 01 12 07; CG 00 01 04 13.

8. The exclusion reads: "This insurance does not apply to . . . 'Bodily injury' or 'property damage' for which the insured is obligated to pay damages by reason of the assumption of liability in a contract or agreement. . . ."

9. In the 1985 and 1986 ISO Forms, the exception provides: "This exclusion does not apply to liability for damages: (1) Assumed in a contract or agreement that is an 'insured contract;' or (2) That the insured would have in the absence of the contract or agreement." (Exclusion b(1) and (2).) In the 1988 and 1993 ISO Forms, the exception provides: "This exclusion does not apply to liability for damages: (1) Assumed in a contract or agreement that is an 'insured contract, provided the 'bodily injury' or 'property damage' occurs subsequent to the execution of the contract or agreement; or (2) That the insured would have in the absence of the contract or agreement.'" (Exclusion b(1) and (2).) In the 1996, 1998, 2001, 2004, 2007, and 2013 ISO Forms, subsections b(1) and b(2) are inverted, but are otherwise the same.

10. In the 1985 and 1986 ISO Forms, "Insured Contract" means, among other things, "[t]hat part of any other contract or agreement pertaining to your business under which you assume the tort liability of another to pay damages because of 'bodily injury' or 'property damage' to a third person or organization, if the contract or agreement is made prior to the 'bodily injury' or 'property damage.'" Tort liability means a liability that would be imposed by law in the absence of any contract or agreement.

In the 1988, 1993, 1996, 1998, 2001, 2004, 2007, and 2013 ISO Forms, "Insured Contract" means, among other things, "[t]hat part of any other contract or agreement pertaining to your business (including an indemnification of a municipality in connection with work performed for a municipality) under which you assume the tort liability of another party to pay for 'bodily injury' or 'property damage' to a third person or organization." Tort liability means a liability that would be imposed by law in the absence of any contract or agreement.

The parenthetical reference in the 1988 Form appears as a separate item in the definition of "insured contract" in the 1985 Form.

11. *See* fn. 10, *supra*.

the policy from the third-party indemnitor under the insured's right to indemnity from that third party.[12]

The ultimate question, then, is whether the indemnity agreement is enforceable and what impact it has on the insurance obligation. This is the context of this survey. A uniform format is followed in each of the state summaries:

- **Section 1 – General Rules of Contractual Indemnity:** A preliminary discussion of indemnity agreements.
- **Section 2 – Exceptions to General Rules of Contractual Indemnity:** Identifies statutory or judicially created exceptions to the general rules applicable to contracts of indemnity.
- **Section 3 – Indemnity Agreements as Insured Contracts:** Addresses the extent to which an insured's agreement to indemnify a third party constitutes an "insured contract" under the state law, negating the exclusion for contractually assumed liability to the extent of the indemnity.
- **Section 4 – Operation of an Agreement to Indemnify Referring to or Requiring Insurance:** Addresses the interplay between an insured's agreement to indemnify a third party, which is combined with a reference to first- or third-party insurance.

While this is principally a survey of the intersection between general liability insurance and an insured's separate agreement to indemnify, the discussion of relevant case law is not always limited to general liability policies where discussion and analysis of other coverage is relevant to the subject matter of this survey.

12. An insurer may also potentially recover on a theory of contribution or indemnity in the absence of a written indemnity, but such actions are typically limited to the applicable state's law regarding joint tortfeasor liability.

Alabama

Christopher Frost
Maynard, Cooper & Gale, P.C.

1. GENERAL RULES OF CONTRACTUAL INDEMNITY

Express contracts of indemnity are enforceable under Alabama law.[1] If the parties to an agreement "knowingly, evenhandedly, and for valid consideration intelligently enter into an agreement whereby one party agrees to indemnify the other,"[2] the agreement will be enforced if expressed in *clear and unequivocal language*.[3]

That rule applies to indemnify the indemnitee's own unintended wrongs.[4] "While 'talismanic language' is not a necessity, the intention to indemnify for the indemnitee's own negligence must be clear from the instrument."[5] The language must clearly and unequivocally contemplate indemnification for the sole negligence of the indemnitee.[6] Applying this rule, an agreement to indemnify providing that it "shall apply regardless of the cause and even in the event of the sole, gross or concurrent negligence of [indemnitee]" was enforceable and did not run afoul of public policy, even though the indemnitor could not control the indemnitee's activity giving rise to the claim.[7] The potential inequity of such an outcome is tempered by the indemnitor's ability to expressly *exclude* liability for the sole negligence of the indemnitee, which he can do through the clear and unambiguous terms of his indemnity provision.[8]

An agreement that provided an indemnitor would hold harmless another "from all damage suits and claims" gave rise to the duty to indemnify for the indemnitee's negligence.[9] But an agreement to indemnify that provided indemnification "from *all liability*, claims, lawsuits and demands" was ambiguous enough to prevent the Alabama Supreme Court from finding it clearly and unequivocally agreed to indemnify losses arising out of the indemnitee's acts of negligence.[10]

---

1. *See* Holcim (US), Inc. v. Ohio Cas. Ins. Co., 38 So. 3d 722, 727 (Ala. 2009); Royal Ins. Co. of Am. v. Whitaker Contracting Corp., 824 So. 2d 747, 753 (Ala. 2002); Nationwide Mut. Ins. Co. v. Hall, 643 So. 2d 551, 555 (Ala. 1994); Indus. Tile, Inc. v. Stewart, 388 So. 2d 171, 175–76 (Ala. 1980).

2. *Indus. Tile*, 388 So. 2d at 176; *Holcim*, 38 So. 3d at 727.

3. *Indus. Tile*, 388 So. 2d at 176; *Holcim*, 38 So. 3d at 727.

4. *Indus. Tile*, 388 So. 2d at 176; *Royal Ins.*, 824 So. 2d at 753.

5. Humana Med. Corp. v. Bagby Elevator Co., Inc., 653 So. 2d 972, 975 (Ala. 1995) (quoting *Nationwide*, 643 So. 2d at 557).

6. *See* Mobil Oil Corp. v. Schlumberger, 598 So. 2d 1341, 1346 (Ala. 1992) (internal quotations omitted).

7. *Id.* at 1344–46 (internal quotations omitted).

8. *See* McDevitt & Street Co. v. Mosher Steel Co., 574 So. 2d 794, 796–97 n.3 (Ala. 1991) (citing with approval *Stewart* and acknowledging the validity of an indemnity provision that disclaims the duty to indemnify when the negligent act "is caused by the sole negligence of a party indemnified hereunder").

9. *Nationwide*, 643 So. 2d at 556–57 (agreement to indemnify property owner "from all damage suits and claims arising in connection with the property" and "from all liability for injuries to persons or property while in, on, or about the premises").

10. Brown Mech. Contractors, Inc. v. Centennial Ins. Co., 431 So. 2d 932, 945–46 (Ala. 1983) (emphasis in original).

2. EXCEPTIONS TO GENERAL RULES OF CONTRACTUAL INDEMNITY

Alabama law appears to have only one significant exception to the general rule that express contracts of indemnity are enforceable: "Agreements that purport to indemnify another for the other's intentional conduct are void as a matter of public policy."[11] Where agreements do not purport to indemnify intentional conduct, however, Alabama courts will strive to effectuate the bargained-for intent of the parties contracting for indemnity. Therefore, non-public policy-related limitations on the scope of the indemnity arise out of the terms and conditions of the indemnity agreement and are subject to the rule articulated in *Industrial Tile, Inc. v. Stewart*—that clear and unequivocal language controls the scope of the agreement.[12]

While Alabama still adheres to a rule precluding contribution or common law indemnity between tortfeasors,[13] Alabama courts will enforce written agreements between tortfeasors, where one agrees to indemnify another even for claims based on the other's own negligence.[14]

3. INDEMNITY AGREEMENTS AS INSURED CONTRACTS

Often liability insurance policies exclude coverage for injuries or damage that the insured assumed in a contract or agreement.[15] This "'contractual exclusion' . . . provision 'traditionally serves to exclude indemnity types of liability, whereby the [insured's] liability itself was assumed, rather than [where the insured breached a] warranty[.]'"[16] Such provisions also typically contain exceptions of their own for "insured contracts," allowing coverage where the underlying contract is a lease, license, easement, or warranty.[17] But if the "insured contracts" defined by the policy include a contract through which the insured assumes tort liability over a third party's actions, then the liability insurance policy will also indemnify the insured's obligations to indemnify the third party, subject to other policy conditions and exclusions.[18]

---

11. City of Montgomery v. JYD Int'l Inc., 534 So. 2d 592, 594 (Ala. 1988) (citing Pruet v. Dugger-Holmes & Assocs., 162 So. 2d 613, 615 (Ala. 1964)); *see also* Price-Williams Assocs., Inc. v. Nelson, 631 So. 2d 1016, 1019 (Ala. 1994).

The decision in Titan Indemnity Co. v. Riley, 679 So. 2d 701 (Ala. 1996), arguably calls into question the sturdiness of this exception to the general rule that an indemnity agreement's clear and unequivocal language controls. In *Titan*, the Alabama Supreme Court found that "Alabama public policy does not prohibit the enforcement of a contract in which an insurer agrees to pay for injuries suffered by third parties as a result of intentional acts of the insured." *Titan*, 679 So. 2d at 707. However, the ruling is likely limited to policies of insurance. *Id.* at 706. After all, the holding was based on the court's earlier decision in Burnham Shoes, Inc. v. West American Insurance Co., 504 So. 2d 238 (Ala. 1987), in which the Alabama Supreme Court held that an insurer was obligated to provide defense and coverage consistent with the terms of its policy, regardless of whether the policy purported to cover losses arising out of an insured's intentional torts. *Burnham*, 504 So. 2d at 241 (overruled on other grounds). *Titan* extends the *Burnham* court's reasoning only slightly to enforce an insurer's contractual duty to indemnify an insured for its intentional acts, suggesting that it did not appreciate a difference between an insurer's duty to defend and an insurer's duty to indemnify. *Titan*, 679 So. 2d at 707; *cf.* Ladner & Co. v. S. Guar. Ins. Co., 347 So. 2d 100, 102 (Ala. 1977) (insurer's duty to defend is broader than its duty to indemnify).

12. *Indus. Tile*, 388 So. 2d at 176.

13. Parker Towing Co. v. Triangle Aggregates, Inc., 143 So. 3d 159, 167 (Ala. 2013); *accord Ex parte Stenum Hosp.*, 81 So. 3d 314, 318 (Ala. 2011) (citation omitted); *Bagby Elevator*, 653 So. 2d at 974; Parker v. Mauldin, 353 So. 2d 1375, 1377 (Ala. 1977) (citations omitted).

14. *Bagby Elevator*, 653 So. 2d at 974.

15. *See, e.g.*, Townsend Ford, Inc. v. Auto-Owners Ins. Co., 656 So. 2d 360, 364 (Ala. 1995).

16. *Id.* (some internal quotation marks and alterations omitted).

17. *Id.* at 364 n.1.

18. *See generally id.* at 364.

Alaska

Jennifer Wasson
Potter Anderson & Corroon LLP

1. GENERAL RULES OF CONTRACTUAL INDEMNITY

Absent an applicable statutory prohibition, Alaska courts construe a contractual indemnity provision to "effectuate the objectively reasonable expectations of the parties."[1] With regard to an indemnification agreement that purports to indemnify a party for its own negligence, the interpretation of such a clause varies, depending upon the nature of the contract.

With respect to commercial contracts, Alaska courts have not adopted the general rule that indemnity clauses are to be strictly construed.[2] Instead, when interpreting an indemnity provision in a commercial contract indemnifying a party for its own negligence, courts apply the "reasonable construction rule."[3] Under this rule of interpretation, the unambiguous language of an indemnity clause is given effect, and the indemnitee may be indemnified for its own negligence even if the provision does not specifically grant it, if that outcome is consistent with a reasonable construction of the provision.[4] Other than certain statutory restrictions set forth below, there is no public policy impediment to an indemnitor undertaking to indemnify the indemnitee for the indemnitee's own negligence.[5]

For example, a broad interpretation was given to an indemnity agreement providing that a contractor must indemnify the state from all claims brought because of injuries received by any person "on account of the [contractor's] operations."[6] The court found the indemnity obligation applied to injuries occurring as a result of the state's own negligence.[7] Similarly, an agreement indemnifying a contractor for all claims "arising out of, in connection with, or incident to" the subcontractor's performance of its duties was held to include claims based on the contractor's own negligence.[8]

An express indemnity clause is enforceable in an action for indemnity against an injured party's employer, despite the general worker's compensation bar.[9]

---

1. Duty Free Shoppers Group Ltd. v. State, 777 P.2d 649, 652 (Alaska 1989).

2. Stephan & Sons, Inc. v. Municipality of Anchorage, 629 P.2d 71, 74 (Alaska 1981). Outside of the commercial context, however, the Supreme Court of Alaska has held that contractual provisions purporting to exculpate a party from its own negligence are disfavored. *See, e.g.*, Kissick v. Schmierer, 816 P.2d 188, 191,193 n.4 (Alaska 1991) (declining to apply the "reasonable construction" approach employed in the commercial setting to disclaimers of liability in exculpatory provisions used in the recreational, noncommercial setting).

3. Manson-Osberg Co. v. State, 552 P.2d 654, 659 (Alaska 1976).

4. *Duty Free Shoppers*, 777 P.2d at 652.

5. Burgess Constr. Co. v. State, 614 P.2d 1380, 1382 (Alaska 1980). *Burgess* also carves out a very limited exception for public utilities and common carriers, whose duties run to the public and whose contracts with its customers are typically contracts of adhesion. *Id.* at 1381; *see also* Section 2 *infra*.

6. *Id.*

7. *Id.* at 1382–83 (noting that most modern authorities hold that similar indemnity clauses are effective to shift responsibility for an accident where the indemnitee is negligent and the indemnitor is not because financial responsibility for the risk of injury is often shifted by the primary parties to their insurance carriers).

8. C.J.M. Constr., Inc. v. Chandler Plumbing & Heating, Inc., 708 P.2d 60, 62 (Alaska 1985). The court explained that "an indemnity clause is no longer so unusual in modern commerce as to require such specific mention of the indemnitee's conduct as being within the scope of the indemnifying obligation." *Id.* (citations and quotations omitted). The court further noted that if "[the Indemnitor] wanted to limit its liability to its own negligence, [it] could have inserted limiting language in its indemnity clause." *Id.* at 64.

9. *Manson-Osberg Co.*, 552 P.2d at 658. In Alaska, worker's compensation is the exclusive remedy available to a claimant to secure compensation for injuries sustained as a result of a work-related incident. *Id.*

2. EXCEPTIONS TO GENERAL RULES OF CONTRACTUAL INDEMNITY

Alaska Statutes § 45.45.900 provides:

> A provision, clause, covenant, or agreement contained in, collateral to, or affecting a construction contract that purports to indemnify the promisee against liability . . . from the sole negligence or willful misconduct of the promisee or the promisee's agents, servants or independent contractors who are directly responsible to the promisee, is against public policy and is void and unenforceable; however, this provision does not affect the validity of an insurance contract, workers' compensation, or agreement issued by an insurer subject to the provisions of AS 21, or a provision, clause, covenant, or agreement of indemnification respecting the handling, containment, or cleanup of oil or hazardous substances defined in AS 46.[10]

In the context of Alaska Statutes § 45.45.900, willful misconduct means "volitional action taken either with a knowledge that serious injury to another will probably result, or with wanton and reckless disregard of the possible results."[11] This statute promotes the public policy that all wronged persons should have a remedy for injuries suffered as a result of another's negligence.[12]

As used in Alaska Statutes § 45.45.900, the word "indemnity" has been read to mean "exempt," and thus, the statute has been construed to restrict limitation-of-liability clauses as well as indemnity agreements.[13] Additionally, the statute has been read broadly to apply to indemnification clauses contained in construction *equipment* leases, on the grounds that such leases are "contained in, collateral to, or affecting a construction contract."[14] Importantly, however, indemnification clauses in construction contracts that could *potentially* encompass claims caused by the indemnitee's sole negligence or willful misconduct are not void simply because they could be read broadly. Alaska Statutes § 45.45.900 does not invalidate an indemnity clause merely because there is a theoretical possibility that the clause could be applied to indemnify the indemnitee for conduct governed by the statute.[15] Instead, the statute only applies to invalidate an indemnity clause if the clause is actually applied, as between the parties, to indemnify an indemnitee for the indemnitee's own sole negligence or willful misconduct.[16]

In addition to the restrictions placed on indemnity agreements in Alaska Statutes § 45.45.900, Alaska courts also recognize a public duty exception, which is generally applicable to public utilities and common carriers.[17] This public duty exception is based on two principles: (1) the exception applies to entities that must guard against negligence at all times, since indemnity agreements would create improper incentives for them to breach a duty owed to the public; and (2) public service entities should not be able to impose liability on those they are supposed to serve, since the recipients of the public service would have no choice but to accept that liability.[18]

---

10. Alaska Stat. § 45.45.900 (2015).
11. Aetna Cas. & Sur. Co. v. Marion Equip. Co., 894 P.2d 664, 671 (Alaska 1995).
12. City of Dillingham v. CH2M Hill Nw., Inc., 873 P.2d 1271, 1276 (Alaska 1994).
13. *Id.* at 1277.
14. *Aetna*, 894 P.2d at 667–70.
15. Hoffman Constr. Co. of Alaska v. U.S. Fabrication & Erection, Inc., 32 P.3d 346, 358 (Alaska 2001).
16. *Id.*; *see also* Rogers & Babler v. State, 713 P.2d 795, 798 (Alaska 1986).
17. *Burgess*, 614 P.2d at 1381; Kuhn v. State, 692 P.2d 261, 266–67 (1984).
18. *Burgess*, 614 P.2d at 1382.

3. INDEMNITY AGREEMENTS AS INSURED CONTRACTS

The Alaska Supreme Court has recognized that an agreement to indemnify another is within the definition of "liability assumed in a contract." Standard commercial general liability insurance policies often include an exclusion for this type of contractually assumed liability. The court has not definitively determined whether agreeing to indemnify for another's tort liability falls within a common exception, called the "insured contract exception," to the standard policy exclusion for contractual liability.[19] An Alaska federal court acknowledged that an agreement to indemnify another for tort liability may fall within the definition of "insured contract," but could not determine the scope of the indemnity agreement on the evidence before it.[20]

4. OPERATION OF AN AGREEMENT TO INDEMNIFY REFERRING TO OR REQUIRING INSURANCE

Alaska courts generally recognize that parties are allowed to freely negotiate the allocation of tort liability regardless of fault so long as the contract terms are not unconscionable.[21] Where one party is responsible for procuring full insurance for both parties, that intent must be stated in express terms.[22] In such a case, that party becomes responsible for the total risk of loss by affirmatively undertaking the duty to provide full insurance coverage for the mutual benefit of the parties.[23]

Alaska courts will broadly construe additional insured endorsements purportedly affording broader coverage than the named insured's underlying agreement to indemnify or to obtain insurance coverage. In *State v. Underwriters at Lloyds, London*,[24] a lease between an airline and airport required the airline to indemnify the airport and to maintain insurance to protect the airport against comprehensive public liability, products liability, and property damage. However, the insurance procured by the airline provided coverage that was broader than what the lease required.[25] The court held that "[t]he obligation of a liability insurer is contractual and is generally determined by the terms of the policy."[26] Finding nothing in the contract between the parties that limited the insurance coverage to the minimums required under the lease, and no legal doctrine to support such a limitation, the court decided that the airline's insurer was responsible for the full coverage in the policy with the airline, although this was greater than the airline's agreement to indemnify.[27]

Where an additional insured endorsement in a policy identifies all subcontractors of the named insured as additional insureds, but only with regard to the subcontractors' property interest, the court held that an insurer cannot seek subrogation against those subcontractors for any claim of negligence, even if such a claim is beyond the scope of the subcontractor's property interest.[28] To the Alaska Supreme Court, because a subcontractor has been identified as an additional insured, the insurer has no right to enforce a contractual indemnity agreement between its insured and the subcontractor.[29] In subrogation actions, an insurer

---

19. Olympic, Inc. v. Providence Wash. Ins. Co. of Alaska, 648 P.2d 1008, 1010–11 (Alaska 1982) (referring to incidental contracts as an exception to contractual liability exclusion); *see also* Alaska Nat'l Ins. Co. v. Indus. Indem. Co., 757 P.2d 1052, 1055 (Alaska 1988).

20. United States v. CNA Fin. Corp., 168 F. Supp. 2d 1109, 1120–21 (D. Alaska 2001).

21. Dressler Indus., Inc. v. Foss Launch & Tug Co., 560 P.2d 393, 395 (Alaska 1977).

22. *Id.*

23. *Id.* (holding that in the bailment context, an agreement to purchase insurance for the benefit of both parties is sufficient to shift the risk of loss for the bailed goods).

24. 755 P.2d 396 (Alaska 1988).

25. *Id.* at 400.

26. *Id.*

27. *Id.*

28. Baugh-Belarde Constr. Co. v. College Utilities Corp., 561 P.2d 1211, 1214 (Alaska 1977).

29. *Id.* at 1213–15.

cannot recover its losses from a negligent actor if that actor is an additional insured under the applicable policy.[30] The language in the policy limiting coverage will not prevent courts from viewing subcontractors as insureds in order to prevent them from being liable in subrogation claims.[31] For example, although the policy may limit coverage for the subcontractor "only as regards [their] property," or "as their interests may appear," the subcontractor is still protected from subrogation claims for damages beyond this coverage.[32]

However, if the insured has agreed to indemnify a third party who is not named as an additional insured in the insured's policy, the insurer may recover from that third party amounts paid under the policy pursuant to the indemnification agreement.[33] In so doing, the court looks to and applies the plain language of the indemnification clause.[34]

In *Alaska Insurance Co. v. RCA Alaska Communications, Inc.*,[35] the Alaska Supreme Court decided that a party could be an implied additional or co-insured and still obtain the benefit of the named insured's coverage. In *RCA*, a fire destroyed a building that RCA rented from the owner.[36] The written lease between the parties provided that the owner would maintain insurance that would provide protection against all risks, including fire.[37] The owner's insurer paid for the fire loss and then commenced a subrogation action against RCA, contending that RCA had negligently caused the fire.[38] To the court, RCA was an implied co-insured and it would "contradict the reasonable expectations of a commercial tenant to allow the landlord's insurer to proceed against it after the landlord had contracted in the lease to provide fire insurance on the leased premises . . . ."[39] In these circumstances, it would be undesirable as a matter of public policy to permit the risk of loss from a fire negligently caused by a tenant to fall upon the tenant rather than the landlord's insurer.[40]

Alaska courts have not discussed whether an agreement to procure insurance to cover an indemnity obligation violates Alaska Statutes § 45.45.900. The courts' general approach suggests that indemnity agreements would not be subject to the statute if they provide that the indemnitor will procure insurance sufficient to cover the risk involved, although this issue has not been specifically addressed.

---

30. Graham v. Rockman, 504 P.2d 1351, 1356–58 (Alaska 1972).

31. *Baugh-Belarde*, 561 P.2d at 1213–15 (holding that the builder's risk policy protected each insured party against his own negligence, whether the property lost belonged to him or to some other insured party).

32. *Id.*

33. United Airlines, Inc. v. State Farm & Cas. Co., 51 P.3d 928, 932–33 (Alaska 2002).

34. *Id.*

35. 623 P.2d 1216 (Alaska 1981).

36. *Id.* at 1217.

37. *Id.* at 1219.

38. *Id.* at 1217.

39. *Id.* at 1219.

40. *Id.*

Arizona

E. Tanner Warnick
Polsinelli, P.C.

1. GENERAL RULES OF CONTRACTUAL INDEMNITY

A party may contractually relieve itself from liability to another for damages or ordinary negligence through a contract for indemnity.[1] The duty to indemnify is determined by the contract itself, rather than by common law principles, if expressly agreed in a contract.[2]

Indemnity agreements may be considered "specific" or "general." A specific indemnity agreement obligates one party to indemnify another for the other party's own negligent acts.[3] Specific indemnity agreements do not violate public policy.[4] However, indemnity of this nature is strictly construed and is not enforced unless the indemnitor's obligation to protect the indemnitee against its own negligence is expressed in "clear and unequivocal terms."[5]

A general indemnity agreement is silent as to its application to the negligence of the indemnitee.[6] One example of a general indemnity provision is an agreement to "protect and indemnify [c]ontractor from any claims, liability, or losses suffered by anyone wholly or partially through the negligence of subcontractor or any of its agents or employees."[7]

Under a general indemnity agreement, an indemnitee is usually entitled to indemnification for a loss resulting in part from an indemnitee's passive negligence, but not active negligence.[8] "Active negligence" is where an indemnitee personally participated in an affirmative act of negligence, was connected with negligent acts or omissions by knowledge or acquiescence, or failed to perform a precise duty the indemnitee agreed to perform. By contrast, "passive negligence" is mere nonfeasance, such as where an indemnitee failed to discover a dangerous condition, perform a duty imposed by law, or take adequate precautions against certain hazards inherent in employment.[9]

While Arizona courts ordinarily follow the rule that a party will not be indemnified for its own active negligence under a general indemnity agreement,[10] courts avoid applying this rule mechanically when determining the parties' intent regarding contractual indemnification provisions.[11] As the Arizona Supreme Court explained, "[r]elying exclusively on the active/passive distinction in determining whether an indemnity agreement applies in a given case may prevent an agreement from being enforced as the parties intended."[12]

1. *See* Schweber Elecs. v. Nat'l Semiconductor Corp., 850 P.2d 119, 123 (Ariz. Ct. App. 1992).
2. *See* INA Ins Co. of N. Am. v. Valley Forge Ins. Co., 722 P.2d 975, 979 (Ariz. Ct. App. 1986); Grubb & Ellis Mgmt. Servs., Inc. v. 407417 B.C. LLC, 138 P.3d 1210, 1213 (Ariz. Ct. App. 2006).
3. *See Grubb & Ellis*, 138 P.3d at 1214.
4. *See* Wash. Elem. Sch. Dist. No. 6 v. Baglino Corp., 817 P.2d 3, 6 (Ariz. 1991).
5. *Id.*, citing Pioneer Roofing Co. v. Mardian Constr. Co., 733 P.2d 652, 671 (Ariz. Ct. App. 1986).
6. *Id.*
7. Estes Co. v. Aztec Constr., Inc., 677 P.2d 939, 940–41 (Ariz. Ct. App. 1983).
8. *See Wash. Elem.*, 817 P.2d at 6, citing *Pioneer Roofing*, 733 P.2d at 671.
9. *See Grubb & Ellis*, 138 P.3d at 1213 n.3, citing *Estes Co.*, 677 P.2d at 942.
10. *See Wash. Elem.*, 817 P.2d at 6.
11. *See id.*
12. *Id.*

2. EXCEPTIONS TO GENERAL RULES OF CONTRACTUAL INDEMNITY

Contractual indemnity provisions can also be construed as a limited-form indemnity agreement, an intermediate-form indemnity agreement, or a broad-form indemnity agreement. A limited-form indemnity provision obligates the indemnitor to save and hold harmless the indemnitee for the indemnitor's own negligence. An intermediate-form indemnity provision obligates the indemnitor to hold harmless the indemnitee for all liability that does not arise out of the indemnitee's sole negligence. A broad-form indemnity provision requires the indemnitor to save and hold harmless the indemnitee from all liabilities arising from the project, regardless of which party's negligence causes the liability.[13]

In the context of certain construction contracts, courts may void intermediate-form or broad-form indemnity provisions on the basis of public policy. In construction contracts involving private entities, Arizona Revised Statutes § 32-1159 voids broad-form indemnity provisions as against public policy:

> A covenant, clause or understanding in, collateral to or affecting a construction contract or architect-engineer professional service contract that purports to indemnify, to hold harmless or to defend the promisee from or against liability for loss or damage resulting from the sole negligence of the promisee or the promisee's agents, employees or indemnitee is against the public policy of this state and is void.[14]

In construction contracts involving public entities, Arizona Revised Statutes § 34-226 permits only limited-form indemnity provisions and voids both broad-form and intermediate-form indemnity provisions as a matter of public policy.[15] Importantly, these statutory exceptions to the general rules of indemnity apply ***only*** in the construction context.

3. INDEMNITY AGREEMENTS AS INSURED CONTRACTS

Arizona courts do not appear to have addressed the extent to which an agreement to assume another's tort liability through an indemnity agreement is an "insured contract" within the meaning of the exception to the exclusion for contractually assumed liability in the form commercial general liability (CGL) policy. In an unpublished opinion, however, an Arizona federal court addressed this issue and treated an indemnity provision as an "insured contract" for purposes of this exception.[16]

4. OPERATION OF AN AGREEMENT TO INDEMNIFY REFERRING TO OR REQUIRING INSURANCE

In some circumstances, the parties to a contract agree to waive their respective rights against one another, including the right of indemnification, and instead look to the insurance procured by one or both of the parties in order to cover a particular loss.[17] This type of waiver-of-subrogation clause arises, for example, in construction contracts where the contractor agrees to indemnify an owner for losses occasioned by the negligence or partial negligence of the contractor. That same contract may also include provisions providing that (1) the owner will procure insurance for a particular type of loss, most commonly fire damage; and

13. 3 Conn. Ins. L.J. 169, 179 (1996).

14. Ariz. Rev. Stat. § 32-1159 (2017).

15. Ariz. Rev. Stat. § 34-226 (2017).

16. *See* James v. B.N.S.F. Ry. Co., No. CV05-04106-PCT-NVW, 2007 WL 2461685, at *5–6 (D. Ariz. Aug. 27, 2007).

17. *See, e.g.*, U.S. Fid. & Guar. Co. v. Farrar's Plumbing & Heating Co., Inc., 762 P.2d 641, 642 (Ariz. Ct. App. 1988); Fire Ins. Exch. v. Thunderbird Masonry, Inc., 868 P.2d 948, 952–53 (Ariz. Ct. App. 1993).

(2) the owner and contractor waive all rights against each other and against subcontractors and separate contractors for damages arising out of that particular type of loss. Regardless of its duty to indemnify, if the contractor's negligence results in the specific type of covered loss, the courts will look to the owner's insurance to cover the loss.[18]

A waiver-of-subrogation is useful in construction projects because it avoids disruption and disputes among the contracting parties, yet protects them by bringing all property damage under the owner's property insurance.[19] Courts may read an indemnity provision that refers to or requires procurement of a specific type of insurance as a "loss shifting" mechanism designed to impose liability solely on the insurer, rather than the parties, in the event of a specific loss. Thus, the controlling language may not be the reference to indemnity, but rather the reference to insurance.

18. *See Farrar's*, 762 P.2d at 642–43 (citing Tokio Marine & Fire Ins. Co. Ltd. v. Employers Ins. of Wausau, 786 F.2d 101, 104 (2d Cir. 1986)).

19. *See Tokio Marine*, 786 F.2d at 104.

Arkansas

Jason A. Frye
Neal, Gerber & Eisenberg, LLP

1. GENERAL RULES OF CONTRACTUAL INDEMNITY

Arkansas courts apply the same rules of interpretation to indemnity agreements that they apply to contracts generally.[1] "In construing a contract, the courts must endeavor to give meaning and effect to every word and may discard words as surplusage only when the intention of the parties clearly makes them such."[2] If, however, "there is no ambiguity in the language of the contract, then there is no need to resort to rules of construction."[3] Like any contract, the interpretation of an indemnity agreement is "determined by the court as a question of law, except where the meaning of the language depends on disputed extrinsic evidence."[4]

Contracts indemnifying a person for their own negligence are enforceable but disfavored;[5] as such, the language must be clear and unequivocal.[6] "Agreements to indemnify an indemnitee against its own negligence are generally disfavored, closely scrutinized, strictly construed against the indemnitee and in favor of the indemnitor, and will not be upheld unless expressed in such clear and unequivocal terms that no other meaning can be ascribed."[7] Courts, however, will not strictly construe an indemnification agreement against the indemnitee when the agreement is entered into by business entities in the context of free and understanding negotiation,[8] or where the language of the agreement is unambiguous, meaning that rules of construction are not necessary to ascertain the contract's meaning.[9]

While any ambiguity in the contract will preclude a finding of indemnification for the indemnitee's own negligence, even an unambiguous agreement may not provide indemnity to an indemnitee for their own negligence. "The language of an indemnity agreement can be unambiguous and still not spell out in clear, unequivocal, unmistakable terms the indemnitor's intention to obligate itself to indemnify for the indemnitee's negligence."[10] While no particular words are required, the liability of an indemnitor for the negligence of an indemnitee is an extraordinary obligation to assume, and an intention to so indemnify must be spelled out in unmistakable terms.[11]

Even with these strict rules of construction, broadly worded indemnity agreements may extend to indemnification for the indemnitee's own negligence, and the indemnity agreement will be limited only to the extent the indemnitee is the sole proximate cause of the injury. For example, an agreement that required the indemnitor to indemnify "from whatever cause to property or persons used or employed on or in connection with his

1. Pickens-Bond Constr. Co. v. North Little Rock Elec. Co., 459 S.W.2d 549, 552 (Ark. 1970); Chevron U.S.A. Inc. v. Murphy Exploration & Prod. Co., 2004 Ark. LEXIS 142, at *6 (Ark. Mar. 4, 2004).

2. *Pickens-Bond*, 459 S.W.2d at 552.

3. Nabholz Constr. Corp. v. Graham, 892 S.W.2d 456, 459 (Ark. 1995). *See also* Ark. Kraft Corp. v. Boyed Sanders Constr. Co., 764 S.W.2d 452, 453 (Ark. 1989).

4. East-Harding, Inc. v. Horace A. Piazza & Assocs., 91 S.W.3d 547, 551 (Ark. Ct. App. 2002).

5. *Nabholz*, 892 S.W.2d at 460.

6. Potlatch Corp. v. Missouri Pac. R.R., 902 S.W.2d 217, 222 (Ark. 1995).

7. *Potlatch*, 902 S.W.2d at 222. *See also* Wal-Mart Stores, Inc. v. Black & Decker U.S., Inc., 2009 U.S. Dist. LEXIS 72838, at *10 (W.D. Ark. Aug. 17, 2009); Paul Hardeman, Inc. v. J.I. Hass Co., 439 S.W.2d 281 (Ark. 1969).

8. *Potlatch*, 902 S.W.2d at 222.

9. *Pickens-Bond*, 459 S.W.2d at 552.

10. *Arkansas Kraft*, 764 S.W.2d at 453.

11. *Id.*

work" was considered broad and sweeping enough as to clearly and unequivocally show the indemnitor's intention to cover the negligence of the indemnitee.[12] But that language was not sufficient to require indemnity for injuries for which the indemnitee's negligence was the sole proximate cause.[13]

In contrast, where an agreement specifically refers to the indemnitee's own negligence, an even broader reading is warranted, and the indemnity agreement will be enforced even if the indemnitee's negligence is the sole proximate cause of the injury.[14] Typically, an indemnity agreement only covers tort liability, and absent express language to the contrary, an indemnity agreement will not cover contractual liabilities.[15]

Additionally, as many of the indemnification cases arise in the construction context, a slightly different analysis may apply in cases involving other types of indemnity agreements.[16] "Generally speaking, the issues in construction contractor-subcontractor cases have centered around whether a subcontractor can be held liable for acts of negligence on the part of the general contractor, when those acts of negligence lead to an instance of personal injury."[17] On the other hand, in an oil and gas lease for example, the concern is with ongoing environmental issues that frequently persist over a span of years and that may or may not be known at the time an oil and gas lease is transferred from one exploration company to another.[18]

Although claims for tort-based or common law indemnity are barred by Arkansas' worker's compensation act, there is "an exception to the exclusivity of the Workers' Compensation remedy when there is a contract or special relation capable of carrying with it an implied obligation to indemnify."[19] Thus, an express contract for indemnity will support a claim against the employer of an injured party.[20]

2. EXCEPTIONS TO GENERAL RULES OF CONTRACTUAL INDEMNITY

Unlike the rule in many states, there is no statutory prohibition on indemnity agreements in the construction context, and the law on indemnity agreements has been developed through cases in which a subcontractor agreed to indemnify a general contractor.[21] Generally such contracts are upheld against the contention that they violate public policy, but the language must be clear, unequivocal and certain.[22]

The general rule is that "[s]ubject to public policy considerations a party may voluntarily agree to hold another harmless against loss by whatever cause it might be sustained."[23] Arkansas courts have not set forth in detail what types of indemnity agreements will violate public policy.

A party may not recover under a broad indemnity provision for "loss based upon an independent indemnity agreement with [a third party], to which [the party seeking indemnity] was neither party or privy" without clear and express language.[24]

---

12. *Pickens-Bond*, 459 S.W.2d at 552.
13. *Id.*
14. Ross v. Smith, 315 F. Supp. 1064, 1068 (E.D. Ark. 970).
15. Weaver-Bailey Contractors, Inc. v. Fiske-Carter Constr. Co., 657 S.W.2d 209, 211 (Ark. Ct. App. 1983).
16. *See, e.g., Chevron*, 2004 Ark. LEXIS 142, at *8.
17. *Id.*
18. *Id.*
19. Mosley Machinery Co. v. Gray Supply Co., 833 S.W.2d 772, 772 (Ark. 1992); *see also* Cherry v. Tanda, Inc., 940 S.W.2d 457, 461 (Ark. 1997).
20. C & L Rural Elec. Coop. Corp. v. Kincaid, 256 S.W.2d 337, 340 (Ark. 1953).
21. *See Nabholz*, 892 S.W.2d at 460.
22. Elk Corp. of Arkansas v. Builders Transport, Inc., 862 F.2d 663, 665 (8th Cir. 1988).
23. JFM, Inc. v. Weddington, 1988 Ark. App. LEXIS 568, at *5 (Ark. Ct. App. Dec. 7, 1988).
24. Weaver-Bailey Contractors, Inc. v. Fiske-Carter Constr. Co., 657 S.W.2d 209, 211 (Ark. App. Ct. 1983).

3. INDEMNITY AGREEMENTS AS INSURED CONTRACTS

An agreement to indemnify falls within the "insured contract" provisions of a commercial general liability policy.[25] The liability for which indemnity is sought from the insured must be tort liability.[26]

Where the claim against the insured sounds both in negligence and breach of contract, coverage for an "insured contract" will only extend to indemnification of the indemnitee for tortious injuries.[27]

4. OPERATION OF AN AGREEMENT TO INDEMNIFY REFERRING TO OR REQUIRING INSURANCE

Although no cases appear to directly discuss the effect of an agreement to obtain insurance on an indemnity agreement, conclusions can be drawn from cases that discuss parallel indemnity agreements and agreements to obtain insurance. For example, "where one party has agreed with another to obtain insurance for their mutual protection, the insurer will not be allowed to recover its losses from the non-insured party by means of subrogation or indemnity."[28]

An indemnity agreement can give context to allocation between various insurers.[29] An agreement that requires indemnity for the indemnitee's own negligence can actually control an insurer's liability and trump an "other insurance clause."[30] "[I]ndemnity agreements determine the allocation of liability in an insurance dispute . . . 'an indemnity agreement between the insureds or a contract with an indemnification clause . . . may shift an entire loss to a particular insurer notwithstanding the existence of an 'other insurance' clause in its policy.'"[31] Thus, in a suit "between two insurers with identical and dueling 'other insurance' clauses, the indemnity agreement [is] paramount."[32]

Finally, an agreement that contains both an agreement to indemnify and an agreement to procure insurance does not transform the indemnitor into an "insurer."[33] In such a case, the indemnity agreement and the agreement to obtain insurance are typically incidental to the actual object of the contract (e.g., a construction project).[34] Therefore, by entering into parallel indemnity and insurance agreements, the indemnitor is not undertaking to become an insurer.

25. *See* United States Fid. & Guar. Co. v. Cont'l Cas. Co., 2003 Ark. LEXIS 397, at *12 (Ark. June 26, 2003); *see also* Clarendon Nat'l Ins. Co. v. United Fire & Cas. Co., 571 F.3d 749, 753 (8th Cir. 2009).

26. *Id.*

27. *Id.*

28. U.S. Fid. & Guar. Co. v. Aetna Cas. & Sur. Co., 418 F.2d 953, 955 (8th Cir. 1969).

29. Wal-Mart Stores, Inc. v. RLI Ins. Co., 292 F.3d 583, 588 (8th Cir. 2002).

30. *Id.* at 590.

31. *Wal-Mart Stores, Inc.*, 292 F.3d at 586, citing Rossmoor Sanitation, Inc. v. Pylon, Inc., 532 P.2d 97 (Cal. 1975) and 15 Couch on Insurance § 219:1.

32. *Id.* at 590.

33. *See Cherry*, 940 S.W.2d at 462.

34. *Id.*

California

Terrance Evans
Duane Morris, LLP

1. GENERAL RULES OF CONTRACTUAL INDEMNITY

Historically, California courts have construed express contractual indemnity provisions using a three-tiered analysis focused on the indemnitee's active or passive negligence.[1] The three tiers are normally referred to as "Type I," "Type II," and "Type III" indemnity provisions.[2] Type I indemnity provisions are the broadest in that the indemnitor "expressly and unequivocally" agrees to indemnify the indemnitee with respect to the indemnitee's own negligence, including its active negligence.[3] Generally, California courts have strictly construed these types of indemnity provisions against the indemnitee.[4] Type II indemnity provisions are provisions that require the indemnitor to indemnify the indemnitee against its passive but not active negligence.[5] California courts have generally placed indemnity provisions that did not specifically address the indemnitee's negligence in this category.[6] Type III indemnity provisions require the indemnitor to indemnify the indemnitee only for liabilities that result solely from the indemnitor's negligence.[7] Under Type III indemnity clauses, the indemnitor is not liable if the indemnitee's negligence contributed to the liability.[8] In other words, if an indemnitor can establish that the indemnitee was contributorily negligent, the indemnitor will not be liable under a Type III indemnity provision. Attorneys representing indemnitors in California should consider asserting contributory negligence as an affirmative defense in response to a claim for indemnity under a Type III indemnity provision.

2. EXCEPTIONS TO GENERAL RULES OF CONTRACTUAL INDEMNITY

Express indemnification agreements are subject to limitations based upon principles of public policy that have been codified in California. "All contracts which have for their object, directly or indirectly, to exempt anyone from responsibility for his own fraud, or willful injury to the person or property of another, or violation of law, whether willful or negligent, are against the policy of the law."[9] However, an indemnity agreement as to a wrongful act already done is valid, unless it was a felony.[10] Additionally, "[a]n insurer is not liable for a loss caused by the willful act of the insured; but he is not exonerated by the negligence of

1. *See* 5 Miller & Starr California Real Estate Forms § 5:404 (July 2016); *see also* MacDonald & Kruse, Inc. v. San Jose Steel Co., 29 Cal. App. 3d 413, 419 (1972).

2. *Id.*

3. *See* 5 Miller & Starr California Real Estate Forms § 5:405 (July 2016).

4. *Id.*

5. *Id.*

6. *Id.*

7. *Id.*

8. *Id.*

9. Cal. Civ. Code § 1668.

10. Lemat Corp. v. Am. Basketball Ass'n, 51 Cal. App. 3d 267, 277 n.9 (1975); *see* Cal. Civ. Code § 2774 ("An agreement to indemnify a person against an act already done, is valid, even though the act was known to be wrongful, unless it was a felony.").

the insured, or of the insured's agents or others."[11] Public policy also proscribes indemnification for punitive damages.[12]

Crawford v. Weather Shield MFG., Inc.[13] is the seminal case regarding contractual indemnity in California. *Crawford* involved a group of homeowners in a housing development in Southern California who brought a construction defect action against a developer, a window subcontractor, a framing subcontractor, and several other subcontractors.[14] The developer cross-complained against all of the subcontractors involved in the development—including the window subcontractor and the framing subcontractor—seeking attorneys' fees incurred while defending the lawsuit brought by the homeowners, and also requesting indemnification.[15]

The developer had subcontracted with the window subcontractor to manufacture and supply wood-framed windows for the development.[16] Additionally, the developer had subcontracted with the framing subcontractor to frame the structures and install the windows at the development.[17] Each of the subcontracts at issue in the case were drafted by the developer and included identical defense and indemnity provisions.[18] Specifically, in their respective subcontracts, each of the subcontractors promised (1) "to indemnify and hold the developer harmless against all claims for damages . . . loss . . . and/or theft . . . growing out of the execution of the window subcontractor's work," and (2) "at [its] own expense to defend any suit or action brought against the developer founded upon the claim of such damage[,] . . . loss or theft."[19]

Each of the subcontractors, except for the window subcontractor and the framing subcontractor, settled before trial.[20] Following the trial, the jury returned general verdicts against the framing subcontractor and in favor of the window subcontractor.[21] The framing subcontractor settled all the claims against it following the jury verdict.

The developer's cross-complaint against the window subcontractor was tried separately.[22] In its cross-complaint, the developer sought both (1) express indemnity for amounts paid to the homeowners in settlement; and (2) under the duty-to-defend provisions of the window subcontractor's subcontract, attorneys' fees and expenses incurred by the developer in defending itself against the homeowners' suit.[23]

With respect to the developer's cross-complaint, the trial court ruled that the subcontract's terms obliged the window subcontractor to indemnify the developer for amounts paid to the homeowners only if the window subcontractor was found negligent.[24] Thus, the court determined, the jury's verdict that the window subcontractor was not negligent absolved the window subcontractor of indemnity liability in this case.[25] On the other hand, the trial court concluded, the subcontract did give the window subcontractor responsibility for the developer's legal defense against the homeowners' claims, insofar as those claims concerned the windows supplied by the window subcontractor regardless of whether the window subcontractor was ultimately found negligent.[26]

---

11. Cal. Ins. Code § 533.
12. PPG Indus., Inc. v. Transamerica Ins. Co., 975 P.2d 652, 658 (Cal. 1999).
13. Crawford v. Weather Shield MFG, Inc., 44 Cal. 4th 541 (2008).
14. *Id.* at 541–51.
15. *Id.*
16. *Id.* at 547–48.
17. *Id.*
18. *Id.*
19. *Id.*
20. *Id.* at 548.
21. *Id.* at 548–49.
22. *Id.* at 549.
23. *Id.*
24. *Id.* at 549.
25. *Id.*
26. *Id.*

Following entry of judgment, both sides filed cross appeals with the California Court of Appeal.[27] A divided California Court of Appeal affirmed the trial court's judgments and orders.[28] The window subcontractor then sought and was granted review by the California Supreme Court.[29]

The California Supreme Court made several determinations regarding the enforceability of contractual defense and indemnity provisions in California.[30] Specifically, the California Supreme Court concluded that parties to a contract, including a construction contract, may define therein their duties toward one another in the event of a third-party claim against one or both arising out of their relationship.[31] The *Crawford* court noted that terms of this kind may require one party to indemnify the other, under specified circumstances, for money paid or expenses incurred by the latter as a result of such claims.[32] The *Crawford* court also concluded that indemnity provisions may assign one party, pursuant to the contract's language, responsibility for the other's legal defense when a third-party claim is made against the latter.[33]

With respect to how express indemnity provisions should be interpreted, the *Crawford* court concluded that such an agreement is construed under the same rules that govern the interpretation of other contracts.[34] As the court explained, "[e]ffect is to be given to the parties' mutual intent (§ 1636), as ascertained from the contract's language if it is clear and explicit (§ 1638)."[35] Unless the parties have indicated a special meaning, the contract's words are to be understood in their ordinary and popular sense.[36]

The *Crawford* court also compared indemnity provisions to insurance policies:

> Though indemnity agreements resemble liability insurance policies, rules for interpreting the two classes of contracts do differ significantly. Ambiguities in a policy of insurance are construed against the insurer, who generally drafted the policy, and who has received premiums to provide the agreed protection. (See, e.g., *Buss, supra*, 16 Cal.4th 35, 47–48; *La Jolla Beach & Tennis Club, Inc. v. Industrial Indemnity Co.*, (1994) 9 Cal.4th 27, 37–38.) In noninsurance contexts, however, it is the *indemnitee* who may often have the superior bargaining power, and who may use this power unfairly to shift to another a disproportionate share of the financial consequences of its own legal fault. (E.g., *Goldman v. Ecco–Phoenix Elec. Corp.*, (1964) 62 Cal.2d 40, 49 (Goldman); see *Regan Roofing Co. v. Superior Court* (1994) 24 Cal.App.4th 425, 436 (Regan Roofing).)[37]

As it relates to public policy, the *Crawford* court stated:

> This public policy concern influences to some degree the manner in which noninsurance indemnity agreements are construed. For example, it has been said that if one seeks, in a noninsurance agreement, to be indemnified for his or her own active negligence, or regardless of the indemnitor's fault—protections beyond those afforded by the doctrines of implied or equitable indemnity—language on the point must be particularly clear and explicit, and will be construed strictly against the indemnitee.

27. *Id.* at 550–51.
28. *Id.*
29. *Id.*
30. *Id.* at 551–69.
31. *Id.* at 551.
32. *Id.*
33. *Id.*; *see also* Mel Clayton Ford v. Ford Motor Co., 104 Cal. App. 4th 46, 49, 55 (2002).
34. *Id.* at 551–52.
35. *Id.*
36. *Id.*
37. *Id.* at 552.

> For similar public policy reasons, statutory law imposes some absolute limits on the enforceability of noninsurance indemnity agreements in the construction industry. At the time Weather Shield contracted with JMP, a party to a construction contract could not validly agree to indemnify the promisee for the latter's sole negligence or willful misconduct.[38]

The California Supreme Court consequently concluded that the duty to defend against claims founded upon damage or loss caused by the window subcontractor's negligent performance of its work, pursuant to the window subcontractor's subcontract, was triggered as soon as a lawsuit was filed against the developer asserting such claims, and regardless of whether the window subcontractor was ultimately determined to be negligent.[39]

In the realm of construction contracts, effective January 1, 2009, the California legislature amended the California Civil Code to address indemnity and defense obligations in "non-wrap" situations; indemnity, contribution, and disclosure requirements in the context of residential construction projects with wrap insurance policies; and contribution and disclosure requirements in the context of nonresidential construction projects with a wrap insurance policy. (The new and modified provisions are sections 2782, 2782.9, 2782.95, and 2782.96.[40]) These revisions and additions apply only to contracts and contract amendments entered into after January 1, 2009.[41]

Nevertheless, revisions to California Civil Code § 2782(c) do not affect the builder's or general contractor's ability to obtain additional insured endorsements for completed operations coverage that covers the builder's or general contractor's negligence from a subcontractor's insurer.[42] In fact, the statute expressly provides that the subdivision does not affect the obligations of insurance carriers under *Presley Homes, Inc. v. Am. States Ins. Co.*[43]

Pursuant to California Civil Code § 2782(d) and (e), in a non-wrap setting, a subcontractor now has no defense obligation on construction defect claims to a builder or general contractor unless and until a written tender is made to the subcontractor that includes all information concerning the claims arising or resulting from the subcontractor's scope of work.[44] After that tender, the subcontractor must then either defend the general contractor with the subcontractor's choice of counsel or pay an allocated share of the general contractor's defense cost (if an itemized invoice of defenses costs has been sent to the subcontractor).[45] If the subcontractor breaches its duty by failing to timely accept the tender, adequately conduct the defense, or pay the allocated attorneys' fees and costs, the subcontractor will be held liable to the builder or general contractor for damages, potentially including attorneys' fees and costs and liquidated damages.[46]

Additionally, California Civil Code § 2782(d) requires a builder or general contractor in a residential setting to tender a claim to a subcontractor before any defense obligation arises.[47] The builder or general contractor must also provide information that directly implicates the subcontractor's scope of work.[48]

After receiving a tender from the builder or general contractor, a subcontractor may either provide a complete defense of the builder or general contractor at its own expense or

38. *Id.* (internal citations omitted).

39. *Id.* at 558–59.

40. *See* California Civil Practice Torts § 4:11 (Nov. 2016).

41. *Id.*

42. *See id.*

43. Presley Homes, Inc. v. Am. States Ins. Co., 90 Cal. App. 4th 571 (2001) (finding subcontractor's commercial general liability insurer was obligated to provide developer with full and complete defense, even though the indemnification obligation was more limited).

44. *See* Cal. Civ. Code § 2782(d), (e); *see also* California Civil Practice Torts § 4:11 (Nov. 2016).

45. *Id.*

46. *Id.*

47. *Id.*

48. *Id.*

pay its reasonable proportion of the defense (also if an itemized invoice of defense costs has been sent to the subcontractor).[49] If the subcontractor elects to defend the builder at its own cost, the subcontractor will be liable for any vicarious liability imposed upon the builder.[50] If the subcontractor elects to pay an allocated portion, the allocation must be reasonable and may be reallocated upon final resolution of the claim.[51] Additionally, the builder, general contractor, and subcontractors have the right to seek equitable indemnity for any claim under section 2782.[52]

Several decisions still control residential indemnity claims that do not concern construction defects after January 1, 2009.[53] The California Supreme Court has declined to find void construction indemnity agreements not containing express disclaimers of any right to indemnification for the promisee's sole negligence or willful misconduct.[54]

It is well established under California law that the issue of whether an indemnity provision requires a showing of negligence to trigger the indemnity obligation is a matter of contract interpretation.[55]

In 2010, approximately two years after the California Supreme Court decided *Crawford*, and one year after the California legislature amended California Civil Code § 2782 (which bans Type I indemnity provisions), the California Court of Appeal applied *Crawford* to a dispute between a developer and a subcontractor regarding the subcontractor's defense and indemnity obligations under a subcontract with comparable defense and indemnity provisions to those at issue in *Crawford*.[56] (Notably, the California Supreme Court refused to review the decision of the California Court of Appeals in that case.[57])

In applying *Crawford*, the Court of Appeal made it clear that *Crawford* is still good law in California, even after the California legislature amended California Civil Code § 2782 in 2009.[58]

In 2011, the California Court of Appeal extended the application of the contractual indemnity principles set forth in *Crawford* in *Searles Valley Minerals Operations Inc. v. Ralph M. Parsons Service Co.*[59] In that case, the California Court of Appeal held—in a case of first impression in California—that

> an assignee of contract indemnification rights stands in the shoes of the indemnitee. Therefore, if an indemnitor refuses to pay an indemnitee's defense costs, the indemnitee, and in turn the assignee, can pay the costs and seek reimbursement from the indemnitor.[60]

---

49. *See* California Civil Practice Torts § 4:11 (Nov. 2016); Cal. Civ. Code § 2782(e)(1), (2).

50. *See* California Civil Practice Torts § 4:11 (Nov. 2016); Cal. Civ. Code § 2782(d)(1).

51. *See* California Civil Practice Torts § 4:11 (Nov. 2016); Cal. Civ. Code § 2782(d)(2).

52. California Civil Practice Torts § 4:11 (Nov. 2016); *see also* Cal. Civ. Code § 2782(f).

53. *See* California Civil Practice Torts § 4:11 (Nov. 2016).

54. *See* California Civil Practice Torts § 4:11 (Nov. 2016); *see also* Gonzales v. R.J. Novick Constr. Co., 20 Cal. 3d 798 (1978); Armco Steel Corp. v. Roy H. Cox Co., 103 Cal. App. 3d 929 (1980); Smoketree-Lake Murray, Ltd. v. Mills Concrete Constr. Co., 234 Cal. App. 3d 1724 (1991).

55. *See* California Civil Practice Torts § 4:11 (Nov. 2016); *see also*, e.g., Heppler v. J.M. Peters Co., 73 Cal. App. 4th 1265 (1999) (finding the indemnity provision required a finding of negligence to trigger the indemnity obligation), *declined to follow by* Crawford v. Weather Shield Mfg. Inc., 44 Cal. 4th 541 (2008); Cont'l Heller Corp. v. Amtech Mech. Servs., Inc., 53 Cal. App. 4th 500 (1997) (finding the indemnity agreement's "arising out of" language did not require a finding of negligence prior to enforcement of the indemnity provision); Centex Golden Constr. Co. v. Dale Tile Co., 78 Cal. App. 4th 992 (2000) (finding the indemnity provision's language was stronger than that in *Cont'l Heller* and thus, the tile subcontractor was required to indemnify the general contractor prior to a finding of negligence); California Civil Practice Torts § 4:11 (Nov. 2016).

56. UDC-Universal Dev., L.P. v. Ch2M Hill, 181 Cal. App. 4th 10, 10–29 (2010).

57. *Id.* at 10.

58. *Id.* at 10–29.

59. Searles Valley Minerals Operations, Inc. v. Ralph M. Parsons Service Co., 191 Cal. App. 4th 1394 (2011).

60. *Id.* at 1396–97.

It is worth noting that the California Supreme Court refused to review the decision of the California Court of Appeal in *Searles Valley Minerals Operations*. Moreover, the California Court of Appeal's decision in *Searles Valley Minerals Operations* is important because it reaffirms and extends the *Crawford* analysis to apply to assignees of express contractual indemnity agreements.

In 2013, California again reduced the exposure of subcontractors under Type I indemnity agreements. Effective January 1, 2013, the California legislature amended portions of California Civil Code §§ 2782 and 2783, and added § 2782.05 to place additional limitations on the enforceability of Type I indemnity provisions in California.[61]

In particular, these revisions provide that for nonresidential construction contracts and amendments executed on or after January 1, 2013, a direct contract with a public agency or the owner of private property, as specified in California Civil Code § 2782.05(b), that seeks to indemnify or insure, including the cost to defend, a general contractor, construction manager, or other subcontractor, by a subcontractor against liability for claims for death, bodily injury to persons, injury to property, or other loss, damage, or expense, are unenforceable, but only to the extent the claims relate to the active negligence or willful misconduct of the party seeking to be indemnified or insured, or for defects in the designs furnished by those persons, or to the extent that the claims fall outside the scope of work of the subcontractor as stated in the written contract.[62]

Additionally and importantly for subcontractors and suppliers with limited bargaining power, these provisions cannot be waived and cannot be circumvented by employing a choice of law provision requiring that the laws of a state that enforces Type I indemnity provisions be the governing law on contract interpretation issues.[63] Furthermore, these amendments do not affect the validity of any existing insurance contract or agreement or an agreement issued before January 1, 2013.[64]

Furthermore, the 2013 amendments set forth detailed procedures for the tender of defense and payment of defense fees for indemnity provisions affected by the statutory revisions and new statute. With respect to defense obligations, no subcontractor has a defense obligation on an indemnity claim to a general contractor, pursuant to California Civil Code § 2782.05(e), unless and until a written tender is made to the subcontractor that includes information provided by the claimant concerning the claims arising or resulting from the subcontractor's scope of work.[65] The general contractor must also provide a written statement regarding how the reasonably allocated share of fees and costs was determined.[66]

After receiving a tender from the builder or general contractor, a subcontractor must then either defend the general contractor with the subcontractor's choice of counsel or pay an allocated share of the general contractor's defense cost (if an itemized invoice of defense costs has been sent to the subcontractor).[67] In the event that a subcontractor breaches its duty by either failing to timely accept the tender, adequately conducting the defense, or failing to pay the allocated attorneys' fees and costs, the subcontractor will be held liable to the builder or general contractor for damages, potentially including attorneys' fees and costs and liquidated damages.[68]

If the subcontractor elects to defend the builder at its own cost, the subcontractor will be liable for any vicarious liability imposed on the builder.[69] In the event that a subcontractor elects to pay an allocated portion, that allocation must be reasonable and may be

---

61. *See* California Civil Practice Torts § 4:11 (Nov. 2016).

62. *See* California Civil Practice Torts § 4:11 (Nov. 2016).

63. *Id.*

64. *Id.*

65. *Id.*

66. *Id.*; *see also* Cal. Civ. Code § 2782.05(e) (stating that the written tender shall have the same force and effect as a notice of commencement of legal proceedings).

67. *See* California Civil Practice Torts § 4:11 (Nov. 2016); *see also* Cal. Civ. Code § 2782.05(e)(1), (2).

68. *See* California Civil Practice Torts § 4:11 (Nov. 2016).

69. *See id.*; *see also* Cal. Civ. Code § 2782.05(e)(1).

reallocated upon final resolution of the claim.[70] Finally, a general contractor may also seek equitable indemnity for any claims under California Civil Code § 2782.05.[71]

3. INDEMNITY AGREEMENTS AS INSURED CONTRACTS

California recognizes an agreement to indemnify a third party by an insured as an "insured contract" within the meaning of the exclusion for contractually assumed liability.[72]

4. OPERATION OF AN AGREEMENT TO INDEMNIFY REFERRING TO OR REQUIRING INSURANCE

Because insurance contracts are expressly excepted from the statutory provision voiding certain indemnity agreements in the construction context,[73] if an indemnitee is named as an additional insured under a liability policy, California courts will enforce an otherwise unenforceable indemnity agreement by construing the agreement as a contract for the purchase of insurance.[74] California has not addressed the operation of an additional insured endorsement that purports to extend greater coverage to the indemnitee than the underlying agreement of the named insured to indemnify.

---

70. *See* California Civil Practice Torts § 4:11 (Nov. 2016); *see also* Cal. Civ. Code § 2782.05(e)(2).

71. *See* California Civil Practice Torts § 4:11 (Nov. 2016); *see also* Cal. Civ. Code § 2782.05(j).

72. N.H. Ins. Co. v. Ridout Roofing Co., Inc., 68 Cal. App. 4th 495, 500–01 (1988).

73. *See* Cal. Civ. Code § 2782.

74. *See* Chevron U.S.A., Inc., v. Bragg Crane & Rigging Co., 180 Cal. App. 3d 639, 644–47 (1986); *see also* Shell Oil Co. v. Nat'l Union Fire Ins. Co. of Pittsburgh, PA, 44 Cal. App. 4th 1633, 1641–43 (1996).

Colorado

E. Tanner Warnick
Polsinelli, P.C.

1. GENERAL RULES OF CONTRACTUAL INDEMNITY

Colorado courts generally uphold indemnity agreements as long as the parties' intent to indemnify is clear and unambiguous.[1] Indemnity agreements are subject to the same rules of construction that govern contracts generally.[2] Courts thus interpret indemnity agreements in their entirety to give effect to all of their provisions and enforce them according to the plain and generally accepted meaning of the language used.[3] Like other contracts, indemnity agreements can arise orally, but broad statements such as "Don't worry about it; we will take care of it if anything happens" do not create an indemnity obligation.[4] The word "indemnity" is not required to create an indemnity obligation, and conversely, using the word "indemnity" does not guarantee that an indemnity contract was actually created.[5]

To hold an indemnitee harmless for its ***own*** negligent acts, an indemnity agreement must contain "clear and unequivocal" language to this effect.[6] The clear and unequivocal standard does not, however, require the contract to expressly state that one party will indemnify the other party for the other party's own negligence.[7] In a commercial setting, this intent may be demonstrated by broad language holding another harmless against liability generally, such as "party A will indemnify and hold harmless party B from and against all claims and liabilities[.]"[8]

In worker's compensation actions, courts will allow an action by a third party against an employer for injuries to an employee if based upon an express contractual indemnity provision, despite the immunity provided by the Colorado Workers' Compensation Act.[9]

2. EXCEPTIONS TO GENERAL RULES OF CONTRACTUAL INDEMNITY

For construction contracts involving public entities, Colorado Revised Statutes § 13-50.5-102 states that indemnification agreements that purport to indemnify a party for that party's own negligence are void as against public policy.[10] In 2007, the Colorado Legislature passed Colorado Revised Statutes § 13-21-111.5(6), which states that any provision in *any* construction contract that purports to require a party to indemnity, insure, or defend another party for the other party's own negligence is void as against public policy and unenforceable.[11] A provision requiring indemnification of the indemnitee's negligence, however, might not automatically void the indemnity agreement. In *Sterling Const. Mgmt., LLC v. Steadfast Ins. Co.,*

1. *See* Pub. Serv. Co. of Colo. v. United Cable TV of Jeffco, Inc., 829 P.2d 1280, 1284 (Colo. 1992).
2. *See* May Dep't Stores Co. v. Univ. Hills, Inc., 824 P.2d 100, 101 (Colo. App. 1991).
3. *See* Trosper v. Wilkerson, 764 P.2d 375, 376 (Colo. App. 1988).
4. *See* Williams v. White Mtn. Constr. Co., Inc., 749 P.2d 423, 426 (Colo. 1988).
5. *See id.*
6. *See* Constable v. Northglenn, LLC, 248 P.3d 714, 716 (Colo. 2011).
7. *See id.*; *Pub. Serv.*, 829 P.2d at 1284.
8. *See Constable*, 248 P.3d at 716; *Pub. Serv.*, 829 P.2d at 1284.
9. *See* United Cable TV of Jeffco Inc. v. Montgomery LC, Inc., 942 P.2d 1230, 1233 (Colo. App. 1996); Borroel v. Lakeshore, Inc., 618 F. Supp. 354, 359 (D. Colo. 1985).
10. *See* Colo. Rev. Stat. § 13-50.5-102 (2018).
11. *See* Colo. Rev. Stat. § 13-21-111.5(6)(b) (2018).

the District of Colorado found that an indemnity provision requiring indemnification for the indemnitee's own negligence was not void under § 13-31-111.5(6)(b) because the particular claims at issue in the case were caused by the indemnitor's negligence.[12] No Colorado state court has had a chance yet to address this issue or otherwise interpret § 13-31-111.5(6).

Contractual provisions that purport to indemnify a party for its intentional wrongdoing are against public policy, and Colorado courts will not enforce such provisions, even if one party has detrimentally relied upon the contract.[13] For example, if a person breaches a fiduciary duty, she will not be entitled to enforce an indemnity provision and obtain indemnification for her wrongful acts.[14]

Parental indemnity provisions (i.e., agreements whereby a parent agrees to indemnify another party for injuries or damages suffered by the parent's child) were previously held to violate public policy intended to protect minors and avoid conflicts of interest between a minor and his or her parent or guardian.[15] Parental indemnity provisions are now permitted by statute; however, parental indemnity provisions that purport to waive claims for a willful or wanton, reckless, or grossly negligent act or omission are still void and unenforceable.[16]

3. INDEMNITY AGREEMENTS AS INSURED CONTRACTS

Colorado courts recognize that an indemnity agreement generally falls within the term "liability assumed in a contract" as used in the exclusion for contractually assumed liability in the form commercial general liability (CGL) policy.[17] Colorado courts, however, have not addressed whether an indemnity agreement falls within the "insured contract" or "incidental contract" exception to the exclusion for contractually assumed liability in the form CGL policy.

4. OPERATION OF AN AGREEMENT TO INDEMNIFY REFERRING TO OR REQUIRING INSURANCE

Mutual agreements to shift the risk of loss to insurance are valid under Colorado law.[18] This type of agreement can take various forms.

In *Steamboat Development Corp. v. Bacjac Industries, Inc.*, the court found that an agreement between an owner and a contractor that required the owner to provide insurance for the full value of the work was sufficient to shift the loss to the owner's insurer, as the agreement "mirrors the parties' intent to provide mutual exculpation" from the incurred loss.[19]

In *Town of Silverton v. The Phoenix Heat Source System, Inc.*, the court found that a waiver-of-subrogation provision that referred to property insurance obtained by the owner placed the owner and contractor in the position of co-insureds on a policy of first-party property insurance.[20] In that case, the court found that the waiver of subrogation expressed the parties' agreement to exculpate each other from liability and to look solely to the owner's insurance for recovery.[21]

---

12. Sterling Const. Mgmt., LLC v. Steadfast Ins. Co., 2011 WL 3903074, at *8–10 (D. Colo. Sept. 6, 2011).
13. *See* Equitex, Inc. v. Ungar, 60 P.3d 746, 753 (Colo. App. 2002); Bohrer v. Church Mut. Ins. Co., 965 P. 2d 1258, 1262 (Colo. 1998).
14. *See Equitex*, 60 P.3d at 751–53.
15. *See* Cooper v. Aspen Skiing Co., 48 P.3d 1229, 1237 (Colo. 2002).
16. Colo. Rev. Stat. § 13-22-107.
17. Weger v. United Fire and Cas. Co., 796 P.2d 72, 74 (Colo. App. 1990).
18. Steamboat Development Corp. v. Bacjac Industries, Inc., 701 P.2d 127, 129 (Colo. App. 1985).
19. *Id.*
20. Town of Silverton v. The Phoenix Heat Source System, Inc., 948 P.2d 9, 12 (Colo. App. 1997).
21. *Id.*

In *Richmond v. Grabowksi,* the court read a provision that insurance obtained by the owner "shall include the interest of the Owner, the Contractor, Subcontractor . . . and their work" as an intent to include the subcontractor as a beneficiary of the owner's insurance obligation.[22]

In *Hartford Insurance Co. v. CMC Builders, Inc.,* a contractor agreed to indemnify the owner, but the agreement stated that any loss of property would be covered by insurance procured by the owner.[23] The court found that the owner's obligation to obtain insurance to cover a specific loss was an exception to the indemnification agreement. The court reasoned that the exception's purpose was to relieve the contractor of liability for the specific peril insured against and to require the owner to protect itself through insurance.[24]

Colorado law permits a construction contract to require the purchase of additional-insured coverage for the indemnitee.[25] Except in the case of builder's risk insurance, however, a construction contract can only require the purchase of additional-insured coverage for liability arising from the acts or omissions of the indemnitor.[26] Any provision in a construction agreement that requires a party to purchase insurance covering the other party for liability resulting from the other party's own negligence is void as against public policy.[27]

Colorado courts have not directly addressed the extent to which an insurer's obligations to an indemnitee pursuant to an additional-insured endorsement interact with the insured's underlying agreement to indemnify the additional insured.

22. Richmond v. Grabowksi, 781 P.2d 192, 195–96 (Colo. App. 1989).

23. Hartford Ins. Co. v. CMC Builders, Inc., 752 P.2d 590 (Colo. App. 1988).

24. *Id.*

25. *See* Colo. Rev. Stat. § 13-21-111.5(6)(d)(I).

26. *See id.*

27. *See id.* § 13-21-111.5(6)(b), (d)(I); Higby Crane Servs., LLC v. Nat. Helium, LLC, 703 F. App'x 687, 691 (10th Cir. 2017).

Connecticut

John Malloy
LeClair Ryan

1. GENERAL RULES OF CONTRACTUAL INDEMNITY

As a general matter, absent a statutory prohibition to the contrary and subject to limitations on indemnitees being indemnified for their own negligence, Connecticut courts enforce and uphold indemnification agreements. Under Connecticut law, indemnity agreements are those agreements that "protect the indemnitee against claims asserted by third parties against the indemnitee."[1] Connecticut courts draw a distinction between agreements that indemnify for "loss" and agreements that indemnify for "liability," although the courts recognize that an indemnity agreement may require the indemnitor to indemnify the indemnitee for both loss and liability.[2] This distinction is important in determining when a cause of action under an indemnity agreement accrues, and therefore when the statute of limitations begins to run.[3] With respect to indemnity agreements that indemnify against "liability," "the cause of action arises as soon as liability is incurred," while a cause of action to enforce an agreement that indemnifies against "loss" does not arise "until the indemnitee has actually incurred the loss" by paying amounts owed to the third party.[4]

Connecticut law allows a party to be indemnified for its own negligence, but such agreements are disfavored.[5] In order for a party to be indemnified for its own negligence, the contract must express that agreement in clear and unequivocal language.[6] Such agreements generally are not considered to be against public policy, except to the extent they implicate an express statutory prohibition or public interest.[7]

1. Amoco Oil Co. v. Liberty Auto & Elec. Co., 810 A.2d 259, 263–64 (Conn. 2002) ("The logic and rationale underlying our indemnity case law are based on the premise that an action for indemnification is one in which one party seeks reimbursement from another party for losses incurred in connection with the first party's liability to a third party"). *But see* Helming & Co., P.C. v. RTR Techs., Inc., 76 F. Supp. 3d 363, 369 (D. Mass. 2015) (suggesting that *Amoco* did not intend to limit indemnity agreements to third-party claims).

2. *Id.* ("[L]oss in the context of indemnity is the payment that discharges a liability . . . . [U]nder an agreement to indemnify against loss only, it is theoretically impossible for an indemnitee to have an actionable claim against the indemnitor until the indemnitee actually has paid something he is legally obligated to pay . . . . Conversely, an action to enforce an agreement to indemnify against liability only would accrue as soon as an indemnitee becomes liable to a third party.").

3. *Id.* Under Conn. Gen. Stat. § 52-598a, "an action for indemnification may be brought within three years from the date of the determination of the action against the party which is seeking indemnification by either judgment or settlement."

4. *Id.*

5. *See* Hanks v. Powder Ridge Rest. Corp., 885 A.2d 734, 739 (Conn. 2005) (discussing exculpatory clauses and noting that they are only enforceable if they are not contrary to public policy and must be set forth "plainly and precisely," and further noting that "[t]he question of whether a contract is against public policy is a question of law dependent on the circumstances of the particular case, over which an appellate court has unlimited review"); Comind, Companhia De Seguros v. Sikorsky Aircraft, 116 F.R.D. 397 (D. Conn. 1987). *See also* Dow-Westbrook, Inc. v. Candlewood Equine Practice, LLC, 989 A.2d 1075, 1082 (Conn. App. 2010) ("[O]ur courts have recognized the enforceability of hold harmless provisions releasing a defendant from liability for his own negligence where the parties to the contract are both commercial entities").

6. *See* Burkle v. Car & Truck Leasing Co., Inc., 467 A.2d 1255, 1257 (Conn. App. 1983) (use of the phrase "any and all" sufficient to allow indemnitee to be indemnified for its own negligence). *See also* Hyson v. White Water Mtn. Resorts of Connecticut, 829 A.2d 827 (Conn. 2003); United Aircraft Corp. v. David H. Mackenzie, Inc., 196 F. Supp. 933, 935 (D. Conn. 1961).

7. *See Hanks*, 885 A.2d at 739; *Burkle*, 467 A.2d at 1257; *see also* Local 1035 v. Pepsi Allied Bottlers, Inc., 99 F. Supp. 2d 219 (D. Conn. 2000) (indemnity agreement void under Fair Labor Standards Act and Connecticut counterpart).

2. EXCEPTIONS TO GENERAL RULES OF CONTRACTUAL INDEMNITY

The one significant exception to the general rule that express contracts of indemnity are enforceable under Connecticut law is a prohibition against certain indemnity provisions in construction agreements.[8] Under Connecticut General Statutes § 52-572k, any agreement in a contract relating to construction that purports to indemnify a party for its own negligence is unenforceable.[9] Section 52-572k provides, in relevant part, as follows:

> Any covenant, promise, agreement or understanding entered into in connection with or collateral to a contract or agreement relative to the construction, alteration, repair or maintenance of any building, structure or appurtenances thereto including moving, demolition and excavating connected therewith, that purports to indemnify or hold harmless the promisee against liability for damage arising out of bodily injury to persons or damage to property caused by or resulting from the negligence of such promisee, such promisee's agents or employees, is against public policy and void, provided this section shall not affect the validity of any insurance contract, workers' compensation agreement or other agreement issued by a licensed insurer.[10]

In 2001, the legislature amended this statute by substituting the word "negligence" for the words "sole negligence," thereby broadening its reach.[11] Since this statutory revision, few cases have examined its application. The courts have yet to determine whether the provisions of the 2001 amendment of § 52-572k will be applied retroactively.[12]

The statute also only applies to negligence claims. Thus, for example, a defendant could seek indemnification pursuant to a written agreement relating to the removal of underground storage tanks because the claims against the defendant (breach of contract, tortious interference, breach of the implied covenant of good faith, and violations of the Connecticut Uniform Trade Practices Act) did not state a claim for negligence, but instead sounded in breach of contract.[13]

3. INDEMNITY AGREEMENTS AS INSURED CONTRACTS

There is very little case law in Connecticut addressing whether contractual indemnity agreements qualify as "insured contracts," and thus are within an exception to the "contractual liability" exclusion commonly found in general liability policies. Several unreported state trial court decisions suggest that Connecticut law appears to consider indemnity agreements to broadly fall within the scope of the exclusion, with indemnity agreements by which one assumes the tort liability of another to fall within the exception. Thus, for example, an agreement to indemnify another for breach of a contract would likely be excluded in Connecticut, whereas a contractual agreement to indemnify another for a tort claim by a third party would be within the scope of the exception to the exclusion.[14]

---

8. CONN. GEN. STAT. § 52-572k (2003).

9. *Id. See* Guild v. Exxon Corp., 81 F. Supp. 2d 377, 381 (D. Conn. 1999) (citing House of Representatives Proceedings, 1997, Vol. 20, Part 10, 3864-4326, p. 4298).

10. CONN. GEN. STAT. § 52-572k(a) (2003).

11. *See* Costin v. Bhandari Constructors & Consultants, Inc., 285 F. Supp. 2d 165 (D. Conn. 2003); Parker v. Konover Constr. Corp., 2003 Conn. Super. LEXIS 1815, No. CV-99-90911-S (Conn. Super. Ct. June 24, 2003) (unpublished).

12. *See Costin*, 285 F. Supp. 2d at 171 n.5.

13. *See Guild*, 81 F. Supp. 2d at 381.

14. *See* Nationwide Mut. Ins. Co. v. Lydall Woods Colonial Vill., Inc., 2003 Conn. Super. LEXIS 1956, No. X04-CV-02-126640-S (Conn. Super. Ct. July 14, 2003) (unreported) ("The contract liability assumption exclusion, as articulated in cases in state and federal courts around the country, is uniformly considered to apply to those situations where an insured agrees to indemnify a third party pursuant to contract, not tortious conduct as it relates to duties pursuant to a contract under which an insured was established and from which it draws its legal existence.").

4. OPERATION OF AN AGREEMENT TO INDEMNIFY REFERRING TO OR REQUIRING INSURANCE

Parties to a contract may waive their rights to recover against each other and agree instead to look to insurance for coverage for any damage or harm resulting from the subject of their agreement.[15] Such a waiver clause bars recovery to the extent of insurance coverage.[16] Additionally, an agreement by contracting parties to waive rights against one another will bar an insurer's subrogation claim absent a contrary provision in the insurance policy.[17] For example, one Connecticut Superior Court decision held that language obligating a contractor to procure liability insurance for damage to a construction project and the owner to purchase property insurance constituted a waiver of "all" claims for damage occurring during a construction project to the extent that the owner had obtained insurance under the contract.[18]

Notably, that decision rejected the argument that the contractor was an additional insured under the contract. According to the court, "[a]bsent any express agreement between the parties, the court will not attach meaning to silence by reading into the contract [i.e., an obligation to procure insurance for the benefit of the other party,] what could have been expressed but was not."[19] In other words, Connecticut courts have recognized the important distinction between an indemnity obligation on the one hand and a contractual obligation to name another party as an additional insured on a policy on the other hand.[20]

15. *See* Stop & Shop Supermarket Co. v. ABCO Refrigeration Supply Corp., 842 A.2d 1194, 1198 (Conn. Super. 2003), *petition to appeal dismissed,* 853 A.2d 523 (Conn. 2004).

16. *See id.*

17. *Id.* at 1198 ("An explicit clause to protect the insurer's right of subrogation at all times could have been included in the policy, but was not.").

18. *See Stop & Shop*, 842 A.2d at 1198 (citing *Burkle, supra* note 6).

19. *Id.* at 1200.

20. *Id.*

Delaware

Jennifer Wasson
Potter Anderson & Corroon LLP

1. GENERAL RULES OF CONTRACTUAL INDEMNITY

Contractual indemnity is enforceable in Delaware where one party expressly contracts to indemnify the other for the liability involved.[1] The indemnity clause must be clear and unequivocal:[2] "[a] contract of indemnity is construed to give effect to the parties' intent; in other words, only losses which reasonably appear to have been intended by the parties are compensable under such contract."[3] Attorneys' fees and expenses are recoverable under an indemnification agreement if they are incurred as a result of defending claims that are the subject of the duty to indemnify.[4] This is true even where the indemnity clause does not expressly mention attorneys' fees, or where the court awards only partial contractual indemnity.[5]

With the exception of construction-related contracts (*see* Section 2, *infra*), agreements under which the indemnitee is indemnified against its own prospective negligence are valid.[6] The contract language, however, must clearly show the indemnitor's specific intent to undertake that obligation. "The test is whether the contract language specifically focused attention on the fact that by the agreement the indemnitor was assuming liability for the indemnitee's own negligence."[7] Moreover, such contracts are not favored at law, and where possible, those contracts will be construed to not confer immunity from liability.[8]

2. EXCEPTIONS TO GENERAL RULES OF CONTRACTUAL INDEMNITY

Delaware Code Annotated tit. 6, § 2704 prohibits parties entering into construction contracts performed in the state from transferring the risk of their own negligence to another party through an agreement to indemnify.[9] The statute provides:

> A covenant, promise, agreement or understanding in, or in connection with or collateral to, a contract or agreement (including but not limited to a contract or

1. Shiles v. Reed Trucking Co., 1995 Del. Super. LEXIS 563, at *7 (Del. Super. Ct. 1995) (quoting Ianire v. Univ. of Delaware, 255 A.2d 687, 692 (Del. Super. Ct. 1969)).

2. All-State Investigation & Sec. Agency, Inc. v. Turner Constr. Co., 301 A.2d 273, 275 (Del. Super. Ct. 1972); *see also* Sweetman v. Strescon, Indus., Inc., 389 A.2d 1319, 1321 (Del. Super. Ct. 1978).

3. Oliver B. Cannon & Son, Inc. v. Dorr-Oliver, Inc., 394 A.2d 1160, 1165 (Del. 1978).

4. Delle Donne & Assocs., LLP v. Millar Elevator Serv. Co., 840 A.2d 1244, 1255 (Del. 2004); *Oliver B. Cannon & Son, Inc.*, 394 A.2d at 1165; E. Mem'l Consultants, Inc. v. Gracelawn Mem'l Park, Inc., 364 A.2d 821, 825 (Del. 1976).

5. *Delle Donne & Assocs.*, 840 A.2d at 1254–55; *see also* Precision Air, Inc. v. Standard Chlorine of Delaware, Inc., 654 A.2d 403, 407–09 (Del. 1995).

6. Del. Code Ann. tit. 6, § 2704(a) (2017); Hollingsworth v. Chrysler Corp., 208 A.2d 61, 64 (Del. Super. Ct. 1965).

7. *Sweetman*, 389 A.2d at 1321; *see also* Riverbend Cmty., LLC v. Green Stone Eng'g, LLC, 55 A.3d 330, 336 (Del. 2012) ("It is still the law in Delaware that a contract provision waiving prospective negligence 'must be crystal clear and unequivocal' to insulate a party from liability for possible future negligence." (citations omitted)).

8. Blum v. Kauffman, 297 A.2d 48, 49 (Del. 1972).

9. Del. Code Ann. tit. 6, § 2704(a) (2017); J.S. Alberici Constr. Co., Inc. v. Mid-West Conveyor Co., Inc., 750 A.2d 518 (Del. 2000). Initially, Del. Code Ann. tit. 6, § 2704(a) was thought only to apply to owners and affiliated preconstruction professionals who furnish plans, designs, and specifications, but in 1988, § 2704(a) was broadened to include anyone in a subcontractor/contractor relationship in the construction context.

> agreement with the State, any county, municipality or political subdivision of the State, or with any agency, commission, department, body or board of any of them, as well as any contract or agreement with a private party or entity) relative to the construction, alteration, repair or maintenance in the State of a road, highway, driveway, street, bridge or entrance or walkway of any type constructed thereon in the State, and building, structure, appurtenance or appliance in the State, including without limiting the generality of the foregoing, the moving, demolition and excavating connected therewith, purporting to indemnify or hold harmless the promisee or indemnitee or others, or their agents, servants and employees, for damages arising from liability for bodily injury or death to persons or damage to property caused partially or solely by, or resulting partially or solely from, or arising partially or solely out of the negligence of such promisee or indemnitee or others than the promisor or indemnitor, or its subcontractors, agents, servants or employees, is against public policy and is void and unenforceable, even where such covenant, promise, agreement or understanding is crystal clear and unambiguous in obligating the promisor or indemnitor to indemnify or hold harmless the promise or indemnity from liability resulting from such promisee's or indemnitee's own negligence. This section shall apply to all phases of the preconstruction, construction, repairs and maintenance described in this subsection, and nothing in this section shall be construed to limit its application to preconstruction professionals such as designers, planners and architects; provided, however, that this section shall not apply to any obligation owed to the Department of Transportation pursuant to a contract awarded under Title 17 or Chapter 69 of Title 29.[10]

Consequently, § 2704(a) renders indemnity-for-negligence provisions in construction contracts unenforceable and void as a matter of public policy, no matter how clearly and unequivocally expressed. However, Delaware Code Annotated tit. 6, § 2704(b), referred to as the "insurance saving provision," exempts from § 2704(a)'s application insurance policies that insure "against losses or damages from any causes whatsoever," including an indemnitee's own negligence.[11] Similarly, § 2704(c) renders § 2704(a)'s anti-indemnification provision inapplicable to partnership agreements, limited liability company agreements, trust agreements, certificates of incorporation, and corporate bylaws.[12]

Although Delaware's worker's compensation law is the exclusive remedy available to a claimant to secure compensation for the injuries sustained as a result of a work-related incident, third-party actions against employers may be brought on a contractual theory of recovery based on express or implied indemnification.[13]

3. INDEMNITY AGREEMENTS AS INSURED CONTRACTS

An insured's agreement to indemnify a third party is an "insured contract" under Delaware law.[14] Whether an indemnitee seeks coverage from an insurer because it is an additional insured on the policy or because the indemnity agreement is an insured contract binding the insurer is a "distinction without a difference."[15] Furthermore, if the policy provides

10. Del. Code Ann. tit. 6, § 2704(a) (2017).

11. *Id.* at § 2704(b) ("Nothing in subsection (a) of this section shall be construed to void or render unenforceable policies of insurance issued by duly authorized insurance companies and insuring against losses or damages from any causes whatsoever."); Chrysler Corp. v. Merrell & Garaguso, Inc., 796 A.2d 648, 653 (Del. 2002); *see also* Section 4, *infra.*

12. Del. Code Ann. tit. 6, § 2704(c) (2017).

13. Farrall v. Armstrong Cork Co., 457 A.2d 763, 766 (Del. Super. Ct. 1983).

14. *See generally* Daimler Chrysler Corp. v. Pa. Nat'l Mut. Cas. Ins. Co., 2004 Del. Super. LEXIS 45 (Del. Super. Ct. 2004); Hercules Inc. v. Amec Virginia, 1999 Del. Super. LEXIS 32 (Del. Super. Ct. 1999); Steadfast Ins. Co. v. Eon Labs Mfg., Inc., 1998 Del. Super. LEXIS 681 (Del. Super. Ct. 1998).

15. *Daimler Chrysler Corp.*, 2004 Del. Super. LEXIS 45, at *7.

coverage for an indemnitor's insured contract, then insurer is obligated to afford that coverage even if the underlying indemnity is void for public policy.[16] "[T]he insurer cannot hide behind § 2704(a) [voiding indemnification by a subcontractor] and refuse to pay coverage 'to any insured, however identified or designated.'"[17] The Delaware Superior Court has found, however, that an insurer should be provided notice of its potential liability for the negligence of a third-party indemnitee so that the additional risk may be taken into account.[18] That notice may be given by naming the indemnitee as an additional insured on the policy or by informing the insurer of the insured contract.[19]

4. OPERATION OF AN AGREEMENT TO INDEMNIFY REFERRING TO OR REQUIRING INSURANCE

Under certain circumstances a contractual requirement to purchase insurance may be unenforceable; however, once such insurance is secured, the terms of the insurance policy are enforceable against the insurer.[20] Specifically, while Delaware Code Annotated tit. 6, § 2704(a) invalidates contract provisions requiring indemnification for another's negligence,[21] § 2704(b)'s insurance saving provision preserves the enforceability of the insurance "against losses or damages from any causes whatsoever."[22]

While this outcome has been challenged as constituting an "end run" around the clear non-indemnification policy set forth in § 2704(a), Delaware courts have concluded that a different outcome would negate the legislative purpose behind § 2704(b)'s insurance savings provisions.[23] The insurance savings provision has meaning "only if it cannot be used as a shield by insurers to decline coverage for insurance once purchased and duly issued to any insured, however identified or designated."[24] Consequently, regardless of the original validity of a contractual provision requiring the purchase of insurance where a policy is obtained and insurance coverage exists, the insurer may be bound to provide coverage.[25]

16. *Id.*; Chrysler Corp. v. Merrell & Garaguso, Inc., 796 A.2d 648, 653 (Del. 2002).
17. *Daimler Chrysler Corp.*, 2004 Del. Super. LEXIS 45, at *6–7 (emphasis and citations omitted).
18. *Id.*
19. *Id.*
20. *Chrysler Corp.*, 796 A.2d at 649–50, 653.
21. Del. Code Ann. tit. 6, § 2704(a) (2017).
22. Del. Code Ann. tit. 6, § 2704(b).
23. *Chrysler*, 796 A.2d at 653.
24. *Id.*
25. *Id.*

District of Columbia

James P. Bobotek
Pillsbury Winthrop Shaw Pittman LLP

1. GENERAL RULES OF CONTRACTUAL INDEMNITY

In the District of Columbia, the parties' intent will be enforced as long as the language of the indemnification clause is sufficiently broad and clear.[1] Indemnity agreements are narrowly construed, however, so as not to read into them obligations that the parties never intended to assume.[2] In order to permit a negligent party to obtain contractual indemnity, a "reviewing court must be firmly convinced that such an interpretation reflects the intention of the parties."[3] This standard emanates from the law governing exculpation agreements, which cannot be enforced unless they are "spelled out with such clarity that the intent to negate the usual consequences of tortious conduct is made plain."[4] For example, if the indemnity agreement is ambiguous regarding an indemnitee's sole negligence, the indemnitee may not seek indemnity.

The determination of whether or not an indemnity agreement is ambiguous is made by the court, and is not submitted to the jury.[5] "[N]o particular form or words are needed" to demonstrate that the contracting parties intended to permit a negligent party to recover contractual indemnity.[6] Rather, the scope of an indemnity agreement "may be so broad and comprehensive that although it contains no express stipulation indemnifying against a party's own negligence, it accomplishes the same purpose."[7] In such cases, "the presumption is that if the parties had intended some limitation of the all-embracing language, it would be expressly stated."[8]

2. EXCEPTIONS TO GENERAL RULES OF CONTRACTUAL INDEMNITY

Indemnification agreements for one's own negligence are enforceable in the District of Columbia as long as they contain clear and unambiguous language. In determining whether indemnity agreements unambiguously apply to liability for an indemnitee's own negligence, District of Columbia courts carefully and closely analyze the agreement's language. The result often hinges on the inclusion or modification of only a few words. For instance, the District of Columbia Court of Appeals found that an agreement requiring indemnification for "any and all claims . . . arising out of or resulting from or in connection with the execution of the work" encompasses the indemnitee's sole or concurrent negligence.[9]

---

1. *See* N.P.P. Contrs. v. John Canning & Co., 715 A.2d 139, 141–43 (D.C. 1998); Grunley Constr. Co. v. Conway Corp., 676 A.2d 477 (D.C. 1996); Rivers & Bryan, Inc. v. HBE Corp., 628 A.2d 631, 635–36 (D.C. 1993); Princemont Constr. Corp. v. B&O R.R. Co., 131 A.2d 877 (D.C. 1957).

2. *See, e.g.*, Am. Building Maint. Co. v. L'Enfant Plaza Prop., 655 A.2d 858, 861 (D.C. 1995) (finding that "[t]here is no liability to indemnify unless it is plainly spelled out in the contract").

3. W.M. Schlosser Co., Inc. v. Maryland Drywall Co., Inc., 673 A.2d 647, 653 (D.C. 1996).

4. Maiatico v. Hot Shoppes, Inc., 287 F.2d 349, 350–51 (D.C. Cir. 1961); Moore v. Waller, 930 A.2d 176, 181 (D.C. 2007). *See also* Moses-Ecco Co. v. Roscoe-Ajax Corp., 320 F.2d 685, 687–88 (D.C. Cir. 1963) (analogizing indemnity agreements to exculpation agreements).

5. *Rivers & Bryan, Inc.*, 628 A.2d at 635; Harris v. Howard Univ., Inc., 28 F. Supp. 2d 1, 14 (D.D.C. 1998).

6. *W.M. Schlosser Co., Inc.*, 673 A.2d at 654 (quoting *Moses-Ecco Co.*, 320 F.2d at 688).

7. Princemont Const. Corp. v. B&O R.R. Co., 131 A.2d 877, 878 (D.C. 1957).

8. *Id.*

9. *N.P.P. Contrs.*, 715 A.2d at 140–42; *W.M. Schlosser Co., Inc.*, 673 A.2d at 653.

Likewise, in *Moses-Ecco Co. v. Roscoe-Ajax Corp.*, a subcontractor was required to indemnify a general contractor under a provision requiring indemnification "against any loss, because of injury or damage to persons or property arising or resulting from the performance of this contract."[10]

As another example, in *Bland v. L'Enfant Plaza North, Inc.*,[11] a general contractor was entitled to indemnification against its own sole negligence based upon the following contractual language:

> The subcontractor agrees to indemnify and save harmless the owner and general contractor against loss or expense by reason of liability imposed upon the owner or general contractor for damage because of bodily injuries . . . accidentally sustained by a person . . . *whether or not such injuries . . . are due or claimed to be due to any negligence of the subcontractor, his employees, his agents or servants*.[12]

The court found that this language encompassed liability for the indemnitee's sole negligence because any other interpretation "would largely strip the clause of any meaning." In other words, since the indemnity agreement applied to a case where the subcontractor was not negligent, and in that case the general contractor could be subject to liability only as a result of its own sole negligence, the indemnity agreement must require the subcontractor to indemnify the general contractor for its own sole negligence.[13]

On the other hand, in *District of Columbia v. Murtaugh*,[14] a contract providing for indemnity "against any and all claims or liability arising from or based on, or as a consequence or result of, any act, omission or default of the Contractor . . . in the performance of, or in connection with, any work required, contemplated, or performed under the contract" was not sufficiently broad to encompass indemnity against the District's own negligence. The court relied on this holding in *District of Columbia v. Royal*,[15] a case interpreting an identical clause and reaching the same result. The *Royal* court, in turn, relied on *District of Columbia v. C. F. & B.*,[16] which held that an agreement requiring a contractor to "indemnify the government from any and all claims . . . to which said government may be subjected at any time . . . on account of any injuries to persons or damage to property or premises that occur as a result of any act or omission of the Principal" did not provide for indemnification against the District's own negligence.

Under District of Columbia law, no party may limit its own liability for gross negligence, willful acts, or fraud; such agreements are void as against public policy.[17] Similarly, District of Columbia courts refuse, on public policy grounds, to enforce indemnity provisions "where there were allegations and showing of gross negligence, recklessness, willful and wanton conduct, intentional misconduct or conduct so serious as to warrant the imposition of punitive damages" on the part of the indemnitee.[18]

---

10. 320 F.2d at 687–88.
11. 473 F.2d 156, 157 (D.C. Cir. 1972).
12. *Id.* (emphasis added).
13. *Id.*; *see also Princemont Const. Corp.*, 131 A.2d 877.
14. District of Columbia v. Murtaugh, 728 A.2d 1237, 1245 (D.C. 1999).
15. District of Columbia v. Royal, 465 A.2d 367 (D.C. 1983).
16. District of Columbia v. C. F. & B., 442 F. Supp. 251, 254 (D.D.C. 1977).
17. Brown v. 1301 K Street Ltd. P'ship, 31 A.3d 902 (D.C. 2011).
18. Nat'l R.R. Passenger Corp. v. Consolidated Rail Corp., 698 F. Supp. 951, 972 (D.D.C. 1988), *vacated on other grounds*, 892 F.2d 1066, 1067 (D.C. Cir. 1989).

3. INDEMNITY AGREEMENTS AS INSURED CONTRACTS

District of Columbia courts have not addressed whether an agreement to indemnify is an "insured contract" for purposes of the exclusion for contractually assumed liability in the ISO form commercial general liability (CGL) policy. In these circumstances, District of Columbia courts look to Maryland law. Although Maryland statutes and case law do not constitute the law of the District of Columbia, courts customarily look to Maryland law as "especially persuasive authority" in determining how the District of Columbia courts would rule on a question of law.[19]

Under Maryland law, an insurer's obligation to defend its insured under the insured contract provision is determined by the allegations in the underlying lawsuit.[20] Any doubts as to whether the allegations of a complaint trigger an insurer's duty to defend should be resolved in favor of the insured.[21] It is also established that courts should construe "insured contract" provisions broadly, in favor of coverage.[22]

4. OPERATION OF AN AGREEMENT TO INDEMNIFY REFERRING TO OR REQUIRING INSURANCE

District of Columbia courts recognize a distinction between indemnity agreements and contractual requirements to obtain insurance. In *Hooks v. Southeast Construction Corp.*,[23] a subcontractor agreed to two separate obligations in the same paragraph of its contract. The first two sentences of the clause dealt, respectively, with (a) the obligations to furnish liability insurance and worker's compensation insurance and (b) the obligation to indemnify. Under the first sentence, the subcontractor was required "to carry public liability insurance protecting [itself] and [the general contractor]." In the second sentence, the subcontractor agreed to indemnify the general contractor against liability growing out of the subcontractor's "act, omission, or negligence." The court found that the two sentences must logically be read as requiring different undertakings by the subcontractor. The first sentence, addressing liability insurance, pledges the subcontractor to provide insurance protecting the general contractor against liability for damage to personal property or for personal injuries to the general contractor's nonemployees, including the public. In the second sentence, the indemnification agreement was imposed to protect the general contractor against losses due to its own negligence that might not be paid under the insurance policies due to the insolvency of the insurer or for some other reason.[24] The court found these two obligations to be separate, and the requirement to indemnify the general contractor for the subcontractor's negligence was not a limitation on the insurance obligation.

---

19. Napoleon v. Heard, 455 A.2d 901, 903 (D.C. 1983); *see also* Conesco Indus., Ltd. v. Conforti & Eisele, Inc., 627 F.2d 312, 315–16 (D.C. Cir. 1980) (finding that "[s]ince there is no District law on point, we should look to Maryland law first . . . because the District of Columbia derives its common law from that state and because District of Columbia courts have in the past looked to Maryland law for guidance"); *see also* Potomac Plaza Terraces v. QSC Prods., 868 F. Supp. 346, 352 (D.D.C. 1994).

20. Brohawn v. Transamerica Ins. Co., 347 A.2d 842 (Md. 1975).

21. Aetna Cas. & Sur. Co. v. Cochran, 651 A.2d 859, 863–64 (Md. 1995); Utica Mut. Ins. Co. v. Miller, 746 A.2d 935, 940–41 (Md. Ct. Spec. App. 2000), *cert. denied*, 753 A.2d 3 (Md. 2000).

22. Mid-Continent Cas. Co. v. Swift Energy Co., 206 F.3d 487, 492–93 (5th Cir. 2000).

23. Hooks v. Se. Constr. Corp., 538 F.2d 431, 432–33 (D.C. Cir. 1976).

24. *Id.* at 433–34.

Florida

Steve Rapp
Weinberg, Wheeler, Hudgins, Gunn & Dial, LLC

1. GENERAL RULES OF CONTRACTUAL INDEMNITY

Contractual agreements to indemnify another are valid and enforceable in Florida under certain circumstances. However, "contracts of indemnification which attempt to indemnify a party against its own wrongful acts are viewed with disfavor in Florida."[1] Further, "Florida public policy prohibits liability insurance coverage for punitive damages assessed against a person because of his own wrongful conduct."[2] However, Florida public policy allows liability insurance coverage for punitive damages when the insured is not personally at fault and is instead vicariously liable.[3]

A contract for indemnity will not be construed to indemnify the indemnitee against losses resulting from his or her own sole negligence unless such intention is expressed in clear and unequivocal terms.[4] This general rule has been extended to include cases where the indemnitor and indemnitee are found to be jointly liable.[5]

An indemnification agreement stated in general terms will not meet the "clear and unequivocal terms" standard and thus will not apply to liability resulting from the sole negligence of the indemnitee.[6] Florida courts have decided that the following clauses are too general to require indemnity for the indemnitee's own negligence: agreements to indemnify "against any and all claims"[7] and in which a lessee assumed "all responsibility for claims asserted by any person" and agreed to hold harmless the lessor.[8] In contrast, Florida courts have ordered indemnification when the indemnitee is partially negligent where a lessee agrees to "indemnify Lessor and save it harmless from suits . . . occasioned wholly or in part by any act or omission of Lessee,"[9] or in an agreement to indemnify for "all suits except those resulting from the indemnitee's sole negligence."[10]

2. EXCEPTIONS TO GENERAL RULES OF CONTRACTUAL INDEMNITY

Florida Statutes § 725.06 bars agreements to indemnify another for its own negligence in the construction context. The statute provides, in pertinent part:

> (2) A construction contract for a public agency or in connection with a public agency's project may require a party to that contract to indemnify and hold

1. Charles Poe Masonry, Inc. v. Spring Lock Scaffolding Rental Equip. Co., 374 So. 2d 487, 489 (Fla. 1979); Royal Palm Hotel Prop., LLC v. Deutsche Lufthansa Aktiengesellschaft, Inc., 133 So. 3d 1108, 1110 (Fla. Dist. Ct. App. 2014).
2. U.S. Concrete Pipe Co. v. Bould, 437 So. 2d 1061, 1064 (Fla. 1983); Morgan Int'l Realty, Inc. v. Dade Underwriters Ins. Agency, 617 So. 2d 455, 459 (Fla. Dist. Ct. App. 1993).
3. *Id.*
4. Univ. Plaza Shopping Ctr., Inc. v. Stewart, 272 So. 2d 507, 509 (Fla. 1973); *Royal Palm Hotel Prop., LLC*, 133 So. 3d at 1110.
5. *Charles Poe Masonry*, 374 So. 2d at 489; Leonard L. Farber Co., Inc. v. Jaksch, 335 So. 2d 847, 848 (Fla. Dist. Ct. App. 1976) (lease requiring indemnity for damage "occasioned wholly or in part by any act or omission of Lessee" required indemnity only where parties were jointly liable).
6. *Univ. Plaza*, 272 So. 2d at 512.
7. Cox Cable Corp. v. Gulf Power Co., 591 So. 2d 627, 629 (Fla. 1992).
8. *Charles Poe Masonry*, 374 So. 2d at 489.
9. Leonard L. Farber Co. v. Jaksch, 335 So. 2d 847 (Fla. Dist. Ct. App. 1976).
10. Dep't of Transp. v. Whitehurst & Sons, Inc., 636 So. 2d 101, 105–06 (Fla. Dist. Ct. App. 1994).

> harmless the other party to the contract, their officers and employees, from liabilities, damages, losses and costs, including, but not limited to, reasonable attorney's fees, *to the extent caused by the negligence, recklessness, or intentional wrongful misconduct of the indemnifying party* and persons employed or utilized by the indemnifying party in the performance of the construction contract.
>
> (3) Except as specifically provided in subsection (2), a construction contract for a public agency or in connection with a public agency's project may not require one party to indemnify, defend, or hold harmless the other party, its employees, officers, directors, or agents from any liability, damage, loss, claim, action, or proceeding, and any such contract provision is void as against public policy of this state.[11]

The implication of the statute is clear: an indemnification agreement to indemnify for the indemnitee's own negligence in public agency construction contracts is void.[12] The statute allows indemnification for the indemnitee's own negligence if a reasonable monetary limitation is placed on the agreement that bears a reasonable relationship to the contract and is part of the project documents or bid specifications, if any.[13]

Closely related to the prohibition in Florida Statutes § 725.06 is a statutory prohibition on the indemnification of design professionals. This statute provides:

> (1) Notwithstanding the provisions of s. 725.06, if a design professional provides professional services to or for a public agency, the agency may require in a professional services contract with the design professional that the design professional indemnify and hold harmless the agency, and its officers and employees, from liabilities, damages, losses, and costs, including, but not limited to, reasonable attorneys' fees, *to the extent caused by the negligence, recklessness, or intentionally wrongful conduct of the design professional* and other persons employed or utilized by the design professional in the performance of the contract.
>
> (2) Except as specifically provided in subsection (1), a professional services contract entered into with a public agency may not require that the design professional defend, indemnify, or hold harmless the agency, its employees, officers, directors, or agents from any liability, damage, loss, claim, action, or proceeding, and any such contract provision shall be void as against the public policy of this state.[14]

3. INDEMNITY AGREEMENTS AS INSURED CONTRACTS

Under a general liability policy that affords coverage for an "insured contract," an insured contract includes an insured's agreement to indemnify another.[15] However, an indemnity agreement purporting to indemnify for the indemnitee's own negligence must be clear and

---

11. FLA. STAT. § 725.06 (emphasis added).

12. United Rentals, Inc. v. Mid-Continent Cas. Co., 843 F. Supp. 2d 1309, 1315 (S.D. Fla. 2012) (holding that scissor lift rental agreement was unenforceable to the extent it required indemnification for the indemnitee's own negligence).

13. *Id.*

14. FLA. STAT. § 725.08 (emphasis added); *see* Auto-Owners Ins. Co. v. Ace Elec. Serv., Inc., 648 F. Supp. 2d 1371, 1380 (M.D. Fla. 2009) (explaining that this statute "prevents a public agency from requiring a design professional to indemnify the agency in instances where the design professional is without fault" and holding that an indemnification provision in a design contract may be enforceable if the designer was at fault and the city was not).

15. Florida Mun. Power Agency v. Ohio Cas. Ins. Co., 714 So. 2d 660, 661 (Fla. Dist. Ct. App. 1998) (contract defined "insured contract" as an agreement under which the insured "assume[d] the tort liability of another party to pay for 'bodily injury' or 'property damage'").

unequivocal, and in the absence of such a finding, the indemnitor does not assume the tort liability of another, and there is consequently no "insured contract" to which liability coverage extends.[16]

4. OPERATION OF AN AGREEMENT TO INDEMNIFY REFERRING TO OR REQUIRING INSURANCE

If the parties agree that one will obtain insurance as part of the bargain to shift the loss from both parties to the insurance carrier solely and a loss occurs, it is irrelevant which party was negligent.[17] For example, where a contract contains both a provision that any loss due to the negligence of a contractor shall be borne by that contractor, and a provision that the contractor shall be a named insured jointly with the owner in all policies, the court interprets the contract as having contemplated the shifting of the risk of any party to an insurer, irrespective of negligence.[18] Further, if an owner agrees to provide a contractor with all "necessary insurance," then the owner is required to obtain insurance to protect the parties from *any and all loss*.[19]

In situations where an indemnitor procures liability insurance in connection with an agreement to indemnify, it is possible that the indemnification will not be expanded by the policy of insurance. For example, where a tenant was required to obtain certain minimum levels of liability insurance to cover the landlord, the "insurance coverage does not extend beyond the tenant's liability."[20] Since the tenant was not liable to indemnify for losses caused by the landlord's negligence, neither was the tenant's insurer.[21]

Similarly, where a supplier agreed to indemnify a franchisee for losses except those caused by the franchisee's own negligence and further to obtain liability insurance, the court limited the franchisee's rights to coverage to the extent of the underlying indemnification agreement.[22] In other words, because the indemnification agreement did not cover losses caused by the franchisee's negligence, the existence of the supplier's liability insurance did not require that the insurance cover the franchisee's negligence.[23]

The result is different if the "indemnity language of the contract does not require [the indemnitor] to hold [the indemnitee] harmless for [the indemnitee's] own negligence" and the indemnitee is named as an additional insured; in that case, "the indemnity language of the contract is [not] dispositive of the coverage issue."[24] Rather, the "language of the policy is controlling"[25] and the indemnitee may be entitled to coverage above and beyond what was promised in the underlying indemnification agreement.

---

16. Allianz Ins. Co. v. Goldcoast Partners, Inc., 684 So. 2d 336, 337 (Fla. Dist. Ct. App. 1996).

17. Cont'l Ins. Co. v. Kennerson, 661 So. 2d 325, 327 (Fla. Dist. Ct. App. 1995).

18. Smith v. Ryan, 142 So. 2d 139 (Fla. Dist. Ct. App. 1962).

19. Hous. Inv. Corp. of Fla. v. Carris, 389 So. 2d 689 (Fla. Dist. Ct. App. 1980).

20. *Univ. Plaza*, 272 So. 2d at 512.

21. *Id.*

22. *Allianz Ins. Co.*, 684 So. 2d at 337.

23. *Id.* The *Allianz* case, unfortunately, raises more questions than it answers. The court limited the indemnitee's coverage from insurance in this case to the limits set forth in the underlying indemnity agreement. However, the agreement between the supplier and the franchisee required the supplier to name the franchisee as *an additional* insured (which based on the *Container Corp.* case discussed *infra*, would seem to change the outcome). For some unknown reason, however, the *Container Corp.* court distinguished *Allianz* by stating that "there was no indication in [*Allianz*] that the claimant had been named in the policy as an additional insured." Container Corp. of Am. v. Md. Cas. Co., 707 So. 2d 733, 735 n.1 (Fla. 1998). This distinction is at odds with the facts in *Allianz*.

24. *Container Corp. of Am.*, 707 So. 2d at 735.

25. *Id.*

Georgia

John Bonnie
Weinberg, Wheeler, Hudgins, Gunn & Dial, LLC

1. GENERAL RULES OF CONTRACTUAL INDEMNITY

Except where prohibited by statute or where a public duty is owed, a party may contractually relieve itself from liability to another for damages or ordinary negligence, and such an agreement is not void as against public policy.[1] Furthermore, a party may bind itself to indemnify another for that party's own future acts of negligence,[2] except where expressly disallowed by statute. As a matter of public policy, however, an agreement to indemnify a party for the indemnitee's own negligence will only be enforced if the indemnitor's intention to do so is expressed in plain, clear and unequivocal terms.[3] Absent an explicitly and expressly stated intent, Georgia courts will not interpret an indemnity agreement as a promise to save the indemnitee from its own negligence.[4] Every presumption is against such intention: if any ambiguity exists, the words of the agreement are construed strictly against the indemnitee.[5] "Georgia courts never imply an agreement to indemnify another for one's own negligence in the absence of express language."[6] The contract will be scrutinized closely to discover whether such an intent is actually revealed.[7]

This rule expresses the reluctance to cast the burden for negligent actions upon those who are not actually at fault;[8] instead, Georgia public policy encourages the exercise of due care for fear of liability, rather than acts of carelessness, cloaked with the knowledge that an indemnity contract will relieve a party's indifference.[9]

Consequently, one party's agreement to indemnify another "against any and all claims" does not "expressly, plainly, clearly and unequivocally" evidence the indemnitor's intent to indemnify the indemnitee for its own negligence, and it will not be read to do so.[10] Similarly, an agreement to indemnify and hold harmless "from and against all claims, damages, losses and expenses" does not require indemnification for the indemnitee's own negligence.[11] The duty to indemnify will only be avoided under this rule where the loss or damage is occasioned by the sole negligence of the indemnitee, not where the indemnitor is solely at fault or where the indemnitor and indemnitee are concurrently negligent.

As noted earlier, indemnity can exist were both parties are negligent. If the negligence of the indemnitor and indemnitee combine to cause injury, e.g., if the parties are

1. Batson-Cook Co. v. Ga. Marble Setting Co., 144 S.E.2d 547, 549 (Ga. Ct. App. 1965).

2. *Id.*

3. *Id.* at 550; Emergency Professionals of Atlanta, P.C. v. Watson, 654 S.E.2d 434, 438 (Ga. Ct. App. 2008); S. Ry. Co. v. Union Camp Corp., 353 S.E.2d 519, 520 (Ga. Ct. App. 1987); Ga. State Tel. Co. v. Scarboro, 251 S.E.2d 309, 310 (Ga. Ct. App. 1978).

4. *Union Camp*, 353 S.E.2d at 519; *Ga. Marble Setting*, 144 S.E.2d at 550; Serv. Merch. Co. v. Hunter Fan Co., 617 S.E.2d 235, 237 (Ga. Ct. App. 2005).

5. *Scarboro*, 251 S.E.2d at 310; *Ga. Marble Setting*, 144 S.E.2d at 552; Scarboro Enter., Inc. v. Hirsh, 169 S.E.2d 182, 185 (Ga. Ct. App. 1969); *Hunter Fan Co.*, 617 S.E.2d at 237.

6. Cent. of Ga. R.R. Co. v. Lester, 165 S.E.2d 587, 592 (Ga. Ct. App. 1968); Ryder Integrated Logistics, Inc. v. BellSouth Telecoms., Inc., 642 S.E.2d 695, 697 (Ga. 2007).

7. *Ga. Marble Setting*, 144 S.E.2d at 550; United Parcel Serv., Inc. v. Colt Sec. Agency, Inc., 676 S.E.2d 22, 24 (Ga. 2009); *BellSouth Telcoms., Inc.*, 642 S.E.2d at 697.

8. Allstate Ins. Co. v. City of Atlanta, 415 S.E.2d 308, 309 (Ga. Ct. App. 1992); *United Parcel Serv., Inc.*, 676 S.E.2d at 24.

9. *Allstate Ins. Co.*, 415 S.E.2d at 310; *Serv. Merch. Co.*, 617 S.E.2d at 240.

10. Park Pride Atlanta, Inc. v. City of Atlanta, 541 S.E.2d 687, 689 (Ga. Ct. App. 2000).

11. Binswanger Glass Co., Inc. v. Beers Constr. Co., 234 S.E.2d 363, 366 (Ga. Ct. App. 1977).

concurrently negligent, the duty to indemnify arises and is enforceable.[12] Consequently, a duty to indemnify in the case of joint negligence arises where the indemnification is for "any and all claims."[13] The same is true if the indemnification is for losses that "arise out of" identified events, regardless of whether the indemnitee's negligence is expressly mentioned, and whether its negligence may have partially caused the loss.[14]

2. EXCEPTIONS TO GENERAL RULES OF CONTRACTUAL INDEMNITY

Georgia Code Annotated § 13-8-2(a) provides that "a contract which is against the policy of the law cannot be enforced." The statute thereafter identifies five types of contracts deemed contrary to public policy, such as contracts in restraint of trade and wagering contracts.[15] Beyond the types of agreements expressly identified by this statute, the Georgia Supreme Court held as unenforceable on public policy grounds a provision in an insurance policy providing coverage for the loss of a leg only if the leg was severed within 90 days of injury.[16]

It has been held that a contract will not be considered contrary to public policy unless the legislature has so declared, the consideration of the contract "is contrary to good morals and contrary to law," or the contract is entered into "for the purpose of affecting an illegal or immoral agreement or doing something which is in violation of law."[17]

A separate statutory provision deems void and unenforceable certain agreements to indemnify relating to the construction, repair, or maintenance of buildings. This anti-indemnity statute states in relevant part:

> A covenant, promise, agreement, or understanding in or in connection with or collateral to a contract or agreement relative to the construction, alteration, repair, or maintenance of a building structure, appurtenances, and appliances, including moving, demolition, and excavating connected therewith, purporting to require one party to such contract or agreement shall indemnify, hold harmless, insure, or defend the other party to the contract or other named indemnitee, including its, his, or her officers, agents, or employees, against liability for claims for damages, losses, or expenses, including attorney fees, arising out of bodily injury to persons, death, or damage to property caused by or resulting from the sole negligence of the indemnitee, or its, his, or her officers, agents, or employees, is against public policy and is void and unenforceable. This subsection shall not affect any obligation under workers' compensation or coverage or insurance specifically relating to workers' compensation, nor shall this subsection apply to any requirement that one party to the contract purchase a project specific insurance policy, including an owner's or contractor's protective insurance, builder's risk insurance, installation coverage, project management protective liability insurance, an owner controlled insurance policy, or a contractor controlled insurance policy.[18]

Georgia courts have given this statute an expansive interpretation, applying it beyond traditional construction contracts to commercial and residential lease agreements having little or no relationship to any ostensible building construction. For example, applying

---

12. *Id.*

13. Cent. of Ga. R.R. Co. v. Ga. Ports Auth., 379 S.E.2d 540, 542 (Ga. Ct. App. 1989).

14. Lawyers Title Ins. Corp. v. New Freedom Mortg. Corp., 645 S.E.2d 536, 543 (Ga. Ct. App. 2007).

15. Ga. Code Ann. § 13-8-2(a)(2). Other types of contracts identified in Ga. Code Ann. § 13-8-2(a) are contracts tending to corrupt legislation or the judiciary, contracts to evade or oppose revenue laws of another country, and contracts of maintenance or champertry.

16. Strickland v. Gulf Life Ins. Co., 242 S.E.2d 148, 149 (Ga. 1978).

17. Dep't of Transp. v. Brooks, 328 S.E.2d 705, 713 (Ga. 1985).

18. Ga. Code Ann. § 13-8-2(b).

Georgia Code Annotated § 13-8-2(b) to a building lease agreement, the Georgia Supreme Court struck as contrary to public policy a provision in the lease agreement in which one party agreed to indemnify and save harmless another "against and from all claims . . . by any cause whatsoever,"[19] reasoning this constituted an agreement to indemnify one party for the party's own sole negligence in connection with a building. In similar reliance upon the statute, the Georgia Court of Appeals struck an exculpatory provision in a lease agreement in which the tenant released and held harmless the landlord "from any and all damages to both person and property . . . whether due to negligence of Landlord."[20] In a case involving the installation of elevators in a building, the court voided an indemnity provision in which a general contractor assumed "complete responsibility for any accident to persons or property, howsoever caused" and agreed to indemnify and hold harmless "against all loss, damage, claims, liability or expense."[21] And in a case involving an indemnity provision in an assignment and assumption agreement transferring to a homeowners' association responsibility for the management and operation of a residential subdivision, the Georgia Supreme Court found the prohibition of the statute similarly applicable.[22]

But Georgia Code Annotated § 13-8-2(b)'s prohibition can be avoided, however, if the indemnitor purchases liability insurance for purposes of satisfying the loss or damage to which the indemnity extends, on the basis that this constitutes mutual exculpation rather than improper indemnity.[23]

Effective June 1, 2016, Georgia's anti-indemnity statute also deems void and unenforceable certain agreements to indemnify in contracts for engineering, architectural, or land surveying services.[24] This provision provides:

> A covenant, promise agreement, or understanding in or in connection with or collateral to a contract or agreement for engineering, architectural, or land surveying services purporting to require one party to such contract or agreement shall indemnify, hold harmless, insure, or defend the other party to the contract or other named indemnitee, including its, his, or her officers, agents, or employees, against liability for claims for damages, losses, or expenses, including attorney fees, is against public policy and void and unenforceable, except for indemnification for damages, losses, or expenses to the extent caused by or resulting from the negligence, recklessness, or intentionally wrongful conduct of the indemnitor or other persons employed or utilized by the indemnitor in the performance of the contract. This subsection shall not affect any obligation under workers' compensation or coverage or insurance specifically relating to workers' compensation, nor shall this subsection apply to any requirement that one party to the contract purchase a project specific insurance policy, or project specific policy endorsement.[25]

No cases have yet been decided under this subsection of the statute.

While an agreement to indemnify another generally for "any and all claims" is not deemed to create an obligation to indemnify for an indemnitee's own sole negligence

19. Frazer v. City of Albany, 265 S.E.2d 581, 584 (Ga. 1980).

20. Country Club Apartments, Inc. v. Scott, 267 S.E.2d 811, 813–14 (Ga. Ct. App. 1980).

21. Morgan v. Westinghouse Elec. Corp., 579 F. Supp. 867, 870 (N.D. Ga. 1980).

22. Kennedy Dev. Co., Inc. v. Camp, 719 S.E.2d 442 (Ga. 2011).

23. Reliance Ins. Co. of Ill. v. Richfield Hospitality Servs., 92 F. Supp. 2d 1329, 1336 (N.D. Ga. 2000); Tuxedo Plumbing & Heating Co. v. Lie-Nielsen, 262 S.E.2d 794, 795–96 (Ga. 1980).

24. In Lanier at McEver, L.P. v. Planners & Eng'rs Collaborative, Inc., 663 S.E.2d 240 (Ga. 2008), decided prior to the effective date of Georgia Code Annotated § 13-8-2(a)(3), the Georgia Supreme Court extended the prohibition of indemnity against sole negligence contained in § 13-8-2(a)(2) to a limitation of liability provision respecting the liability of an engineer under a design contract.

25. Ga. Code Ann. § 13-8-2(a)(3).

absent plain and unequivocal language creating such an obligation,[26] an agreement to indemnify for "all claims" or "any and all claims" that implicates the provisions of Georgia Code Annotated § 13-8-2(b) *is* read as extending to the indemnitee's sole negligence even if the agreement does not so expressly provide,[27] and will be struck down as violating Georgia public policy. This outcome reflects Georgia courts' broad reading of Georgia Code Annotated § 13-8-2,[28] in order to give effect to the legislature's intention in enacting this statute.[29]

The diametrically opposite interpretations applied to general agreements to indemnify on the one hand, and agreements implicating the provisions of Georgia Code Annotated § 13-8-2 on the other, has been described as creating a "catch-22," and an "ambush [on] many unsuspecting indemnitees.[30]

> Under the first line of Georgia authority, the absence of an explicit acknowledgment in the contract that "any claim" includes a claim of negligence dooms the indemnitee's hope for indemnification when it is liable based on its own negligence. Under the line of authority that holds that "any claim" can include a claim of negligence, however, the indemnitee loses because Georgia "public policy" disallows indemnification for [certain] claims of negligence.[31]

3. INDEMNITY AGREEMENTS AS INSURED CONTRACTS

The Georgia Court of Appeals has expressly held that an agreement to indemnify another meets the definition in the standard general liability policy excepting from the exclusion liability assumed in an "insured contract."[32] A Georgia federal court has similarly so held, rejecting a contrary suggestion contained in an earlier decision of the Georgia Court of Appeals.[33]

4. OPERATION OF AN AGREEMENT TO INDEMNIFY REFERRING TO OR REQUIRING INSURANCE

In an early case predating both Georgia Code Annotated § 13-8-2 and its predecessor, the Georgia Court of Appeals considered a subcontractor's obligation to indemnify the general contractor for injuries to a subcontractor's employee under the subcontractor's agreement to indemnify the general contractor for "any and all . . . losses, expenses, damages, demands and claims" arising out of the performance of work by the subcontractor. Consistent with the general rule, the court held the provision evidenced no intent on the part of the subcontractor to indemnify for the contractor's own negligence.[34] As an aside, the court noted that each carried liability insurance that covered its own negligent acts. In the court's view, these

26. *See* note 10 *supra* and accompanying discussion.

27. *Frazer*, 265 S.E.2d at 583; *see also* Fed. Paper Bd. Co., Inc. v. Harbert-Yeargin, Inc., 53 F. Supp. 2d 1361, 1371–73 (N.D. Ga. 1999) and cases cited therein; Morgan v. Westinghouse Corp., 579 F. Supp. 867 (N.D. Ga. 1984); Reliance Ins. Co. of Ill. v. Richfield Hospitality Servs., Inc., 92 F. Supp. 2d at 1335–36.

28. *See* Morgan v. Westinghouse Elec. Corp., 579 F. Supp. at 869–70 (noting earlier Georgia precedent applying a rule of strict construction to the predecessor statute to Georgia Code Annotated § 13-8-2(b) because it was in derogation of the common law).

29. Country Club Apartments, Inc. v. Scott, 271 S.E.2d 841, 842 (Ga. 1980) (overruling numerous decisions of the Georgia Court of Appeals rendered subsequent to the enactment of Georgia Code Annotated § 13-8-2(b) and which "failed to give effect to th[e] [public] policy" stated in the statute); *see also Frazer*, 265 S.E.2d at 583.

30. *Richfield Hospitality Servs.*, 92 F. Supp. 2d at 1336.

31. *Id.*

32. Nuvell Nat'l Auto Fin., LLC v. Monroe Guar. Ins. Co., 736 S.E.2d 463 (Ga. Ct. App. 2012).

33. North Am. Specialty Ins. Co. v. Pen Pals Prods., LLC, 789 F. Supp. 2d 1342 (N.D. Ga. 2011) (addressing Scottsdale Ins. Co. v. Great Am. Assurance Co., 610 S.E.2d 558 (Ga. App. 2005)).

34. *Ga. Marble Setting*, 144 S.E.2d at 552.

facts supported the conclusion that the contract did not contemplate indemnity against the indemnitee's negligent acts and indicated that the contractor was not relying solely, if at all, upon the indemnity agreement with the subcontractor in the event of its own negligent acts.[35]

Clauses in leases and other contracts in which the parties clearly express their mutual intent to shift the risk of loss or damage to insurance do not violate Georgia Code Annotated § 13-8-2(b).[36] In fact,

> where parties to a business transaction mutually agree that insurance will be provided as part of the bargain, such agreement must be construed as providing mutual exculpation to the bargaining parties who must be deemed to have agreed to look solely to the insurance in the event of loss and not to liability on the part of the opposing party.[37]

This rule is premised upon the legal fiction that "exculpation is not indemnification,"[38] even if the agreement provides specifically for indemnification.

Tuxedo v. Lie-Nielsen[39] is a good example of the application of this rule. In that case, a building owner retained a plumber to undertake work, which resulted in a fire loss. The written agreement between the owner and the plumber provided that "Owner shall be responsible for procuring and maintaining fire insurance with extended coverage upon the structures and improvements of the property . . . ."[40] The owner's insurer paid the loss and suit was then initiated in the owner/insured's name against the plumber for that amount. The Georgia Supreme Court concluded that the contractual provision respecting insurance was a "waiver of subrogation," in which insurance coverage was obtained for the benefit of both and in which the owner and plumber waived their claims against each other for any fire loss. The court held the predecessor statute to Georgia Code Annotated § 13-8-2 inapplicable since neither party agreed to indemnify for the other's sole negligence. Rather, the insurance clause shifted the risk of loss to the insurance company regardless of which party was at fault.[41]

In another case, a contractor agreed to indemnify a property owner for injuries to employees of the contractor or its subcontractors, even if the owner was solely negligent. The court found the indemnity enforceable based upon a provision in the agreement in which the contractor agreed to keep insurance in force for the benefit of the owner and contractor "with cross liability clauses."[42] The court found that the two provisions together showed the parties intended coverage by insurance, not ultimate indemnification of the owner against its own negligence,[43] and further, that Georgia Code Annotated § 13-8-2 did not apply because there was no agreement to indemnify for the sole negligence of any party. "Rather, the insurance clause shifts the risk of loss to the insurance company regardless of which party is at fault."[44]

Another case finding Georgia Code Annotated § 13-8-2(b) to be inapplicable involved an agreement between a landlord and tenant containing a "waiver of subrogation" provision providing that the parties "waive any and all rights of recovery against the other . . . for loss or damage to such waiving party or its property . . . arising from any cause insured

35. *Id.*
36. *Lie-Nielsen*, 262 S.E.2d at 795–96.
37. *Id.* (quoting Gen. Cigar Co. v. Lancaster Leaf Tobacco Co., 323 F. Supp. 931, 941 (D. Md. 1971)).
38. McAbee Constr. Co. v. Ga. Kraft Co., 343 S.E.2d 513, 515 (Ga. Ct. App. 1986).
39. *Lie-Nielsen*, 262 S.E.2d at 794.
40. *Id.* at 795.
41. *Id.* at 796.
42. *McAbee*, 343 S.E.2d at 515.
43. *Id.*
44. *Id.*

against under the standard form of fire insurance policy . . . ."[45] The Georgia Court of Appeals rejected the contention that the waiver was unenforceable because there was no specific provision in the agreement actually requiring one or both parties to obtain insurance.[46] Since in the court's view the waiver of subrogation would not apply in the absence of insurance, there was no need to include a mandatory insurance provision to express the parties' intent to look solely to the insurer in the event of a loss.[47]

The Georgia Supreme Court confirms this view:

> [s]ubrogation requires the existence of a contract to pay (insurance) and the actual payment of the claim; in the absence of insurance and payment thereunder, there can be no subrogation and hence no waiver. Accordingly, the absence of an express requirement to maintain insurance does not alone diminish the clarity of the[ ] parties' intent; inasmuch as subrogation arises only upon the payment of an insured claim, the parties' mutually-bargained-for covenant to waive subrogation patently contemplates the existence of insurance coverage and would be rendered meaningless in the absence of the same. A requirement that the parties purchase insurance is a significant indication that they intended to shift the risk of loss, but it is not essential to a valid and legal waiver of subrogation and where their intent so to do is otherwise clear, that agreement will be upheld.[48]

This is true even to the extent the agreement containing the waiver of subrogation clause contains an exception to the waiver of the landlord's own negligence where available insurance does not cover the loss.[49]

Courts will not find that the parties intended to exculpate one another and to look only to insurance if the only evidence is a provision in a lease agreement providing for mandatory insurance covering the risk of loss.[50] Thus, where insurance is addressed, but the agreement further expresses the parties' intention for one party to be liable for damage not covered by insurance if the party's conduct caused or contributed to the loss, no waiver of subrogation will be deemed intended.[51]

If an agreement's exculpatory language is not termed a "waiver of subrogation" and speaks in terms of "insurable hazards" rather than insured causes, that language is unenforceable and violates Georgia Code Annotated § 13-8-2(b) because the language does not necessarily contemplate the purchase of insurance and is not limited to circumstances involving insurance.[52]

45. Glazer v. Crescent Wallcoverings, Inc., 451 S.E.2d 509, 511–13 (Ga. Ct. App. 1994).

46. *Id.* at 512.

47. *Id.* (also holding that the waiver of subrogation between the landlord and tenant precluded an action for contribution against the landlord by the third parties against whom the tenant sought to recover for the loss).

48. May Dep't Store v. Ctr. Developers, Inc., 471 S.E.2d 194, 197–98 (Ga. 1996).

49. *Id.*

50. *See* Alimenta Processing Corp. v. South Ga. Pecan Co., 364 S.E.2d 84, 86 (Ga. Ct. App. 1987).

51. *Id.* at 85.

52. Cent. Warehouse & Dev. Corp. v. Nostalgia, Inc., 435 S.E.2d 230 (Ga. App. 1993), *disapproved on other grounds by Glazer*, 451 S.E.2d at 512; *see also May,* 471 S.E.2d at 196–97 for a further explanation of the limited holding in the case.

Hawaii

Tred Eyerly
Damon Key Leong Kupchak Hastert

1. GENERAL RULES OF CONTRACTUAL INDEMNITY

Contracts of indemnity are enforceable in Hawaii, including those that purport to indemnify the indemnitee for its own negligence.[1] But "contracts of indemnity are strictly construed, particularly where the indemnitee claims that it should be held safe from its own negligence."[2] In such an instance, "the indemnity agreement must be a 'clear and unequivocal' assumption of liability."[3] No "talismanic recitation" is necessary to satisfy this requirement, "and an express statement that the indemnification applied to the indemnitee's own negligence does not appear necessary."[4]

One case suggests a burden on the indemnitor to expressly exclude certain types of indemnity, as opposed to the more common burden on the indemnitee to expand the scope of the indemnity. "[I]f an indemnitor is contractually obligated to indemnify for its negligence, it is obligated to indemnify for both its sole and concurrent negligence unless the indemnity contract clearly and unequivocally specifies otherwise."[5]

2. EXCEPTIONS TO GENERAL RULES OF CONTRACTUAL INDEMNITY

In the construction context, a party cannot be indemnified for its sole negligence.[6] Hawaii Revised Statutes § 431:10-222 provides as follows:

> Any covenant, promise, agreement or understanding in, or in connection with or collateral to, a contract or agreement relative to the construction, alteration, repair or maintenance of a building, structure, appurtenence or appliance, including moving, demolition or excavation connected therewith, purporting to indemnify the promisee against liability for bodily injury to persons or damage to property caused by or resulting from the sole negligence or willful misconduct of the promisee, the promisee's agents or employees, or indemnitee is invalid as against public policy, and is void and unenforceable; provided that this Section shall not affect any valid workers' compensation claim under Chapter 386 or any other insurance contract or agreement issued by an admitted insurer upon any insurable interest under this Code.[7]

Accordingly, Hawaii Revised Statutes § 431:10-222 declares indemnifying the indemnitee's sole negligence in construction contracts void as against public policy. Consequently,

1. *See* Straub Clinic & Hosp., Inc. v. Chicago Ins. Co., 665 P.2d 176 (Haw. Ct. App. 1983).
2. Kamali v. Hawaiian Elec. Co., 504 P.2d 861 (Haw. 1972).
3. Espaniola v. Cawdrey Mars Joint Venture, 707 P.2d 365, 369 (Haw. 1985) (quoting Keawe v. Hawaiian Electric Co., 649 P.2d 1149 (Haw. 1982)).
4. Kole v. AMFAC, Inc., 665 F. Supp. 1460, 1463 (D. Haw. 1987).
5. Straub Clinic & Hosp., Inc. v. Chicago Ins. Co., 665 P.2d 176 (Haw. Ct. App. 1983). Therefore, *Straub* suggests that the contract of indemnity must be clear and unequivocal with respect to the indemnitor's intent to ***exclude*** acts of negligence on the part of the indemnitee from its responsibility to indemnify.
6. *See Espaniola*, 707 P.2d at 370 (discussing Haw. Rev. Stat. § 431-453, predecessor to Haw. Rev Stat. § 431:10-222).
7. Haw. Rev. Stat. § 431:10-222.

pursuant to § 431:10-222, in the construction industry, a contractor is not contractually liable for the sole negligence or willful misconduct of another, or for the defense thereof, as such contractual requirements would cause higher premiums and greater construction costs.[8]

If, however, the indemnitee has an advantage in bargaining power and the parties do not deal at arms-length, the federal district court predicted that Hawaii courts would find the indemnity agreements void.[9] In *Kole v. AMFAC, Inc.*, however, there was no evidence that the indemnitee engaged in misconduct or otherwise coerced agreements from the indemnitors. Consequently, the court concluded that the parties dealt at arms-length with one another, finding that the transaction giving rise to the contract of indemnity did not require the parties to align interests.[10] No case since then has found an indemnity provision to be void due to unequal bargaining power or the parties not dealing at arms-length.

3. INDEMNITY AGREEMENTS AS INSURED CONTRACTS

Limited authority suggests an insurer has a duty to provide coverage for contractual liability assumed by its insured via an indemnity provision with a third party.[11] Courts will look to the terms of the policy in order to determine the extent of coverage.

In *Liberty Mutual Insurance Co. v. United National Insurance Co., Ltd.*, a subcontract agreement contained a provision requiring the subcontractor to indemnify the contractor. The subcontractor had obtained a comprehensive general liability policy covering its activities in connection with the subcontract. While performing work in connection with the subcontract, one of the subcontractor's employees was injured, and in worker's compensation proceedings, the contractor's worker's compensation carrier was found liable for a portion of the injuries sustained by that employee. To recover its payment to the employee, the contractor's worker's compensation carrier sued the subcontractor, and the court found that the subcontractor was liable for all of the worker's compensation damages as an employer.

With that decision in hand, the contractor's carrier then sued the subcontractor's insurer to recover. The subcontractor's insurer was not liable to the contractor's carrier, however, because the subcontractor's policy contained an exclusion for liability assumed by the subcontractor pursuant to any payment of worker's compensation benefits.[12] The court held that the subcontractor's liability arose not from the indemnity provision, but from a separate duty to pay worker's compensation.[13] The court concluded, "[t]he Subcontractor's obligation falls squarely within [the] exception [for payment of worker's compensation benefits]. As a beneficiary of Subcontractor's policy, Contractor's subrogee, [the contractor's carrier], is only entitled to benefits accruing to Subcontractor."[14]

The court continued with a discussion regarding instances in which the contractual liability of an indemnitor flowing to an indemnitee may become a covered loss. For example, where the policy's exclusionary clause applied to "liability imposed upon the insured," the exclusion did not apply to liability imposed upon a third party. In *Liberty Mutual*, however, the exclusion (e) expressly applied to "*any* obligation for which the insured or any carrier as his insurer may be held liable."[15] In other cases discussed in *Liberty Mutual*, the policies had similar language to exclusion (e), but they involved separate negligence actions apart from worker's compensation claims. Therefore, the worker's compensation exclusion did

8. Arthur v. Dept. of Hawaiian Home Lands, 377 P.3d 26, 29 (Haw. 2016).
9. *Kole*, 665 F. Supp. at 1464 (citing Southern Pacific Transp. Co. v. Nielsen, 448 F.2d 121, 123 (10th Cir. 1971)).
10. *Kole*, 665 F. Supp. at 1464.
11. Liberty Mut. Ins. Co. v. United Nat'l Ins. Co., Ltd., 731 P.2d 167 (Haw. 1987).
12. *Id.* at 170.
13. *Id.*
14. *Id.*
15. *Id.* at 41 (discussing C.M. Inc. v. Canadian Indem. Co., 635 F.2d 703 (8th Cir. 1980)) (emphasis in original).

not apply. Here, however, Liberty Mutual's claims were a direct result of the worker's compensation paid to the injured employee.[16]

4. OPERATION OF AN AGREEMENT TO INDEMNIFY REFERRING TO OR REQUIRING INSURANCE

As in many areas of interpretation of comprehensive liability policies by Hawaii courts, how an indemnity agreement impacts coverage under a liability policy is undeveloped by the case law. Consequently, the existence of insurance does not appear to create any greater or lesser duty on the part of the insurer, other than to provide coverage as provided in the policy.

16. *Liberty Mut.*, 731 P.2d at 41 (discussing Utica Mut. Ins. Co. v. Cent. Vermont Ry., Inc., 336 A.2d 200 (Vt. 1975) and Am. Ins. Co. v. Nationwide Mut. Ins. Co., 270 A.2d 907 (N.H. 1970)).

Idaho

Kathryn Kasper
Hancock, Daniel & Johnson, P.C.

1. GENERAL RULES OF CONTRACTUAL INDEMNITY

"Freedom of contract is a fundamental concept underlying the law of contracts and is an essential element of the free enterprise system."[1] Consequently, Idaho law allows parties to contract for indemnification in most circumstances, but the obligation to indemnify is strictly construed, particularly if the indemnitee drafted the agreement. Additionally, the status of indemnitee is interpreted narrowly.[2] The extent of the indemnification obligation based upon an indemnification contract is determined by its provisions.[3]

Idaho law allows a party to indemnify another party for the latter party's sole negligence, even in the context of personal injury. An exception in the context of construction contracts is discussed in Section 2, *infra*. Although there is little case law on the topic, the Supreme Court of Idaho has specifically allowed such indemnification in a lease agreement, and noted several factors that "cut against" the general policy that "a contractual provision should not be construed to permit an indemnitee to recover for his own negligence."[4] The court stated in dicta that an explicit reference to indemnification for the indemnitee's negligence would be dispositive, but was not absolutely required. As the contract did not contain that explicit reference, the court looked to the wording of the indemnification clause, and determined that the "hold harmless" provision, "although not talismanic, is nonetheless indicative of a specific intent to encompass indemnification for the indemnitee's negligence."[5] Additionally, because the language of the clause obligated the tenant to hold the landlord harmless for *any* liability incurred, the court reasoned that obligation further evidenced an intent to indemnify the indemnitee for the indemnitee's sole negligence. The court also determined that placing the indemnity clause directly after a specific provision requiring the indemnitor to purchase insurance indicated an intent to place the onus of indemnification on the tenant by requiring him or her to purchase insurance to fund the indemnity. The court was further persuaded by the fact that there was no disparity of bargaining power between the contracting parties.[6]

When an indemnity obligation requires one party to "indemnify and save harmless" another party, that language has been held to require the indemnitor to fund the indemnitee's defense by either defending or paying the defense costs (including attorneys' fees and investigative expenses).[7]

---

1. Rawlings v. Layne & Bowler Pump Co., 465 P.2d 107, 110 (Idaho 1970).
2. Barnett v. Eagle Helicopters, 831 P.2d 560, 564 (Idaho Ct. App. 1992).
3. Martin v. Lyons, 558 P.2d 1063, 1066 (Idaho 1977).
4. Bonner Cty. v. Panhandle Rodeo Assoc., Inc., 620 P.2d 1102, 1105 (Idaho 1980). The indemnity language stated, "The tenant shall hold harmless the landlord for any liability as a result of the rodeo performances . . . ." *Id.* at 1103.
5. *Id.*
6. *Id.*
7. Farber v. State, 682 P.2d 630, 632 (Idaho 1984).

2. EXCEPTIONS TO GENERAL RULES OF CONTRACTUAL INDEMNITY

Idaho has codified a prohibition on indemnification in construction contracts that purports to indemnify a party against liability for damages arising out of bodily injury or damage to property resulting from the sole negligence of that party. The statute provides:

> A covenant, promise, agreement or understanding in, or in connection with or collateral to, a contract or agreement relative to the construction, alteration, repair or maintenance of a building, structure, highway, appurtenance and appliance, including moving, demolition and excavating connected therewith, purporting to indemnify the promisee against liability for damages arising out of bodily injury to persons or damage to property caused by or resulting from the sole negligence of the promisee, his agents or employees, or indemnitees, is against public policy and is void and unenforceable.

Idaho Code Annotated § 29-114.

3. INDEMNITY AGREEMENTS AS INSURED CONTRACTS

No Idaho cases discuss indemnity agreements as insured contracts, but by implication these appear to be covered insured contracts. The term "insured contracts" has only been written once by Idaho appellate courts (and never by the U.S. District Court of Idaho).[8] In a case involving an insurance policy indicating that there is coverage for underlying written contractual agreements, the Idaho Supreme Court found that these contracts—there a lease agreement—must be covered as "the very object of the contract is for this extended coverage."[9] Idaho law follows the general principle that exclusions are to be construed narrowly and in favor of coverage.[10]

4. OPERATION OF AN AGREEMENT TO INDEMNIFY REFERRING TO OR REQUIRING INSURANCE

The existence of an indemnity clause directly following a provision for insurance indicates the parties' intent to place the burden of indemnification upon the indemnitor for the indemnitee's negligence by requiring the indemnitor to purchase insurance to fund the indemnity.[11]

8. Blackburn v. State Farm Mut. Auto. Ins. Co., 697 P.2d 425, 431 (Idaho 1985).

9. *Bonner Cty.*, 620 P.2d at 1106.

10. *Id.* at 1106–07. *See also* Gordon v. Three Rivers Agency, Inc., 903 P.2d 128, 131 (Idaho 1995).

11. *Bonner Cty.*, 620 P.2d at 1105.

Illinois

Jason A. Frye
Neal, Gerber & Eisenberg, LLP

1. GENERAL RULES OF CONTRACTUAL INDEMNITY

As a general rule, contractual agreements to indemnify are enforceable in Illinois. "Indemnification agreements are contracts, and, as such, are to be construed like any other contract. In construing indemnity contracts, the primary focus is to give effect to the intention of the parties."[1]

While it has been said that indemnity clauses are disfavored and must be strictly construed, that canon of interpretation is limited by two considerations.[2] First, the "strict construction" rule is inapplicable if a contract clearly provides for indemnification or defense, since a court may not strictly construe an indemnity contract in a manner that conflicts with the parties' intent.[3] Second, when a contract does not indemnify a party against its own conduct or negligence, the rule of strict construction cannot be invoked.[4]

Because of the public policy implications of agreements in which one party agrees to indemnify another for the other's own negligence, such agreements are subject to the rule of strict construction.[5] "It is quite generally held that an indemnity contract will not be construed as indemnifying one against his own negligence, unless such a construction is required by clear and explicit language of the contract, or such intention is expressed in unequivocal terms."[6] The Illinois Supreme Court recently interpreted indemnification agreements more broadly and stated that, "when an agreement clearly and explicitly provides indemnification for an indemnitee's own negligence, it should be construed accordingly."[7]

In considering the parties' intent, an indemnity agreement is to "be given a fair and reasonable interpretation based upon a consideration of all of its language and provisions."[8] It is not necessary that there be a specific reference to indemnification for the indemnitee's own negligence, and Illinois courts have read indemnification for "any and all claims" as indicating an intention that the indemnitee be indemnified for his or her own negligence.[9]

1. Scott Stainless Steel, Inc. v. NBD Chicago Bank, 625 N.E.2d 293, 297 (Ill. App. Ct. 1993); *accord* Applied Indus. Materials Corp. v. Mallinckrodt, Inc., 102 F. Supp. 2d 934, 939 (N.D. Ill. 2000).

2. *Applied Indus.*, 102 F. Supp. 2d at 939; Owens v. Midwest Tank & Mfg. Co., 549 N.E.2d 774, 777 (Ill. App. Ct. 1989).

3. *Id.*

4. *Id.* at 943. There is precedent to the effect that all indemnity agreements are subject to a rule of strict construction. *See, e.g.,* Ervin v. Sears, Roebuck & Co., 469 N.E.2d 243, 249 (Ill. App. Ct. 1984). The facts of such cases typically involve an agreement to indemnify for one's own negligence. *See* Ill. Bell Tel. Co. v. Highland Park, 572 N.E.2d 1267, 1275 (Ill. App. Ct. 1991); Bates v. Select Lake City Theater Operating Co., 397 N.E.2d 75, 77 (Ill. App. Ct. 1979). The Illinois state and federal courts continue to articulate different rules of construction for garden-variety indemnity agreements as compared with those involving indemnity for one's own negligence. *See* Burns v. Ford Motor Co., 331 N.E.2d 325, 331 (Ill. App. Ct. 1974); *Applied Indus.*, 102 F. Supp. 2d at 943.

5. McNiff v. Millard Maint. Serv. Co., 715 N.E.2d 247, 249 (Ill. App. Ct. 1999).

6. Barger v. Scandroli Constr. Co., 347 N.E.2d 207, 208 (Ill. App. Ct. 1976); *see also* Tatar v. Maxon Constr. Co., 294 N.E.2d 272, 274 (Ill. 1973) (finding the language insufficient to indemnify the indemnitee for its own negligence); Westinghouse Elec. Elevator Co. v. La Salle Monroe Bldg. Corp., 70 N.E.2d 604, 607 (Ill. 1946); McNiff v. Millard Maint. Serv. Co., 715 N.E.2d 247, 250 (Ill. Ct. App. 1999) (finding the language insufficient to indemnify the indemnitee for its own negligence).

7. Buenz v. Frontline Transp. Co., 882 N.E.2d 525, 535 (Ill. 2008).

8. Hader v. St. Louis Sw. Ry. Co., 566 N.E.2d 736, 742 (Ill. App. Ct. 1991).

9. Economy Mech. Indus., Inc. v. T.J. Higgins Co., 689 N.E.2d 199, 202–03 (Ill. App. Ct. 1997); *see also* Nicor Gas Co. v. Wilmette, 884 N.E.2d 816, 822 (Ill. App. Ct. 2008) (finding "any and all" was sufficient language to be indemnified for the party's own negligence); Haynes v. Montgomery Ward & Co., 198 N.E.2d 548, 551 (Ill. Ct. App. 1964) (same).

The same conclusion was reached about an agreement to indemnify "from any loss, claim demand [or] liability . . . whether or not any negligence . . . by [indemnitee] is alleged to have contributed thereto, in whole or in part."[10] The intent to indemnify for another's negligence has also been found to exist in an agreement to indemnify for "all claims,"[11] and in an agreement to indemnify for injury "regardless of the cause or causes."[12]

But Illinois courts will not always find that an indemnity agreement covers the indemnitee's own negligence. In a construction case involving an agreement to indemnify for "any and all claims and damages . . . arising out of . . . the work, or caused in whole or in part by any fault or neglect of Sub-Contractor . . . ," the Illinois Appellate Court found that the subcontractor did not intend to indemnify a contractor for the contractor's own negligence because the claim did not arise out of the subcontractor's work.[13] (This case predates the Illinois Construction Contract Indemnification for Negligence Act discussed in the next section.) In a contractor's agreement to hold an owner harmless from "all claims for injury . . . and for damages to or loss of property, attributable directly or indirectly to the operations of [Contractor]," the language failed to explicitly and unequivocally cover indemnity for the owner's negligence.[14] Likewise, a subcontractor's agreement "to indemnify [the contractor] against [the subcontractor's] negligence" was not sufficient to provide indemnification for the contractor's negligence for the same reason.[15]

2. EXCEPTIONS TO GENERAL RULES OF CONTRACTUAL INDEMNITY

Agreements to indemnify for another party's negligence in the construction, alteration, repair, or maintenance of a building are void under Illinois's Construction Contract Indemnification for Negligence Act.[16] That Act provides:

> With respect to contracts or agreements, either public or private, for the construction, alteration, repair or maintenance of a building, structure, highway bridge, viaducts or other work dealing with construction, or for any moving, demolition or excavation connected therewith, every covenant, promise or agreement to indemnify or hold harmless another person from that person's own negligence is void as against public policy and wholly unenforceable.[17]

The statute is constitutional and does not violate the equal protection clause.[18] By its express terms, the statute is inapplicable to construction bonds or insurance contracts,[19] and this limitation has been upheld.[20] However, according to the Illinois Supreme Court, the statute is inapplicable to an action seeking contribution from another on the grounds that the other is jointly liable for injuries: pursuing contribution is not tantamount to indemnification for one's own negligence.[21]

---

10. North Am. Van Lines, Inc. v. Pinkerton Sec. Sys., Inc., 1996 U.S. Dist. LEXIS 17838, at *6–11 (N.D. Ill. 1996).

11. Higgins v. Kleronomos, 459 N.E.2d 1048, 1052 (Ill. App. Ct. 1984).

12. *Hader*, 566 N.E.2d at 742–43. This was so notwithstanding the reference to "negligence" in the indemnity provision.

13. Barger v. Scandroli Constr. Co., 347 N.E.2d 207, 208 (Ill. App. Ct. 1976).

14. Kelley v. Marathon Oil Co., 676 F.2d 1388, 1390 (7th Cir. 1982).

15. Dowling v. Otis Elevator Co., 549 N.E.2d 866, 870 (Ill. App. Ct. 1989).

16. 740 Ill. Comp. Stat. § 35/0.01 *et seq.*; *see also* Camper v. Burnside Constr. Co., 998 N.E.2d 1264, 1281 (Ill. App. Ct. 2013) (held indemnity clause was void under the Act); Cox v. Lumbermens Mut. Casualty Co., 439 N.E.2d 126, 129 (Ill. App. Ct. 1982) (same).

17. 740 Ill. Comp. Stat. § 35/1.

18. Davis v. Commonwealth Edison Co., 336 N.E.2d 881, 884 (Ill. 1975).

19. 740 Ill. Comp. Stat. § 35/3.

20. Capua v. W.E. O'Neil Constr. Co., 367 N.E.2d 669, 670 (Ill. 1977).

21. *See* Braye v. Archer-Daniels-Midland Co., 676 N.E.2d 1295, 1304 (Ill. 1997).

An agreement to indemnify another for his or her own willful misconduct is void as against public policy,[22] but this rule is inapplicable to contracts of insurance.[23]

3. INDEMNITY AGREEMENTS AS INSURED CONTRACTS

If a liability insurance policy contains the common exception for "a contract or agreement pertaining to your business . . . under which you assume the tort liability of another," the policy's coverage extends to an insured's agreement to indemnify, even if it also contains an exclusion for an insured's "assumption of liability in a contract or agreement."[24] Under the terms of the insurance policy, an "insured contract" is "one in which one of the contracting parties agrees to indemnify the other from and against that other party's own negligence."[25] However, an indemnification provision that fails to "clearly and explicitly or unequivocally" express an intention to indemnify for the negligence of the indemnitee is not enforceable, and, consequently, there is no assumption of tort liability and no "insured contract" under the insurance policy for purposes of coverage.[26]

More recently, however, the Illinois Appellate Court held that coverage existed for the assumption of "tort liability" in an insured contract endorsement, which liability was broader than merely "negligence liability."[27] To the court, use of the term "tort liability" leaves "open the possibility that its insured could agree to be responsible for another party's liability in a tort action even if that liability was not based on that party's own negligence."[28] The court rejected the insurer's construction of "insured contract" because, in light of the Construction Contract Indemnification for Negligence Act, the insurer's position could mean that coverage would never apply to an insured in the construction business.[29]

In a case in which an insured agreed to indemnify a third party *and* name the third party as an "additional insured" under a liability insurance policy and the third party was not so named in the policy, the "insured contract" exception to the exclusion for contractually assumed liability did not operate to extend a defense to the third party under the insurance policy.[30] In the court's view, the "insured contract" exception created an obligation to defend the named insured for a claim arising under that "insured contract," but not to defend the third party with whom the named insured had contracted.[31]

4. OPERATION OF AN AGREEMENT TO INDEMNIFY REFERRING TO OR REQUIRING INSURANCE

Consistent with the Illinois statute exempting contracts of insurance from the statutory prohibition on indemnity agreements in the construction industry, a party's agreement to obtain liability insurance for the work is valid.[32] Such agreements are permissible because agreeing to obtain insurance is not tantamount to agreeing to indemnify—an insurer, rather than the party obtaining the insurance, bears the risk of injury or damage.[33] However, if the

22. *Davis*, 336 N.E.2d at 885 (citing RESTATEMENT OF CONTRACTS § 575); Dixon Distrib. Co. v. Hanover Ins. Co., 641 N.E.2d 395, 401 (Ill. 1994).

23. *Dixon*, 641 N.E.2d at 401.

24. Hankins v. Pekin Ins. Co., 713 N.E.2d 1244, 1246 (Ill. App. Ct. 1999).

25. *Id.* at 1248.

26. *Id.*

27. Michael Nicholas, Inc. v. Royal Ins. Co. of Am., 748 N.E. 2d 786, 791 (Ill. App. Ct. 2001).

28. *Id.*

29. *Id.* at 791–92.

30. Alliance Syndicate, Inc. v. Parsec, Inc., 741 N.E.2d 1039, 1041–42 (Ill. App. Ct. 2000).

31. *Id.* at 1045–46.

32. *See* USX Corp. v. Liberty Mut. Ins. Co., 645 N.E.2d 396, 400 (Ill. App. Ct. 1994).

33. *Id.* at 401.

party agreeing to obtain insurance uses a self-insurance program, then the agreement is to indemnify and is void under Illinois law.[34]

Further, if the agreement to obtain insurance is inextricably linked to an otherwise void indemnity agreement (for example, an agreement to indemnify a third party for its own negligence in the construction context) both the indemnification and the insurance agreement are void.[35]

An agreement to procure insurance or name another as an additional insured in the construction context need not meet the test of strict construction,[36] and therefore need not explicitly state that the insurance will cover the promisee's own negligence to be effective.[37] This happens because the promisor assumes no responsibility aside from paying the insurance premiums, so there is no public policy implication that the coverage extends to the promisee's own negligence even absent an express statement of such intent.[38] But care needs to be taken in this area. An agreement to name an indemnitee as an additional insured contained within an unenforceable agreement to indemnify is valid only if the agreement to name the party as an additional insured is "not inextricably tied" to the void indemnity agreement.[39]

Additional insured endorsements purporting to afford broader coverage than the named insured's underlying agreement to indemnify or obtain insurance coverage are broadly construed and exclusions to coverage narrowly construed.

In *Mobil Oil Corp. v. Maryland Casualty Co.*,[40] an independent contractor, B.M.W. Constructors, Inc., was hired to repair a flare system at Mobil Oil's refinery. Under the contract, B.M.W. was to obtain liability insurance in the amount of $250,000 for each occurrence, $500,000 aggregate for bodily injury arising from work performed by B.M.W. at the refinery, and liability insurance naming and covering Mobil "as their interests may appear." B.M.W. secured a policy that provided $1 million in coverage per occurrence, and $6 million aggregate. Although the insurer claimed that coverage should be limited to the amount of coverage identified in the underlying agreement, the court found Mobil entitled to the full extent of coverage under the policy. "If [the insurer] truly intended to limit coverage, it readily could have done so by adding its own restrictive language to the insurance policies."[41]

Likewise, as the court stated in *J.A. Jones Constr. Co. v. Hartford Fire Ins. Co.*, where a subcontractor agrees to indemnify a contractor only for damages occasioned by the subcontractor's own negligence and also secures coverage for the contractor as an additional insured not limited to the extent of the subcontractor's agreement to indemnify, the contractor obtains the full benefit of the coverage under the policy.[42] The court concluded that, if the insurer wanted to limit coverage, "it could have done so by stating that the level of insurance provided to additional insureds is only that level which is required under the contract between the additional insured and the named insured."[43]

Further, in *National Union Fire Ins. Co. v. Glenview Park Dist.*,[44] an endorsement was issued by the insurer extending the named insured's coverage to anyone the named insured

---

34. *Id.* at 403.

35. Juretic v. USX Corp., 596 N.E.2d 810, 812–13 (Ill. App. Ct. 1992).

36. *See* Barger v. Scandroli Constr. Co., 347 N.E.2d 207, 208 (Ill. App. Ct. 1976); *See also* Westinghouse Elec. Elevator Co. v. La Salle Monroe Bldg. Corp., 70 N.E.2d 604, 607 (Ill. 1946); Jokich v. Union Oil Co. 574 N.E.2d 214, 218 (Ill. App. Ct. 1991).

37. Duffy v. Poulos Bros. Constr. Co., 587 N.E.2d 1038, 1042 (Ill. App. Ct. 1991); Jokich v. Union Oil Co., 574 N.E.2d 214, 218 (Ill. App. Ct. 1991); *accord* Chicago Hous. Auth. v. Fed. Sec., Inc., 161 F.3d 485, 490 (7th Cir. 1998). *But see* Coverdill v. Lurgi Corp., 496 N.E.2d 1007 (Ill. App. Ct. 1986) and Svenson v. Miller Builders, Inc., 392 N.E.2d 628 (1979). Although there is conflicting law on this issue, it appears that the *Duffy* line of cases is the current state of the law in Illinois.

38. *Duffy*, 587 N.E.2d at 1042.

39. *See* Tanns v. Ben A. Borenstein & Co., 688 N.E.2d 667, 669–71 (Ill. App. Ct. 1997).

40. Mobil Oil Corp. v. Maryland Casualty Co., 681 N.E.2d 552, 555 (Ill. App. Ct. 1997).

41. *Id.* at 559.

42. J.A. Jones Constr. Co. v. Hartford Fire Ins. Co., 645 N.E.2d 980, 981–83 (Ill. App. Ct. 1995).

43. *Id.* at 982–83.

44. National Union Fire Ins. Co. v. Glenview Park Dist., 632 N.E.2d 1039, 1040–41 (Ill. 1994).

had "agreed by contract . . . to include as an Insured with respect to operations performed by or on behalf of the Named Insured." The coverage provided by the endorsement, however, did not apply to "damages arising out of the *negligence* of the Additional Insureds."[45] An employee of the named insured was injured and sued the named and additional insured for a statutory remedy created pursuant to the Illinois Structural Work Act. The insurer denied coverage, contending that the violation of the Structural Work Act "implied" negligence. The court held that the exclusion for negligence reached claims for common law negligence only and not statutory torts, reasoning that if the insurer "intended the term 'negligence' to include allegations that the additional insured had committed a statutory tort, such as a violation of the Structural Work Act, it could have easily modified its insurance policy to so provide."[46]

---

45. *Id.* at 1040–41 (emphasis added).
46. *Id.* at 1042.

Indiana

Brent W. Huber
Ice Miller, LLC

1. GENERAL RULES OF CONTRACTUAL INDEMNITY

Under Indiana law, the obligation to indemnify may arise from an express contract.[1] "The scope of the indemnity clause limits a party's duty to indemnify . . . but an indemnity contract should be construed to cover all losses and damages to which it reasonably appears that the parties intended it to apply."[2]

Indemnification provisions covering a party's own negligence are strictly construed and are valid only if "knowingly and willingly made."[3] Such contracts will not be interpreted to apply to the indemnitee's own negligence unless expressed in "clear and unequivocal terms."[4]

To determine whether a party has knowingly and willingly agreed to indemnify another for the other's own negligence, Indiana courts follow a two-step analysis:

> First, the indemnification clause must expressly state in clear and unequivocal terms that negligence is an area of application where the indemnitor . . . has agreed to indemnify the indemnitee . . . . The second step determines to whom the indemnification clause applies.[5]

Because courts disfavor clauses relieving the indemnitee of its own negligence and those obligate one party to pay for another's negligence,[6] the language of an indemnity clause must both define the area of application—the negligence—as well as to whom the clause applies.[7]

1. In re Ind. State Fair Litig., 49 N.E.3d 545, 549 (Ind. 2016); R. N. Thompson & Assocs. v. Wickes Lumber Co., 687 N.E.2d 617, 619 (Ind. Ct. App. 1997); Indianapolis Power & Light Co. v. Brad Snodgrass, Inc., 578 N.E.2d 669, 670 (Ind. 1991).

2. Allied-Signal, Inc. v. Acme Serv. Corp., 1992 WL 165816, at *15 (N.D. Ind. May 9, 1992) (internal citations omitted). *See also* Mead Johnson & Co. v. Kenco Grp., Inc., 899 N.E.2d 1, 3 (Ind. Ct. App. 2009); Am. States Ins. Co. v. Williams, 278 N.E.2d 295, 300 (Ind. Ct. App. 1972).

3. Plan-Tec, Inc. v. Wiggins, 443 N.E.2d 1212, 1221 (Ind. Ct. App. 1983). *See also* Moore Heating & Plumbing, Inc. v. Huber, Hunt & Nichols, 583 N.E.2d 142, 145 (Ind. Ct. App. 1991) ("[T]he language of the indemnification clause must reflect the indemnitor's knowing and willing acceptance of the burden and must express the burden in clear and unequivocal terms.").

4. Fresh Cut, Inc. v. Fazli, 650 N.E.2d 1126, 1132 (Ind. 1995); N. Am. Roofing Servs., Inc. v. Menard, Inc., 997 N.E.2d 1087, 1091 (Ind. Ct. App. 2013), *trans. denied*, 4 N.E.3d 664 (Ind. 2014); *see also Plan-Tec*, 443 N.E.2d at 122; *Moore Heating*, 583 N.E.2d at 145; WellPoint, Inc. v. National Union Fire Ins. Co. of Pittsburgh, PA, 29 N.E.3d 716, 724 (Ind. 2015).

5. GKN Co. v. Starnes Trucking, Inc., 798 N.E.2d 548, 552 (Ind. Ct. App. 2003) (citing Hagerman Constr. Corp. v. Long Elec. Co., 741 N.E.2d 390, 392 (Ind. Ct. App. 2000)).

6. Ogilvie v. Steele by Steele, 452 N.E.2d 167, 170 (Ind. Ct. App. 1983) (Although a person may contract to be indemnified for his or her own negligence, "courts disfavor such indemnification clauses because it is a harsh burden to obligate one party to pay for the negligence of the other party.") (internal citations omitted)). *See also* Ft. Wayne Cablevision v. Ind. & Mich. Elec. Co., 443 N.E.2d 863, 868 (Ind. Ct. App. 1983) ("This policy of disfavor is directed at indemnification duties which the indemnitor did not knowingly assume. It does not invalidate such clauses simply because they might provide broad protection for the indemnitee.").

7. *Hagerman*, 741 N.E.2d at 392. *See also* Henthorne v. Legacy Healthcare, Inc., 764 N.E.2d 751, 757 (Ind. Ct. App. 2002).

> For example, if a clause simply states that a subcontractor shall indemnify a general contractor for any negligence which arises from the job, it is sufficient to show that the clause applies to negligence but is insufficient to inform the subcontractor that it must indemnify the general contractor for acts of the general contractor's own negligence. The claim of negligence which arises from the job could have been caused by the negligence of the general contractor, the subcontractor, third persons, or a combination of them.[8]

While the agreement does not need to specifically reference the term "negligence,"[9] it must nevertheless include "language of negligence"—terms like "liability, claims and suits" and/or contract provisions that contemplate "losses, fines, and expenses . . . ."[10] Course of dealing, absent express language, is insufficient to evidence indemnification.[11] The primary concern is to ensure the indemnitor is "aware of the burden it [is] accepting" when entering into the agreement.[12]

For instance, in a railroad agreement, an agreement to indemnify each other for damage or injury arising from "the trains, locomotives, cars or equipment of one party only being involved" was sufficient to require indemnification for the indemnitee's own negligence as long as the loss only involved the indemnitor's property.[13]

In contrast, an indemnity agreement referring only to the indemnitor's negligence and limiting its scope to the fault of the indemnitor or its agents will not be read to cover the indemnitee's sole negligence.[14] Thus, if the agreement covers losses "only to the extent" they are caused in whole or in part by the indemnitor, it will not reach the indemnitee's negligence.[15]

However, including a clause that states that the agreement will apply regardless of "whether or not it is alleged that [the indemnitee] in any way contributed to the alleged wrongdoing or is liable due to a nondelegable duty" is sufficient to cover indemnity for at least the indemnitee's concurrent negligence.[16]

Furthermore, there may be no right to indemnity if the parties have unequal bargaining power or if the contract is otherwise unconscionable.[17] Accordingly, if there is prodigiously unequal bargaining power between the parties, the party with more bargaining power must prove that the provision was explained to the other party and that there was a meeting of the minds.[18] Similarly, if there is evidence of unequal bargaining power and an inconspicuous "fine print" indemnity clause not identified to the indemnitor, the clause may be unenforceable and the right to indemnity may be foreclosed.[19] This rule simply extends the requirement that an indemnitor appreciate the burden it is undertaking.[20]

8. *Moore Heating*, 583 N.E.2d at 145–46.

9. *Id.* at 146.

10. Exide Corp. v. Millwright Riggers, Inc., 727 N.E.2d 473, 480 (Ind. Ct. App. 2000) (citing *Moore Heating*, 583 N.E.2d at 146). *See also Allied-Signal*, 1992 WL 165816, at *7 ("[U]se of words such as 'growing out of the performance of this order' or 'resulting from or arising in connection with' in indemnification agreements is evidence that the parties intended the indemnity agreement to provide broad protection.") (internal citations omitted).

11. *State Fair Litig.*, 49 N.E.3d at 552–53.

12. *Ft. Wayne Cablevision*, 443 N.E.2d at 868.

13. *Ogilvie*, 452 N.E.2d at 171.

14. *Hagerman*, 741 N.E.2d at 393–94.

15. *Id.*

16. *Moore Heating*, 583 N.E.2d at 146–47. The agreement in *Moore Heating* expressly excluded claims arising from the indemnitee's own negligence, thereby only covering the joint or concurrent negligence.

17. *See* Weaver v. Am. Oil Co., 276 N.E.2d 144, 148 (Ind. 1971).

18. *Id.*

19. *Id.* at 147 ("The evidence also reveals that the clause was in fine print and contained no title heading which would have identified it as an indemnity clause. It seems a deplorable abuse of justice to hold a man of poor education, to a contract prepared by the attorneys of American Oil, for the benefit of American Oil which was presented to Weaver on a 'take it or leave it basis.'"); *see also State Fair Litig.*, 49 N.E.3d at 546.

20. *See id.*

Determining unequal bargaining power is a question of fact, and "the mere fact that one party has submitted a form contract in sophisticated business transactions between sophisticated business entities [does not establish] a disparity in bargaining power."[21]

If an indemnification clause providing indemnity for "all losses and liability" includes a provision for attorneys' fees, it will be construed broadly to encompass fees for prosecuting the claim for indemnification.[22] The clause will not be narrowly construed so as to limit the defense obligation to fees incurred in defending the original action for which indemnity is sought.[23]

2. EXCEPTIONS TO GENERAL RULES OF CONTRACTUAL INDEMNITY

According to Indiana Code § 26-2-5-1, indemnity agreements in construction contracts in which a party seeks indemnification from another for the consequences of its own sole negligence are void as against public policy.[24] That statute states:

> All provisions, clauses, covenants, or agreements contained in, collateral to, or affecting any construction or design contract except those pertaining to highway contracts, which purport to indemnify the promisee against liability for:
>
> (1) Death or bodily injury to persons;
>
> (2) Injury to property;
>
> (3) Design defects; or
>
> (4) Any other loss, damage or expense arising under either (1), (2) or (3);
>
> from the sole negligence or willful misconduct of the promisee or the promisee's agents, servants or independent contractors who are directly responsible to the promisee, are against public policy and are void and unenforceable.

This statute applies only if the indemnity agreement purports to relieve the indemnitee of its sole negligence.[25] Thus, an agreement in the construction context indemnifying the indemnitee for its concurrent or contributory negligence is permissible.[26]

Also, the statute by its terms applies only to construction contracts, a term that has been narrowly construed. The purpose of the statute "is to protect employees in the construction industry and the public from irresponsible contractors who have shifted their own liability onto a subcontractor whose insurance does not cover contract liability."[27] "[A] construction contract involves hazardous construction work requiring safe working conditions and ultimately a safe product . . . . Construction work means to build, erect,

21. Sink & Edwards, Inc. v. Huber, Hunt & Nichols, Inc., 458 N.E.2d 291, 296 (Ind. Ct. App. 1984). *See also* Maxon Corp. v. Tyler Pipe Indus., Inc., 497 N.E.2d 570, 577 (Ind. Ct. App. 1986) ("When, as here, the imposition of a broad indemnification clause is attempted without the express assent of the proposed indemnitor, and when that clause is placed in relative obscurity on the back of an invoice, it is unconscionable.").

22. Tacks Steel Corp. v. ARC Constr. Co., 821 N.E.2d 883, 890 (Ind. Ct. App. 2005); *see also* Putz v. Allie, 785 N.E.2d 577, 582 (Ind. Ct. App. 2003) (stating that an Indiana contract that allows for the recovery of reasonable attorneys' fees will be enforced according to its terms unless it violates public policy) (citing Harrison v. Thomas, 761 N.E.2d 816, 821 (Ind. 2002)).

23. *Tacks Steel*, 821 N.E.2d at 890.

24. Ind. Code § 26-2-5-1 (2014).

25. *Moore Heating*, 583 N.E.2d at 147–48.

26. *Id.*

27. *Ogilvie*, 452 N.E.2d at 169–70 (citing *Ft. Wayne Cablevision*, 443 N.E.2d at 868).

or create."[28] Accordingly, the statute applies to any construction contract, whether or not it is for "new" construction.[29] However, a contract for maintenance of an existing structure would not fall within the scope of the statute,[30] nor would a lease agreement,[31] or a licensing agreement.[32]

In certain situations, Indiana has recognized a public policy prohibition on indemnity agreements in favor of common carriers:

> [W]e believe the rule to be well established that a railway company acting as a *common carrier* may not contract for indemnity against its own tort liability when it is performing either a public or quasi public duty such as that owing to a shipper, passenger, or servant, and *that such contracts are void as against public policy*.[33]

This rule is largely based on the railroad acting as a common carrier, and "[a]n indemnification clause in a lease is not void or voidable as against public policy simply because the indemnitee is charged with a nondelegable duty to the public or third persons."[34] "[A] railroad company when called upon to perform a service which it is not compelled to perform by the very nature of its operation as a common carrier, may, under proper conditions, contract against its liability for negligence for the reason that it is then acting in the capacity of a private carrier."[35]

3. INDEMNITY AGREEMENTS AS INSURED CONTRACTS

Standard commercial general liability (CGL) policies often include a provision excluding liability assumed by the insured under a separate contract or agreement, which Indiana courts have found enforceable.[36] For instance, a father's homeowner's insurance carrier is not responsible for liability assumed by the father in signing a financial responsibility agreement for his son to obtain a driver's license as long as the father's homeowner's insurance policy contains such an exclusion.[37] The exclusion likewise applies to assumptions of liability for "property damage" and "bodily injury." However, Indiana has not addressed whether this exclusion for contractual liability applies to subsequent agreements to indemnify, which would provide insurance coverage for indemnity agreements, i.e., making the indemnity agreement an "insured contract." The policy definition of an "insured contract" has been cited in an insurance policy as an exception to exclusions otherwise applicable to claims for "property damage" and "bodily injury," but the case in which the exception was cited involved a claim under the policy's "personal injury" coverage, which did not contain an "insured contract" exception to the contractual liability exclusion.[38] As such, the "insured contract" exception is an unsettled area of Indiana's jurisprudence on contractual

---

28. *Id.* (citing *Ft. Wayne Cablevision*, 443 N.E.2d at 868; other internal citations omitted).

29. LTV Steel Co. v. Nw. Eng'g & Constr., 845 F. Supp. 1295, 1298 (N.D. Ind. 1994).

30. Bethlehem Steel Corp. v. Sercon Corp., 654 N.E.2d 1163, 1167 (Ind. Ct. App. 1995).

31. Orville Milk Co. v. Beller, 486 N.E.2d 555, 561 (Ind. Ct. App. 1985).

32. *Ft. Wayne Cablevision*, 443 N.E.2d at 871. *See also* Portside Energy Corp., Inc. v. N. Ind. Commuter Transp. Dist., 913 N.E.2d 221 (Ind. Ct. App. 2009) (holding that an agreement granting an energy company a license to use railroad crossing was not a "construction or design contract," and therefore transportation district's action against the company under indemnification provision for damages arising out of a train collision was not barred).

33. Pa. R. Co. v. Kent, 198 N.E.2d 615, 619 (Ind. Ct. App. 1964) (emphasis in original; internal citations omitted).

34. Sequa Coatings Corp. v. N. Ind. Commuter Transp. Dist., 796 N.E.2d 1216, 1223 (Ind. Ct. App. 2003).

35. *Kent*, 198 N.E.2d at 619.

36. *See* Selleck v. Westfield Ins. Co., 617 N.E.2d 968 (Ind. Ct. App. 1993).

37. *Id.*

38. *See* Exec. Builders, Inc. v. Motorists Ins. Cos., 2001 WL 548391 (S.D. Ind. Mar. 30, 2001). *See also* W. Bend Mut. Ins. Co. v. MacDougall Pierce Const., Inc., 11 N.E.3d 531 (Ind. Ct. App. 2014), *trans. denied sub nom.* W. Bend Mut. Ins. Co. v. MacDougall Pierce Const., Inc., 25 N.E.3d 746 (Ind. 2015).

indemnity, which could provide insured individuals and entities broader coverage for contractual liabilities.

4. OPERATION OF AN AGREEMENT TO INDEMNIFY REFERRING TO OR REQUIRING INSURANCE

The standards applicable to agreements to indemnify are not applied in the context of an agreement to obtain insurance.

> [W]here neither party has a legal duty to insure but each foresees the potential of a loss occurring by negligence or accident, the reasonable expectation of both in expressly imposing the duty to insure against the loss upon one of them is that the other will be protected as fully as if he had assumed the duty himself. There is no need to apply to such agreements the standard applied to indemnity agreements. With agreements to insure, the risk of loss is not intended to be shifted to one of the parties; it is intended to be shifted to an insurance company in return for a premium payment. Neither party intends to assume a potential liability; rather both are demonstrating "normal" business foresight in avoiding liability and allocating it to an insurer.[39]

Unlike agreements to indemnify, agreements to procure insurance or name another party as an "additional insured" do not require clear and explicit terms.

> As a matter of interpretation, indemnification agreements that require one party to compensate the other party for the other party's own negligence are construed much more strictly than insurance agreements. A stricter reading is given to such indemnification clauses because indemnification for another party's own negligence is a harsh burden that a party would not lightly accept . . . . Therefore, such indemnification provisions will not be held to provide complete indemnity unless the indemnity is expressed in clear and unequivocal terms.
>
> In contrast, an agreement to insure is an agreement to provide both parties with the benefits of insurance regardless of the cause of the loss (excepting wanton and willful acts) . . . . An agreement to insure differs from an agreement to indemnify in that, with an agreement to insure, the risk of loss is not intended to be shifted to one of the parties, but is instead intended to be shifted to an insurance company . . . . Therefore, standard rules of contract interpretation apply to insurance agreements, rather than the strict construction given to self-indemnification clauses.[40]

As such, an agreement to obtain insurance may be valid and enforceable, while a parallel indemnity agreement in the same instrument is not.[41]

Since an agreement to obtain insurance does not invoke the same concerns as an agreement to indemnify another for the other's own negligence, an agreement to obtain insurance should not be invalidated under Indiana Code § 26-2-5-1 (which governs indemnity agreements in the construction context).[42] In dicta, the U.S. Court of Appeals for the Seventh Circuit has stated that "[t]he potential invalidity of the indemnification provision does not

39. Morsches Lumber, Inc. v. Probst, 388 N.E.2d 284, 286–87 (Ind. Ct. App. 1979). *See also* S.C. Nestel, Inc. v. Future Constr., Inc., 836 N.E.2d 445 (Ind. Ct. App. 2005).

40. *Exide Corp.*, 727 N.E.2d at 482 (internal citations omitted).

41. *Id.*

42. *See* Doherty v. Davy Songer, Inc., 195 F.3d 919, 923 n.1 (7th Cir. 1999).

affect the enforceability of the insurance provision because, under Indiana case law, the two are separate provisions applying in separate circumstances."[43]

An agreement to obtain insurance is typically considered a "waiver of subrogation" between the contracting parties.[44] "In an arrangement where one party agrees to purchase insurance for the benefit of both parties, the first party in effect agrees to waive the intended insured's liability . . . . Thus, the party who agreed to purchase insurance has no cause of action against the party for whose benefit the insurance was intended regardless of the fault of this intended insured."[45] As a result, the insurer for the named insured loses its subrogation rights against the "intended insured," and "the first party's insurance carrier has no subrogation cause of action against the intended insured."[46]

"[A]n agreement to provide insurance constitutes an agreement to limit the recourse of the party acquiring the policy solely to its proceeds even though the loss may be caused by the negligence of the other party to the agreement."[47] The implicit waiver of subrogation is based on the assumption that the parties intended the insurance to cover certain risks, and "the foregoing assumption is valid only if the agreement to insure includes the risk which results in the loss and at the time the loss occurs, i.e., there is a meeting of the minds on the risks against which the parties are to be insured and the period of time the parties are to be so insured."[48]

An agreement to obtain insurance will not be read to waive subrogation rights to one not privy to the contract.[49] Thus, an agreement to obtain insurance between an owner and a general contractor will not extend to waive subrogation rights against a subcontractor, if insurance in favor of that subcontractor is not contemplated by the terms of the agreement.[50]

43. *Id.* (citing Ind. Erectors, Inc. v. Trs. of Ind. Univ., 686 N.E.2d 878, 880 (Ind. Ct. App. 1997); *Morsches Lumber*, 388 N.E.2d at 287)).

44. *Ind. Erectors*, 686 N.E.2d at 880 (citing LeMaster Steel Erectors Inc. v. Reliance Ins. Co., 546 N.E.2d 313, 317 (Ind. Ct. App. 1989)).

45. *Id.* (citing *LeMaster Steel Erectors*, 546 N.E.2d at 317).

46. *Id.* (citing *LeMaster Steel Erectors*, 546 N.E.2d at 317; S. Tippecanoe Sch. Bldg. Corp. v. Shambaugh & Son, Inc., 395 N.E.2d 320, 331–34 (Ind. Ct. App. 1979)).

47. *Morsches Lumber*, 388 N.E.2d at 285.

48. Midwestern Indem. Co. v. Leffler Constr. Co., 463 N.E.2d 1130, 1132 (Ind. Ct. App. 1984).

49. *See Ind. Erectors*, 686 N.E.2d at 880.

50. *Id.* at 882. *See also LeMaster Steel Erectors*, 546 N.E.2d at 316–17.

Iowa

Kathryn Kasper
Hancock, Daniel & Johnson, P.C.

1. GENERAL RULES OF CONTRACTUAL INDEMNITY

Indemnity agreements are enforceable in Iowa[1] according to the terms of the agreement.[2] "Generally, no particular language is required to support indemnification, and a written agreement can be established without specifically expressing the obligation as indemnification."[3] "If a contractual provision for indemnity is present, liability is controlled by this provision, and not by the issue of whether the tortious conduct of the respective parties was 'active' or 'passive,' primary or secondary."[4]

Intent is the controlling consideration. An indemnification agreement is created when the words used in the agreement "express an intention by one party to reimburse or hold the other party harmless for any loss, damage, or liability."[5] And while a contract for indemnification is ordinarily subject to the same rules of construction as other contracts,[6] several unique rules apply in construing indemnity contracts.[7] Where "an indemnification is not given by one in the insurance business but is given incident to a contract whose main purpose is not indemnification, the indemnity provision must be construed strictly in favor of the indemnitor."[8] "Also, an indemnity contract is strictly construed against the drafter . . . ."[9]

Courts have also "crafted a special rule of construction for indemnification contracts when [ ] such contracts purport to relieve the indemnitee from liability for its own negligence."[10] In those circumstances, courts will not "permit an indemnitee to recover for its own negligence unless the intention of the parties is clearly and unambiguously expressed."[11]

In applying this rule, courts look to two aspects of the agreement to determine whether a party is to be indemnified for its own negligence. First, courts look for specific language in the contract regarding the fault of the indemnitee.[12] For instance, language indicating that the indemnitor agreed to indemnify the indemnitee "from any and all claims . . . even though the [indemnitee] may have caused or contributed thereto" clearly and unambiguously covers the indemnitee's own negligence.[13] Conversely, language that provides that

1. Herter v. Ringland-Johnson-Crowley Co., 492 N.W.2d 672, 674 (Iowa 1992). *See also* Evans v. McComas-Lacina Constr. Co., 641 N.W.2d 841, 844 (Iowa 2002) ("Contractual indemnity is not disfavored . . . .").

2. *McComas-Lacina Constr.*, 641 N.W.2d at 844. *See also* BVS, Inc. v. CDW Direct, LLC, 88 F. Supp. 3d. 965 (N.D. Iowa 2015).

3. McNally & Nimergood v. Neumann-Kiewit Constructors, Inc., 648 N.W.2d 564, 570 (Iowa 2002) (citing Jenckes v. Rice, 93 N.W. 384 (Iowa 1903)).

4. Hysell v. Iowa Pub. Serv. Co., 534 F.2d 775, 785 (8th Cir. 1976).

5. McNally & Nimergood, 648 N.W.2d at 570.

6. *See* Evans v. Howard R. Green Co., 231 N.W.2d 907, 916 (Iowa 1975).

7. *See* Pugh v. Prairie Constr. Co., 602 N.W.2d 805, 809 (Iowa 1999).

8. *Id.* (internal citations omitted).

9. *Id.*

10. Cochran v. Gehrke Constr., 235 F. Supp. 2d 991, 994 (N.D. Iowa 2002) (citing *McNally & Nimergood*, 648 N.W.2d at 571).

11. *McNally & Nimergood*, 648 N.W.2d at 571. *See also* Thornton v. Guthrie Cty. Rural Elec. Coop. Ass'n, 467 N.W.2d 574, 576 (Iowa 1991) ("The general rule is that an indemnity agreement will not be construed to relieve the indemnitee from the effect of its own negligence unless the agreement provides for it in 'clear and unequivocal' language."); *Herter*, 492 N.W.2d at 674 ("The enforceability of such contracts [purporting to relieve the indemnitee of its own negligence] turns on whether the indemnifying language is 'clear and unequivocal.'").

12. *McNally & Nimergood*, 648 N.W.2d at 571.

13. Employers Mut. Cas. Co. v. Chi. & N.W. Transp. Co., 521 N.W.2d 692, 694 (Iowa 1994). *See also Thornton*, 467 N.W.2d at 576–77 (indemnification imposed "regardless of whether [damages were] caused in part by [the indemnitee]").

the indemnitor will indemnify the indemnitee "from and against . . . all claims . . . caused by, arising from, incident to, connected with or growing out of the work to be performed under this contract regardless of whether such claim is alleged to be caused, in whole or in part, by negligence or otherwise on the part of the [indemnitor]" is insufficient to impose liability for the indemnitee's negligence.[14]

Second, and in addition to looking for specific language addressing the fault or negligence of the indemnitee, courts will construe indemnity contracts to include indemnification for an indemnitee's own negligence if the intent of the contract contemplates such indemnification, regardless of the terms used.[15] Iowa's rule of construction thus does not actually require the contract to mention the indemnitee's negligence or fault specifically as long as this intention is otherwise clearly expressed by the words of the agreement.[16]

Ultimately, the courts' tendency to find broad indemnification clauses to be insufficient to create indemnity for an indemnitee's own negligence is "only a guideline, not a strict principle."[17] "In each case, the intent of the parties will control as revealed by the language of the agreement," and the courts will not "impose any special requirement that specific language be used to express that intent."[18]

An indemnity agreement can support a claim by a third party against an employer for indemnification where the indemnitee has been held liable for an employee's injury.[19] The Iowa Supreme Court has adopted the view that an employer's immunity under the Iowa Workers Compensation Act "is only against actions for damages on account of the employee's injury; a third party's action for indemnity is not exactly for 'damages' but for reimbursement, and it is not 'on account of' the employee's injury, but on account of breach of an independent duty owed by the employer to the third party."[20] "Thus, an indemnity claim by a third party against the injured plaintiff's employer is viable under Iowa law, if it is based on an 'independent duty' of the employer to the third party claiming indemnity."[21] The independent duty cannot be a general duty of care; without some specific duty or a contractual obligation owed to the indemnitee/third party, indemnity from the employer will not be permitted.[22]

A party may also obtain indemnity for damages that it occasioned, including recovering for its own damages as opposed to recovering amounts paid to a third party.[23] In other words, the indemnitee could recover for its own damages under an indemnity agreement, even when it caused part of those damages and even though there was no third-party claim against the indemnitee.[24]

---

14. *See, e.g.*, Trushcheff v. Abell-Howe Co., 239 N.W.2d 116, 134 (Iowa 1976).

15. *Herter*, 492 N.W.2d at 674. *See also* Wells Dairy, Inc. v. Am. Indus. Refrigeration, Inc., 762 N.W.2d 463, 470–71 (Iowa 2009).

16. *See, e.g.*, Payne Plumbing & Heating Co. v. Bob McKiness Excavating & Grading, Inc., 382 N.W.2d 156, 160 (Iowa 1986) (finding that contract in which subcontractor agreed to indemnify for damages "caused in part by a party indemnified hereunder" covered indemnitee's own negligence).

17. *McNally & Nimergood*, 648 N.W.2d at 572 (stating that it "is not our rule" that an indemnity contract needs "to contain a specific reference to the indemnitee's own negligence" before indemnification of the indemnitee would be permitted).

18. *Id. See also Cochran*, 293 F. Supp. 2d at 995 (describing the rule set out in *McNally & Nimergood, supra*, as "the current formulation of the rule in Iowa for contracts purporting to provide indemnity for an indemnitee's own negligence . . ."); N. Natural Gas Co. v. Roth Packing Co., 323 F.2d 922 (8th Cir. 1963) ("If the intention to indemnify is apparent from the whole instrument, it will be construed as a contract of indemnity, although it is called by some other name by the parties.").

19. *See McComas-Lacina Constr.*, 641 N.W.2d at 844.

20. Woodruff Constr. Co. v. Barrick Roofers, Inc., 406 N.W. 2d 783, 785 (Iowa 1987).

21. *Cochran*, 235 F. Supp. 2d at 1001. The "independent duty" must be a duty that is of "a specific, defined nature," not simply a "general duty" such as the duty not to harm another through tortious acts. *Id.* at 1103.

22. *Hysell*, 534 F.2d at 783.

23. *See Payne Plumbing*, 382 N.W.2d at 160.

24. *Id.*

2. EXCEPTIONS TO GENERAL RULES OF CONTRACTUAL INDEMNITY

The Iowa Comprehensive Petroleum Underground Storage Tank Fund Act limits the use of indemnity agreements by providing that an insurance, indemnification, or similar risk-sharing or risk-shifting agreement "shall not be effective to transfer any liability for costs recoverable" for corrective actions taken under the Act.

> An insurance, indemnification, hold harmless, conveyance, or similar risk-sharing or risk-shifting agreement shall not be effective to transfer any liability for costs recoverable under this section. The fund, board, or department of natural resources may proceed directly against the owner or operator or other allegedly responsible party. This section does not bar any agreement to insure, hold harmless, or indemnify a party to the agreement for any costs or expenditures under this chapter, and does not modify rights between the parties to an agreement, except to the extent the agreement shifts liability to an owner or operator eligible for assistance under the remedial account for any damages or other expenses in connection with a corrective action for which another potentially responsible party is or may be liable. Any such provision is null and void and of no force or effect.[25]

A "corrective action" is one to minimize, eliminate, or clean up a release to protect the public health and welfare or the environment. Corrective action includes, but is not limited to, excavation of an underground storage tank for the purposes of repairing a leak or removal of a tank, removal of contaminated soil, and cleansing of groundwaters or surface waters.[26] The prohibition on indemnification agreements, however, is not absolute: it bars those agreements only to the extent they shift liability to an owner or operator "eligible for assistance under the remedial account for any damages or other expenses in connection with a corrective action for which another potentially responsible party is or may be liable."[27] In all other cases, an agreement to insure, hold harmless, or indemnify a party for any costs or expenditures under the Act is allowed.[28] The statutory prohibition has been narrowly construed, and the Iowa Supreme Court has rejected the argument that the prohibition evidences any legislative intent to impose liability on oil producers who are not otherwise responsible parties.[29]

Under the Iowa Business Corporation Act, a corporation may typically ***indemnify*** an individual who is a party to a proceeding because the individual is a director of the corporation, and where the director acted in good faith for the best interests of the corporation[30] but a corporation is generally prohibited from ***indemnifying*** a director in two situations:

> a. In connection with a proceeding by or in the right of the corporation, except for reasonable expenses incurred in connection with the proceeding if it is determined that the director has met the relevant standard of conduct under subsection 1.
>
> b. In connection with any proceeding with respect to conduct for which the director was adjudged liable on the basis that the director received a financial benefit to which the director was not entitled, whether or not involving action in the director's official capacity.[31]

---

25. Iowa Code § 455G.13(8).
26. Iowa Code § 455G.2(6).
27. Iowa Code § 455G.13(8).
28. *Id.*
29. Iowa Comprehensive Petroleum Underground Storage Tank Fund Bd. v. Mobil Oil Corp., 606 N.W.2d 359 (Iowa 2000).
30. Iowa Code § 490.851(1).
31. Iowa Code § 490.851(4). *See also* Iowa Code § 501.412(4) (applying above-described prohibition on indemnification to directors of closed cooperatives); Iowa Code § 512B.9(2) (prohibiting the indemnification of officers and members of fraternal benefit societies under certain defined circumstances).

Courts have also recognized a common law prohibition on agreements to indemnify involving public utilities, finding Iowa law to be in accord with the Restatement (Second) of Contracts § 575:

> A bargain for exemption from liability for the consequences of a willful breach of duty is illegal, and a bargain for exemption from liability for the consequences of negligence is illegal if . . . one of the parties is charged with a duty of public service, and the bargain relates to negligence in the performance of any part of its duty to the public, for which it has received or been promised compensation.[32]

This rule does not apply if the entity charged with public service is not rendering the public service to the other party to the indemnity contract.[33] The same public policy considerations that counsel against indemnity agreements by public utilities apply to agreements in which a common carrier (such as a railroad) attempts to relieve itself from liability for its own negligence.[34] But nothing prohibits a common carrier from obtaining an indemnity agreement from another party "when the railroad is not acting in its public capacity."[35]

With respect to indemnity agreements in the construction context, while the Iowa Supreme Court has described as "sound policy" statutes in other jurisdictions prohibiting certain indemnification agreements in construction contracts,[36] neither the state legislature nor the courts have created any such prohibition.

3. INDEMNITY AGREEMENTS AS INSURED CONTRACTS

An agreement to indemnify may constitute an "insured contract" if it meets a particular insurance policy's definition of "insured contract."[37] This includes an oral agreement to indemnify.[38]

For an "insured contract" to be covered under a liability policy, the underlying indemnity agreement must be sufficiently specific to create an indemnification obligation on the insured.[39] And coverage for an "insured contract" may exist, absent policy language to the contrary, where the liability assumed by the insured would otherwise be imposed by law on the insured.[40]

4. OPERATION OF AN AGREEMENT TO INDEMNIFY REFERRING TO OR REQUIRING INSURANCE

It does not appear that Iowa courts have addressed the interplay between an indemnity agreement and a parallel agreement to obtain insurance. Since intent is the primary concern in construing indemnity contracts, an indemnity agreement accompanied by an agreement to obtain insurance for the benefit of the indemnitee are likely to be read together to discern the parties' intent as to the scope of the indemnity agreement.

---

32. *N. Natural Gas*, 323 F.2d at 927–28. *See also* Fire Ass'n of Philadelphia v. Allis Chalmers Mfg. Co., 129 F. Supp. 335, 351 (D. Iowa 1955) (finding § 575 to be the law of Iowa).

33. *Fire Ass'n of Philadelphia*, 129 F. Supp. at 352.

34. *Emp'rs Mut. Cas.*, 521 N.W.2d at 695.

35. *Id. See also* Chi. G. W. R. Co. v. Farmers Produce Co., 164 F. Supp. 532 (D. Iowa 1958).

36. *Pugh*, 602 N.W.2d at 809.

37. John Deere Ins. Co. v. De Smet Ins. Co., 650 N.W.2d 601, 606 (Iowa 2002) (quoting Smithway Motor Xpress v. Liberty Mut., 484 N.W.2d 192, 196 (Iowa 1992)) (interpreting the term "incidental contract" to include one in which the insured assumes another's liability); and *see, e.g., John Deere Ins. Co.*, 650 N.W.2d at 607.

38. *Id.* at 606.

39. *See* Rapid Leasing, Inc., v. Nat'l Am. Ins. Co., 263 F.3d 820 (8th Cir. 2001) (finding a lease agreement not to be an "insured contract" because it was not specific enough to create an obligation on the insured to indemnify the indemnitee for its own negligence).

40. *John Deere Ins. Co.*, 650 N.W.2d at 607.

Iowa courts have addressed agreements in which one party agrees to name another as an "additional insured" under the named insured's policy of insurance.[41] Courts carefully examine whether the particular loss that is argued to be included within the scope of the "additional insured" agreement is actually covered by the terms of the policy.[42] If the policy does not cover the loss and does not provide the coverage the indemnitee believed it bargained for with the indemnitor, courts will deny coverage and will require the indemnitee/additional insured to look to the indemnitor/named insured for recourse.[43]

Where an indemnitor is not a named defendant in an injured party's successful action against an indemnitee (for instance, where an employee brings suit against a third party but not against his employer), courts will not allow the indemnitor to escape its duty to indemnify under an indemnity agreement or its contractual duty to provide "additional insured" coverage to the indemnitee until a finding of fact is made with respect to the indemnitor's own negligence.[44]

41. *See generally* Regent Ins. Co. v. Estes Co., 564 N.W.2d 846 (Iowa 1997).

42. In *Regent*, a subcontractor's employee was injured when tresses installed by the contractor collapsed. After the employee collected a judgment against the contractor, the subcontractor's insurer brought a declaratory judgment action seeking a determination that the policy did not afford coverage for the employee's claim against the contractor because the injuries were the sole result of the contractor's negligence. In finding in favor of the insurer, the court ruled that the insurer was not liable to the contractor under the indemnification clause or as an additional insured because the language of the two provisions specifically limited coverage to liability arising out of the subcontractor's work. *Id.* at 847–49.

43. *Id.* at 849. *See also* City of Cedar Rapids v. Ins. Co. of N. Am., 562 N.W.2d 156, 157–59 (Iowa 1997) (noting that if the indemnitor failed to procure for the indemnitee the full extent of liability coverage that was required under the lease agreement (pursuant to the indemnitor's agreement to name the indemnitee as an additional insured), the party seeking indemnification must look to the indemnitor for recourse, not the insurance company).

44. *See* IBP, Inc. v. DCS Sanitation Mgmt. Serv., Inc., 498 N.W.2d 425, 428 (Iowa Ct. App. 1993). In *IBP, Inc.*, the indemnitor's employee was injured while working at the indemnitee's place of business. After the employee recovered from the indemnitee, the indemnitee brought an action against the employer and its insurer. The appeals court found that a question of fact as to whether the indemnitee or the indemnitor caused the employee's injury precluded summary judgment since the issue of whether the indemnitor/employer was responsible for the employee's injury was not previously litigated.

Kansas

Christina Arnone and Katherine Bechina
Stinson Leonard Street LLP

1. GENERAL RULES OF CONTRACTUAL INDEMNITY

Express contracts of indemnity are generally valid and enforceable.[1] Contracts of indemnity are construed in accordance with the general rules of contract construction.[2] In constructing a contract of indemnity, a Kansas court ascertains the parties' intention and gives effect to that intention if it can be determined consistently with legal principles.[3] However, a contract exempting a party from liability or negligence is not favored by the law and is strictly construed against the party relying on it.[4] A party who has fairly and voluntarily entered an express contract of indemnity is bound by it, notwithstanding whether it was unwise or disadvantageous to him or her.[5] Further, a contract clause that limits liability does not have to be supported by separate consideration.[6]

A party may even contract away responsibility for its own negligence[7] if the parties do not have a vast disparity in bargaining power.[8] Courts disfavor exculpation of liability for a party's own negligence and will strictly construe against a yardstick of "clear and unequivocal language."[9] An acceptable example of "clear and unequivocal" language was set forth in *Corral v. Rollins Protective Services Co.*,[10] and cited with approval in *Zenda Grain & Supply Co. v. Farmland Indus., Inc.*[11] and *Elite Prof'ls, Inc. v. Carrier Corp.*[12]

1. Unified Sch. Dist. 467 v. Leland A. Gray Architects, LLC, 112 F. Supp. 3d 1223, 1239 (D. Kan. 2015) (applying Kansas law); Nolde v. Hamm Asphalt, Inc., 202 F. Supp. 2d 1257, 1267 (D. Kan. 2002) (applying Kansas law); *see also, e.g.*, Griffin v. Rogers, 653 P.2d 463, 467–68 (Kan. 1982) (concessionaires bound to indemnify park authority under "hold harmless" clause in contract); Dennis v. Se. Kan. Gas Co., Inc., 610 P.2d 627, 633 (Kan. 1980) (plaintiffs bound by judgment for indemnity).

2. Bartlett v. Davis Corp., 547 P.2d 800, 807 (Kan. 1976); Emprise Bank v. Rumisek, 215 P.3d 621, 632 (Kan. Ct. App. 2009).

3. *Id.*

4. Midwest Concrete Placement, Inc. v. L & S Basements, Inc., Case No. 07-2316-JAR, 2009 WL 1162391, at *4 (D. Kan. Apr. 29, 2009) (applying Kansas law); Cason v. Geis Irrigation Co. of Kan., 507 P.2d 295, 299 (Kan. 1973); Zenda Grain & Supply Co. v. Farmland Indus., Inc., 894 P.2d 881, 887 (Kan. Ct. App. 1995).

5. Moler v. Melzer, 942 P.2d 643, 645 (Kan. Ct. App. 1997); Estate of Bryant v. All Temperature Insulation, Inc., 916 P.2d 1294, 1298 (Kan. Ct. App. 1996) (quoting Kan. Power & Light Co. v. Mobil Oil Co., 426 P.2d 60, 64 (Kan. 1967)).

6. *Moler*, 942 P.2d at 645.

7. Ki Ron Ko v. Bally Total Fitness Corp, Case No. Civ.A. 02-2360GTV, 2003 WL 22466193, at *3 (D. Kan. Sept. 16, 2003) (applying Kansas law); Johnson v. Bd. of Cty. Comm'rs of Pratt Cty., 913 P.2d 119, 136 (Kan. 1996); *Zenda Grain*, 894 P.2d at 887.

8. Neustrom v. Union Pac. R.R. Co., 156 F.3d 1057, 1062 (10th Cir. 1998) (applying Kansas law); Belger Cartage Serv., Inc. v. Holland Constr. Co., 582 P.2d 1111, 1119 (Kan. 1978) (quoting Kan. City Power & Light Co. v. United Tel. Co., 458 F.2d 177, 179 (10th Cir. 1972)).

9. Dixon v. CertainTeed Corp., 944 F. Supp. 1501, 1506 (D. Kan. 1996); Elite Prof'ls, Inc. v. Carrier Corp., 827 P.2d 1195, 1203 (Kan. Ct. App. 1992).

10. *See* Corral v. Rollins Protective Servs. Co., 732 P.2d 1260, 1263 (Kan. 1987). The "clear and unequivocal" language included, in pertinent part:

> The parties agree that if loss or damage should result from the failure of performance or operation or from defective performance or operation or from improper installation or servicing of the [Rollins] System, that Rollins' liability, if any, for the loss or damage thus sustained shall be limited . . . and that the provisions of this paragraph shall apply if loss or damage . . . results . . . from negligence . . . of Rollins, its agents or employees.

11. "We conclude that in order to protect itself from its own negligence, malfeasance, or mismanagement, an entity must employ language similar to the clause in *Corral*. Those drafting hold harmless clauses in the future should look to that language and follow it carefully." *Zenda Grain*, 894 P.2d at 888.

12. The indemnity clause in *Corral* "in our view, is a clear and unequivocal expression of exemption from liability for negligence. It is a statement of exculpatory purpose beyond any peradventure of a doubt. No comparable clear and unequivocal language appears in the printed warranty and disclaimer here involved." *Elite Prof'ls, Inc.*, 827 P.2d at 1203.

There must be no possibility that any other meaning can be ascribed to a contract for indemnity; "mere general broad and seemingly all-inclusive language in the indemnifying agreement is not sufficient to impose liability for the indemnitee's own negligence."[13] Indemnification clauses that seek to indemnify an indemnitee for its own negligence must specifically address the issue of the indemnitee's negligence ("clear and unequivocal language") if it is to apply to negligent acts of the indemnitee.[14]

Because the Kansas Workers' Compensation Act "expressly precludes any liability of the employer for . . . negligence when the employer and employee are covered by the Act," the Act typically "abrogates a passively negligent third party's common law right to indemnity from an actively negligent employer."[15] However, the "exclusive remedy" provision of the Kansas Workers' Compensation Act[16] does not bar a third-party indemnity claim against an employer based on an express indemnification agreement where the liability claim bears no relation to the Acts.[17]

2. EXCEPTIONS TO GENERAL RULES OF CONTRACTUAL INDEMNITY

Indemnity agreements that violate a Kansas statute or public policy[18] are void and unenforceable.[19] An indemnity contract would therefore be unenforceable if, by statute, a party owes a duty to the general public and then, by contract, attempts to relieve itself from its negligent acts in violation of the statute.[20] That hypothetical statute must be for the protection of the public welfare or safety, which would impose a duty toward the public.[21] An indemnity contract contrary to such public policy will be unenforceable if it interferes with public welfare or safety.[22]

3. INDEMNITY AGREEMENTS AS INSURED CONTRACTS

Kansas courts have not determined whether an express indemnification agreement constitutes an "insured contract" within the meaning of the exception to the commercial general liability policy exclusion for contractually assumed liability.

4. OPERATION OF AN AGREEMENT TO INDEMNIFY REFERRING TO OR REQUIRING INSURANCE

Kansas courts have permitted agreements that require procuring insurance for the benefit of a party with respect to its obligation to indemnify for any and all liability.[23] Moreover, Kansas statutes, common law, and public policy do not prohibit contracting to procure

13. George K. Baum Advisors, L.L.C. v. Sprint Spectrum, L.P., Case No. 11-2442-JTM, 2013 WL 5719506, at *14 (D. Kan. Oct. 21, 2013) (applying Kansas law) (quoting Butters v. Consol. Transfer & Warehouse Co., Inc., 510 P.2d 1269, 1273 (Kan. 1973)).

14. *George K. Baum*, 2013 WL 5719506, at *14; *Zenda Grain & Supply Co.*, 894 P.2d at 888; *Elite Prof'ls, Inc.*, 827 P.2d at 1203.

15. McCleskey v. Noble Corp., 577 P.2d 830, 835 (Kan. Ct. App. 1978).

16. KAN. STAT. ANN. § 44-501b(d) (2011) ("Except as provided in the workers compensation act, no employer, or other employee of such employer, shall be liable for any injury for which compensation is recoverable under the workers compensation act nor shall an employer be liable to any third party for any injury or death of an employee which was caused under circumstances creating a legal liability against a third party and for which workers compensation is payable by such employer.").

17. *Estate of Bryant*, 916 P.2d at 1301 (reversing trial court and directing judgment be entered for crane owner because the indemnification was a contractual obligation completely independent of the general contractor's status of a statutory employer under the Workers' Compensation Act).

18. By "public policy," we have referred to a principle of law that holds that no citizen can lawfully do that which injures the public good. *See* Master Builders Ass'n v. Carson, 296 P. 693, 694 (Kan. 1931).

19. *Belger Cartage*, 582 P.2d at 1119; Osterhaus v. Toth, 187 P.3d 126, 135 (Kan. Ct. App. 2008).

20. Hunter v. Am. Rentals, 371 P.2d 131, 133 (Kan. 1962).

21. *Id.*

22. *In re Marriage of Traster*, 339 P.3d 778, 790 (Kan. 2014) (quoting *Hunter*, 371 P.2d at 133).

23. N.H. Ins., Co. v. Fox Midwest Theatres, Inc., 457 P.2d 133, 136 (Kan. 1969); TMD Southglen II, LLC v. Parker, No. 109,484, 2014 WL 2589768, at *2-3 (Kan. Ct. App. May 30, 2014) (table opinion).

insurance as long as such a contract is not illegal or directly against public policy (in which case the contract is void).[24]

In *McIntosh v. Scottsdale Insurance Co.*, applying Kansas law, the United States Court of Appeals for the Tenth Circuit decided that the named insured's policy covered an additional insured and that the coverage did not depend upon determining who was negligent.[25] Although Kansas state courts have not issued any rulings directly pertaining to this issue, other courts have applied *McIntosh* to similar factual scenarios.[26] In reaching its conclusions, the court implied that if a conflict may exist between an express contract of indemnity requiring certain coverage and a competing insurance policy within which an indemnitee is named as an additional insured, the coverage afforded by the policy controls.[27]

24. *Belger Cartage*, 582 P.2d at 1118.

25. McIntosh v. Scottsdale Ins. Co., 992 F.2d 251, 255–56 (10th Cir. 1993) (applying Kansas law).

26. *See, e.g.*, Dillon Cos., Inc. v. Royal Indem. Co., 369 F. Supp. 2d 1277, 1288 (D. Kan. 2005) (applying Kansas law).

27. *McIntosh*, 992 F.2d at 255.

Kentucky

Jason A. Frye
Neal, Gerber & Eisenberg, LLP

1. GENERAL RULES OF CONTRACTUAL INDEMNITY

Agreements to indemnify are construed to cover only such losses, damages, or liability that the parties reasonably appear to have intended.[1] A contract of indemnity will not indemnify the indemnitee against losses resulting from its own negligence unless the contract expresses that intent in unequivocal terms.[2] Furthermore, courts will not interpret a contract of indemnity to apply to losses resulting from one's own negligence unless no other meaning can be ascribed to it; every presumption is against such an interpretation.[3] Nonetheless, agreeing to indemnify another for that party's sole negligence is not against Kentucky public policy.[4]

Kentucky courts will uphold an indemnity obligation in favor of a negligent indemnitee even if the provision does not state specifically that the indemnity will cover "negligence."[5] Rather, the broad language should manifest clear intent to cover even negligent acts of the indemnitee as a matter of law.[6]

2. EXCEPTIONS TO GENERAL RULES OF CONTRACTUAL INDEMNITY

Kentucky has no statutory prohibition on the enforceability of contractual agreements to indemnify. Thus, in Kentucky, a contractor or owner may be indemnified even if the contractor or owner was indisputably negligent.[7] As noted, Kentucky does not favor clauses that provide indemnity for one's own negligence, but its courts will uphold such provisions "where it is not improbable that a party would undertake such an indemnification of another . . . ."[8] Indemnification provisions "applied to defend against the indemnitee's own negligence, are not against public policy generally, but they are when agreed to by a party in a clearly inferior bargaining position."[9] Additionally, if an indemnification provision shifts the liability for damages caused by a party's failure to follow safety statutes onto another party, then Kentucky courts will not enforce it as against public policy.[10]

1. 42 C.J.S. Indemnity § 12; Employer's Mut. Liab. Ins. Co. of Wis. v. Griffin Constr. Co., 280 S.W.2d 179, 182 (Ky. 1955).
2. *Id.*; 27 Am. Jur. Indemnity § 15.
3. *Employer's Mut. Liab. Ins.*, 280 S.W.2d at 182; Mitchell v. S. Ry. Co., 74 S.W. 216, 217 (Ky. 1903).
4. Fosson v. Ashland Oil & Ref. Co., 309 S.W.2d 176, 178 (Ky. 1957); *see also* Jones v. Hanna, 814 S.W.2d 287, 288 (Ky. Ct. App. 1991) (discussion of the mixed precedent concerning Kentucky's public policy in this area).
5. *Id.*
6. *Id.*; *cf Employers Mut. Liab. Ins. Co.*, 280 S.W.2d at 183 (finding the terms of the contract not sufficiently broad or unequivocal to impose upon the contractor liability for injuries to employees caused by the electric company's negligence and holding proper interpretation of the contract to mean that the contractor would hold the electric company harmless if the contractor's negligence was the sole or primary cause of the injury).
7. Blue Grass Rest. Co., Inc. v. Franklin, 424 S.W.2d 594, 599 (Ky. 1968) (affirming trial court's ruling that a restaurant lessee fully indemnify the motel pursuant to language in the lease agreement even though the motel constructed the subject area in violation of an ordinance and was therefore negligent per se).
8. *Fosson*, 309 S.W.2d at 178.
9. Speedway Superamerica, LLC v. Erwin, 250 S.W.3d 339, 344 (Ky. Ct. App. 2008).
10. Martin Cty. Coal Corp. v. Universal Underwriters Ins. Co., 727 F.3d 589, 595–96 (6th Cir. 2013).

3. INDEMNITY AGREEMENTS AS INSURED CONTRACTS

Kentucky courts have not yet had occasion to determine whether an insured's contractual agreement to indemnify another constitutes an "insured contract" within the meaning of the exception to the exclusion for contractually assumed liability in the form commercial general liability (CGL) policy.

4. OPERATION OF AN AGREEMENT TO INDEMNIFY REFERRING TO OR REQUIRING INSURANCE

Kentucky law places significance on requirements for insurance when courts evaluate the intent of contractual indemnity provisions. In *Fosson v. Ashland Oil & Refining Co.*, a contractor's employee was electrocuted while working on Ashland's property.[11] The electrocuted employee was employed by the contractor at the time of the accident. The decedent's estate sued the owner and obtained a verdict, and the owner filed a third-party complaint against the contractor pursuant to the indemnity provision in the construction contract.[12]

In defense, the contractor argued that agreements to indemnify against the negligence of the indemnitee (here the owner) were valid only in "switch contracts" or "siding agreements," neither of which applied to *Fosson*'s facts.[13] The Kentucky Supreme Court disagreed, stating that indemnity provisions that provide indemnity for one's own negligence, while disfavored, are not against public policy.[14] "It is significant also that the contractor was required to carry liability insurance *satisfactory to the owner*."[15] The court stated that it was not basing its decision on the type of insurance carried by the contractor, however, and elected not to discuss the contractor's contention that the presence of insurance not be considered part of the record.[16]

11. *Fosson*, 309 S.W.2d at 177.

12. The subject clause read: "The Contractor shall indemnify the Owner against all claims, demand, liens, taxes, loss or damages of any character suffered by the Owner and shall save the Owner harmless from all liability growing out of *or* incurred in the prosecution of said work or arising from any operations, acts, or omissions of Contractor." *Id.* (emphasis supplied by the court).

13. *Fosson*, 309 S.W.2d at 178.

14. *Id.*

15. *Id.*

16. *Id.*

Louisiana

Matt Woolf and Kristen Hayes
Baker, Donelson, Bearman, Caldwell & Berkowitz, P.C.

1. GENERAL RULES OF CONTRACTUAL INDEMNITY

In Louisiana, contracts of indemnity are generally enforceable, with some limitations.[1] The general rules governing contract interpretation apply in construing a contract of indemnity.[2] Generally, when the parties' common intent is clear from the terms of the contract, and the contract's wording is clear and leads to no absurd consequences, no further interpretation may be made in search of the parties' intent.[3]

An obligation to indemnify must arise from an unequivocal, express contractual agreement.[4] In determining whether an indemnity agreement is enforceable, the controlling question is "whether the risk that resulted in the injury was one contemplated by the parties to the contract."[5] The party seeking to enforce the agreement bears the burden of proof.[6]

A contract of indemnity may include a provision whereby an indemnitor agrees to indemnify an indemnitee for losses arising from the indemnitee's own negligence, as long as the intent to do so is expressed in unequivocal terms.[7] If doubt exists as to whether an indemnitor has agreed to indemnify an indemnitee against his or her own negligence, "liability, usage, custom, or equity may not be used to interpret a contract expansively in favor of the indemnitee."[8] After applying the general rules of contract construction and interpreting the provision in conjunction with the contract as a whole, if there is still doubt as to the agreement to indemnify, "there is a presumption that the parties did not intend to indemnify an indemnitee against losses resulting from his own negligent act."[9]

Louisiana follows the majority view that general words such as "any and all liability" do not necessarily constitute an intent to obligate one party to indemnify the other party for damages caused by that other party's sole negligence.[10]

2. EXCEPTIONS TO GENERAL RULES OF CONTRACTUAL INDEMNITY

Four statutory prohibitions on agreements to indemnify exist in Louisiana.

First, any agreement pertaining to a well for oil, gas, or water, or drilling for minerals that occur in a solid, liquid, gaseous, or other state that requires indemnification for negligence or fault (strict liability) on the part of the indemnitee or its agents and employees is

1. *See* Adams v. Falcon Equip. Corp., 30,754, pp. 7–8 (La. App. 2 Cir. Aug. 21, 1998); 717 So. 2d 282, 287.

2. *Id.*; Range Ins. Co. v. Shop Rite, Inc., 05-452, p. 5 (La. App. 5 Cir. Jan. 17, 2006); 921 So. 2d 1040, 1043.

3. *Id.*; McGill v. Cochran-Sysco Foods, 35,898, p. 5 (La. App. 2 Cir. May 8, 2002); 818 So. 2d 301, 305–06; La. Civ. Code Ann. art. 2046.

4. Bagwell v. S. La. Elec. Coop. Assoc., 228 So. 2d 555, 561 (La. App. 3 Cir. 1969); Soloco, Inc. v. Dupree, 99-1476, p. 7 (La. App. 3 Cir. Feb. 9, 2000); 758 So. 2d 851, 856.

5. *Id.* at 855 (quoting Perkins v. Rubicon, Inc., 563 So. 2d 258, 259 (La. 1990)); *see* Kelly v. Sneed, 27,171, pp. 3–4 (La. App. 2 Cir. Aug. 23, 1995); 660 So. 2d 118, 120–21.

6. *McGill*, 818 So. 2d at 306 (internal citations omitted).

7. *Adams*, 717 So. 2d at 287; Polozola v. Garlock, Inc., 343 So. 2d 1000, 1003 (La. 1967); *Perkins*, 563 So. 2d at 259; *see McGill*, 818 So. 2d at 306.

8. *Adams*, 717 So. 2d at 287.

9. *Id.*; Sovereign Ins. Co. v. Tex. Pipeline Co., 488 So. 2d 982, 985–86 (La. 1986).

10. Arnold v. Stupp Corp., 205 So. 2d 797, 799 (La. App. 1967); Berry v. Orleans Parish Sch. Bd., 2001-3283, pp. 4–5 (La. June 21, 2002), 830 So. 2d 283, 285.

null and void as against public policy.[11] This statutory prohibition is known as the Louisiana Oilfield Indemnity Act or the Louisiana Oilfield Anti-Indemnity Act (LOIA).[12] LOIA voids indemnity agreements only to the extent that the contractual indemnitee's negligence or fault contributed to the third party's injury.[13] This statute has its genesis in Louisiana's commitment to protect subcontractors from the "inequity" foisted on such entities by indemnity provisions and work agreements pertaining to wells for oil and gas.[14]

Second, similar to LOIA, in contracts related to motor carrier transportation or construction to be performed in Louisiana, any agreement that requires indemnification for damages "resulting from the negligence or intentional acts or omissions of the indemnitee, its agent or employee, or a third party over which the indemnitor has no control is null and unenforceable as against public policy."[15]

Third, a Louisiana statute prohibits certain indemnity provisions in public contracts, including:

> any provision contained in a public contract, other than a contract of insurance, providing for a hold harmless or indemnity agreement, or both, (1) From the contractor to the public body for damages arising out of injuries or property damage to third parties caused by the negligence of the public body, its employees or agents, or, (2) From the contractor to any architect, landscape architect, engineer, or land surveyor engaged by the public body for such damages caused by the negligence of such architect, landscape architect, engineer, or land surveyor, is contrary to the public policy of the state [of Louisiana], and any and all such provisions in any and all public contracts are null and void.[16]

Fourth, any provision or requirement of any agreement that purports to provide for the defense, indemnification, or other relief of liability on behalf of any sheriff directed to seize property under any writs of *fieri facias*,[17] seizure and sale, or other writ issued by a court of competent jurisdiction or venue, commanding and directing that the property be seized, is also null and void and against public policy.[18] This provision is based upon the inequities and injustices resulting from the refusal of sheriffs to seize certain immovable property despite issuance of a writ directing the sheriff to do so without advance grant of blanket indemnification.[19]

---

11. La. Stat. Ann. § 9:2780; *See* Knapp v. Chevron USA, Inc., 781 F. 2d 1123 (5th Cir. 1986); Hodgen v. Forest Oil Corp., 87 F.3d 1512 (5th Cir. 1996); Roberts v. Energy Dev. Corp., 235 F. 3d 935 (5th Cir. 2000); Am. Home Assur. Co. v. Chevron, USA, Inc., 400 F.3d 265, 268–70 (5th Cir. 2005).

12. *Roberts*, 235 F.3d. at 937; *Chevron*, 400 F.3d at 266.

13. *Chevron*, 400 F.3d at 266.

14. *Id.* at 269. As discussed *infra*, courts have created a narrow exception to the LOIA, called the "*Marcel* Exception," which allows parties to secure indemnity obligations for an indemnitee's negligence by procuring insurance, as long as the indemnitee pays the premiums on the insurance. *See* Marcel v. Placid Oil Co., 11 F.3d 563 (5th Cir. 1994).

15. La. Stat. Ann. § 9:2708.1(B), (C).

16. La. Stat. Ann. § 38:2216(G); *see* Sys. Contractors Corp. v. Williams & Assocs. Architects, 99-1221, pp. 6–7 (La. App. 5 Cir. Sept. 26, 2000); 769 So. 2d 777, 781.

17. A writ of *fieri facias* directs the sheriff to seize a debtor's property to satisfy a money judgment.

18. La. Stat. Ann. § 13:3889(B).

19. La. Stat. Ann. § 13:3889(A).

3. INDEMNITY AGREEMENTS AS INSURED CONTRACTS

Louisiana courts have recognized that an insured's contractual agreement to indemnify a third party constitutes an insured contract within the meaning of an insurance policy covering an insured's agreement to assume the tort liability of another.[20] As such, agreements to indemnify fall outside the general exclusion for contractually assumed liability.[21]

4. OPERATION OF AN AGREEMENT TO INDEMNIFY REFERRING TO OR REQUIRING INSURANCE

"Additional insured" and other contractual arrangements designed to circumvent the prohibition of the LOIA are unenforceable.[22] "The LOIA is aimed at preventing the shifting of the economic burden of insurance coverage or liability onto an independent contractor."[23] In fact, the LOIA states that any provision in any agreement subject to its scope that includes a waiver of subrogation, an additional named insured endorsements, or any other form of insurance protection which frustrate or circumvent LOIA's prohibitions is null and void.[24] A recognized exception exists if the indemnitor purchases insurance for both itself and the indemnitee, and the indemnitee reimburses the indemnitor for the portion of the premium corresponding to the cost of covering the indemnitee.[25] In this instance, the court reasoned that "if the principal pays for its own liability coverage . . . no shifting occurs."[26]

While the statute prohibiting the indemnification of a public body for its own negligence does not expressly provide that the shifting of such a risk to insurance is void, such a prohibition has been read into the statute based upon the language of the LOIA.[27] However, where the public body is not being indemnified for its own negligence, but only for the negligence of a third party, the indemnification is not a violation of the statute.[28] Presumably, efforts to shift the risk where both parties bear the cost of the insurance are valid in the context of this statute.

---

20. Hutchins v. Hill Petroleum Co., 609 So. 2d 306, 312 (La. App. 3 Cir. 1992), *aff'd*, 623 So. 2d 649 (La. 1993).
21. *Id.*
22. La. Stat. Ann. § 9:2780(G).
23. *Marcel*, 11 F.3d at 569.
24. La. Stat. Ann. § 9:2780(G).
25. *Hodgen*, 87 F.3d 1512, 1529 (5th Cir. 1996) (citing *Marcel*, 11 F.3d at 569).
26. *Id.* (quoting *Marcel*, 11 F.3d at 569).
27. Dominque v. H & S Constr. Co., 546 So. 2d 913, 918–19 (La. App. 1989), *rev'd on other grounds*, 551 So. 2d 622 (La. 1989).
28. *Id.*

Maine

Julianna Malogolowkin
Hinckley, Allen, & Snyder LLP
Kurt Mullen and Sydney Pritchett
Nixon Peabody, LLP

1. GENERAL RULES OF CONTRACTUAL INDEMNITY

Contractual agreements for indemnification, including agreements covering an indemnitee's own negligence, are generally recognized and enforceable in Maine, as long as the parties' intent is expressed clearly and explicitly in the contract.[1] When interpreting indemnity agreements, the general rules of contract interpretation apply.[2] Courts look for clear terms such as "indemnify," "reimburse," and "hold harmless."[3] "Like any other contractual provision, an indemnification clause should be interpreted according to its plain, unambiguous language. Thus, indemnification claims based on contracts must rest upon a 'clear, express, specific and explicit contractual provision' under which the indemnitor has agreed to assume the duty to indemnify."[4]

As a general rule, courts do not favor indemnity agreements covering loss caused by an indemnitee's own negligence.[5] Courts, however, have enforced agreements where the parties' mutual intention is clear.[6] Broad terms such as "any and all claims," "in connection with," or "arising from or out of any occurrence" are not sufficient.[7] Without an express written intent to indemnify a party for its own negligence, the courts will not obligate one party to indemnify the other for that other party's negligence:

> Indemnity clauses to save a party harmless from damages due to negligence may lawfully be inserted in contracts . . . . But, when purportedly requiring indemnification of a party for damage or injury caused by that party's own negligence, such contractual provisions, with virtual unanimity, are looked upon with disfavor by the courts, and are construed strictly against extending the indemnification to include recovery by the indemnitee for his own negligence. It is only where the contract on its face by its very terms clearly and unequivocally reflects a mutual intention on the part of the parties to provide indemnity for loss caused by negligence of the party to be indemnified that liability for such damages will be fastened on the indemnitor, and words of general import will not be read as expressing such an intent and establishing by inference such liability.[8]

In *McGraw v. S.D. Warren Co.*, the owner of a paper mill hired a contractor to "provide demolition and construction services on a project to rebuild its pulp mill."[9] The contract

1. *See* Emery Waterhouse Co. v. Lea, 467 A.2d 986 (Me. 1983); *see also* Hardy v. St. Clair, 739 A.2d 368 (Me. 1999), *overruled on other grounds*, Brown v. Crown Equip. Corp., 960 A.2d 1188, 1195 (Me. 2008).
2. *See* Int'l Paper Co. v. A & A Brochu, 899 F. Supp. 715 (Me. 1995).
3. Doyle v. Bowdoin College, 403 A.2d 1206, 1208 (Me. 1979) (as explained in *Hardy*, 739 A.2d at 369).
4. *Int'l Paper*, 899 F. Supp. at 717; *see also* Devine v. Roche Biomedical Lab., Inc., 637 A.2d 441 (Me. 1994).
5. *Emery*, 467 A.2d at 993; *see also Int'l Paper*, 899 F. Supp. at 719.
6. *Id.*
7. *Id.*
8. *Id.* (internal citations omitted); *see also Hardy*, 739 A.2d 368; McGraw v. S.D. Warren Co., 656 A.2d 1222 (Me. 1995); *see generally Doyle*, 403 A.2d 1206.
9. *McGraw*, 656 A.2d at 1223.

between the owner and contractor contained an indemnity provision, which made the contractor "responsible for and shall continuously maintain protection of all the work and property in the vicinity of the work from damage or loss from any cause arising in connection with the contract and any work performed thereunder."[10] One of the contractor's employees brought an action against the owner of the paper mill after becoming sick from exposure to toxic emissions from a smoke stack.[11] The owner sought indemnity from the contractor under the indemnity clause in the contract.[12] The Supreme Judicial Court of Maine, relying on its holding in *Emery Waterhouse v. Lea*, held that the contractor was not obligated to indemnify the owner for its own negligence "[b]ecause there is no clear and unequivocal language in the contract at issue that reflects 'a mutual intention . . . to provide indemnity for loss caused by [contractor's] negligence.'"[13]

2. EXCEPTIONS TO GENERAL RULES OF CONTRACTUAL INDEMNITY

Indemnity agreements subjecting an employer to liability beyond what is prescribed in the Maine Workers' Compensation Act[14] are generally void, absent a clear and explicit waiver of the statutory right to immunity from suit by the employer.[15]

Under the Maine Workers' Compensation Act, employers who provide worker's compensation coverage for their employees are generally immunized from suits arising out of workers' injuries.[16] The applicable statute provides that "[a]n employer who has secured the payment of compensation . . . is exempt from civil actions . . . involving personal injuries sustained by an employee arising out of and in the course of employment, or for death resulting from those injuries."[17] The statutory right to immunization from suit, however, may be waived by the employer pursuant to an indemnity agreement.[18]

Fowler v. Boise Cascade illustrates the requirement of a clear waiver provision. In *Fowler*, the operator of a paper mill contracted with a painting company to paint portions of the mill.[19] One of the painting company's employees fell into a hole at the mill, was injured, and received worker's compensation benefits.[20] The employee thereafter sued the operator of the paper mill, who tendered the defense to the painting company pursuant to "an indemnity clause, an insurance procurement clause and a subrogation clause" in their contract.[21] The operator argued that the indemnity and insurance procurement clauses entitled him to indemnity from the employer.[22] The court held that an indemnity clause is only enforceable against an employer if it specifically and explicitly waives the immunity of the Workers' Compensation Act.[23] Determining that the language of the clauses pertaining to the procurement of insurance and indemnity did not state specifically that the employer agreed to waive its immunity under the statute, the court denied the operator's request for indemnification.[24]

---

10. *Id.* at 1224.
11. *Id.*
12. *Id.*
13. *Id*; *Emery*, 467 A.2d at 993; *see also* Gatley v. United Parcel Service, Inc., 662 F. Supp. 200, 203 (D. Me. 1987) (as there was "no clear and unequivocal agreement regarding indemnification for intentional torts," the court refused to enforce the indemnification agreement).
14. ME. REV. STAT. ANN. tit. 39-A, § 104 (2005).
15. *See* Fowler v. Boise Cascade, 948 F.2d 49, 55 (1st Cir. 1991).
16. ME. REV. STAT. ANN. tit. 39-A, § 104; Diamond Int'l Corp. v. Sullivan, 493 A.2d 1043, 1045 (Me. 1985); *see also Int'l Paper*, 899 F. Supp. at 718.
17. ME. REV. STAT. ANN. tit. 39-A, § 104.
18. *Fowler*, 948 F.2d at 55.
19. *Id.* at 52.
20. *Id.*
21. *Id.*
22. *Id.*
23. *Id.* at 57; *Diamond*, 493 A.2d at 1048.
24. *Id.* at 54.

Employers can contractually waive the state worker's compensation immunity, provided the waiver meets strict standards by either specifically stating the intent to waive immunity or stating that the indemnitor assumes any potential liability for actions by the employees.[25] For example, an indemnification clause hidden on the back of a non-contract document under an obfuscatory title will not waive the statutory employer immunity, while the language "Purchaser shall in no way be liable for any claims for personal injuries (including death) whether the same be injuries to its employees or to other persons . . . ." in the body of a contract under the title "Independent Contractor Status and Indemnification" would waive immunity.[26]

3. INDEMNITY AGREEMENTS AS INSURED CONTRACTS

The courts of Maine have not addressed whether an agreement to indemnify is an "insured contract" within the meaning of the exception to the exclusion for contractually assumed liability in the form commercial general liability policy.

4. OPERATION OF AN AGREEMENT TO INDEMNIFY REFERRING TO OR REQUIRING INSURANCE

The courts have held that the common law principle disfavoring a party from being excused for its own negligence without express written agreement is as applicable to insurance procurement clauses as it is to indemnity clauses.[27] If there is no provision in a procurement clause that explicitly provides that one party will be responsible for the other's sole negligence, then the indemnification and procurement clauses must be read together, and the clear intent of the parties will govern.[28]

In general, insurance procurement clauses operate as waivers of insurer subrogation rights.[29] Unlike an indemnity agreement wherein one party agrees to indemnify another for its own negligence, "allocation of risk to insurers through waivers of subrogation are encouraged by the law."[30]

It is universally held that "upon payment of a loss the insurer is entitled to pursue those rights against a third party whose negligence or wrongful act caused the loss."[31] The courts allow an insured to "defeat the insurance company's rights of subrogation by entering into an agreement of release with the wrongdoer before the policy is issued, or after the policy is issued but prior to the loss."[32] Such a release agreement destroys an insurer's right to subrogation, even in situations where the insurer is unaware of the release agreement.[33]

In *Emery Waterhouse Co. v. Lea*, a tenant sued the landlord for damages suffered as a result of a break in the building's main water lines.[34] The lease agreement had both an indemnity provision and a mutual exculpation clause.[35] Under the indemnity provision, the tenant agreed to indemnify the landlord for any and all damages to the property, but under the exculpatory clause, the parties, in general terms, released each other to the extent of their own insurance coverage and agreed that subrogation claims by their respective

25. *See Int'l Paper*, 899 F. Supp. at 718.

26. *Id.* (citing *Diamond*, 493 A.2d at 1048).

27. *See Fowler*, 948 F.2d at 57.

28. *Id.* at 58.

29. *See* Acadia Ins. Co. v. Buck Constr. Co., 756 A.2d 515, 519–20 (Me. 2000); Reliance Nat'l Indemnity v. Knowles Indus. Serv., Corp, 868 A.2d 220 (Me. 2005).

30. *Id.* at 520.

31. *Emery*, 467 A.2d at 994.

32. *Id.*

33. *Id.*

34. *Id.* at 988.

35. *Id.* at 992–94.

insurers were precluded.[36] The court ruled that the landlord was not entitled to recover from the tenant because the indemnity provision did not apply to the landlord's own negligence.[37] With regard to the tenant, despite his failure to "secure from its insurer the necessary modification of its insurance policy to bring it in compliance" with the release agreement, the court precluded recovery on the basis that "the [tenant] was not in fact impeded in any way from recovering its loss under the insurance contract."[38] Recognizing an insured's right to contract away its insurer's entitlement to subrogation,[39] the court held that "exculpatory agreements releasing a party to the agreement from liability caused by that party's own negligence do not contravene public policy and are enforceable on the occasion of a subsequent loss even though the agreement itself was entered into after the issuance of the policy."[40]

As it pertains to agreements to procure insurance, "clauses in construction contracts imposing insurance procurement responsibility operate as waivers of subrogation against builders even for damage occasioned by the builders' negligence, unless the contract provides otherwise."[41] In *Acadia Insurance Co. v. Buck Construction Co.*, the insurer of a property owner brought a subrogation claim against a construction company for money paid to a property owner resulting for property damage from a fire.[42] The terms of the construction contract required the owner to maintain fire insurance and the construction company was to maintain general liability insurance, worker's compensation, and builders' risk insurance.[43] In precluding the insurer's subrogation claim, the court held, "[b]y agreeing to carry a particular type of insurance, an owner has agreed to look solely to the insurer and releases the builder from responsibility when there is loss or damage flowing from the insured, it has no right to recover from the builder."[44]

36. *Id.* at 992–93.

37. *Id.* at 992–93.

38. *Id.* at 994.

39. *Id.* ("[A]n insured may defeat the insurance company's rights of subrogation by entering into an agreement of release with the wrongdoer before the policy is issued, or . . . after the policy is issued, but prior to loss.").

40. *Id.* at 995.

41. *Acadia*, 756 A.2d at 519–20.

42. *Id.* at 515.

43. *Id.* at 516.

44. *Id.*

Maryland

Kathryn Kasper
Hancock, Daniel & Johnson, P.C.

1. GENERAL RULES OF CONTRACTUAL INDEMNITY

Contractual agreements to indemnify are enforceable.[1] Public policy favors freedom of contract.[2] "Contracts made by promisors, other than commercial insurers, to indemnify for loss 'arising out of' a given activity of the indemnitor are interpreted and applied in the same manner as commercial insurance contracts made by commercial insurers."[3] Unlike many states, Maryland does not recognize the common rule that insurance policies are to be interpreted more strictly against the insurer.[4] Exculpatory clauses in contracts will be enforced absent legislation to the contrary.[5]

Additionally, indemnity may be implied by law in certain circumstances. "Quasi-contractual" indemnification, or indemnification "arising out of a 'contract implied by law,'" may be imposed based upon the circumstances.[6] Implied indemnification may arise between persons liable for tort.[7] However, one who is actively negligent cannot obtain tort indemnification.[8]

Contracts to indemnify a party for its sole negligence are also enforceable.[9] However, the contract must clearly indicate the parties' intention to do so.[10] And "[t]he general rule is that contracts will not be construed to indemnify a person against his own negligence unless an intention to do so is expressed in those very words or in other unequivocal terms."[11] Yet no "magic words" are required. Maryland courts have held that general provisions can include a party's own negligence. A provision to hold a party harmless from "liability of every kind" has been held to include liability based solely on the indemnified party's own negligence.[12]

2. EXCEPTIONS TO GENERAL RULES OF CONTRACTUAL INDEMNITY

There are three general exceptions or circumstances under which public policy will not permit an exculpatory clause in a contract.[13] "A party will not be permitted to excuse its liability for intentional acts or for the more extreme forms of negligence, i.e. reckless, wanton or gross [negligence]."[14] Additionally, a contract "cannot be the product of unequal

1. *See generally* Mass Transit Admin. v. CSX Transp., 349 Md. 299, 304 (1998).
2. Wolf v. Ford, 335 Md. 525, 531 (1994).
3. *Mass Transit Admin.*, 349 Md. at 317.
4. G.E. Tingall & Co., Inc. v. Reliance Nat'l Ins. Co., 102 F. Supp. 2d 300, 304 (D. Md. 2000) (citations omitted).
5. *Wolf*, 335 Md. at 531.
6. Franklin v. Morrison, 350 Md. 144, 154–55 (1998) (citations omitted).
7. *Id.*
8. *Id.* at 163.
9. *Mass Transit Admin.*, 349 Md. at 308–09; Crockett v. Crothers, 264 Md. 222, 227 (1972).
10. *Mass Transit Admin.*, 349 Md. at 309.
11. *Crockett*, 264 Md. at 227.
12. *Mass Transit Admin.*, 349 Md. at 300–03, 307. MTA agreed to "indemnify, save harmless, and defend CSXT from any and all casualty losses, claims, suits, damages or liability of every kind arising out of the Contract Service under this Agreement. . . ." The court found that "the indemnification provision in the instant matter applies to CSXT's liability based solely on its own negligence."
13. *Wolf*, 335 Md. at 531–32.
14. *Id.*

bargaining power."[15] Finally, exculpatory agreements will not be enforced in transactions affecting public interest.[16]

This third category—transactions affecting the public interest—includes performance of public services such as public utilities, common carriers, and innkeepers.[17] This category is also a catch-all and includes transactions not easily definable for categorization but so important to the public that an exculpatory clause would be "offensive" such that the community would pronounce it invalid.[18] The courts consider the totality of the circumstances to determine if such an exception applies.[19]

Two statutory provisions explicitly nullify certain agreements to indemnify. First, construction contracts purporting to indemnify for injury caused solely by the indemnitee's negligent conduct are unenforceable. The applicable code section provides:

> A covenant, promise, agreement or understanding in, or in connection with or collateral to, a contract or agreement relating to the construction, alteration, repair, or maintenance of a building, structure, appurtenance or appliance, including moving, demolition and excavating connected with it, purporting to indemnify the promisee against liability for damages arising out of bodily injury to any person or damage to property caused by or resulting from the *sole negligence* of the promisee or indemnitee, his agents or employees, is against public policy and is void and unenforceable. This section does not affect the validity of any insurance contract, workers' compensation, or any other agreement issued by an insurer.[20]

This code section does not nullify agreements for indemnification, however, when the loss or injury is due only in part to the indemnitee's negligent conduct.[21]

Maryland has enacted a similar statute in the landlord-tenant context:

> If the effect of any provision of a lease is to indemnify the landlord, hold the landlord harmless, or preclude or exonerate the landlord from any liability to the tenant, or to any other person, for any injury, loss, damage, or liability arising from any omission, fault, negligence, or other misconduct of the landlord on or about the leased premises or any elevators, stairways, hallways, or other appurtenances used in connection with them, and not within the exclusive control of the tenant, the provision is considered to be against public policy and void. An insurer may not claim a right of subrogation by reason of the invalidity of the provision.[22]

By its express terms, this code section does not apply if the property is within the exclusive control of the tenant.[23]

---

15. *Id.* Maryland has codified two such exceptions that will be discussed herein.

16. *Id.*

17. *Wolf*, 335 Md. at 531–32.

18. *Id.*

19. *Id.* at 534–35.

20. Md. Code Ann., Courts and Judicial Proceedings § 5-401 (emphasis added). This section was previously codified as § 5-305.

21. Bethlehem Steel Corp. v. G.C. Zarnas and Co., Inc., 304 Md. 183, 195 (1985).

22. Md. Code Ann., Real Property § 8-105.

23. Prince Phillip P'ship v. Cutlip, 321 Md. 296, 302–03 (1990). The definition of what constitutes "property within the exclusive control" of the tenant is not always obvious. In *Cutlip*, a landlord did not comply with building codes when he failed to construct handicapped restrooms in common areas of an office building. The tenant, a physician, had a handicapped patient who fell while using a restroom in the lobby of the physician's office. The patient sued the landlord only. The landlord impleaded the physician, seeking to enforce a provision in the lease requiring the physician to indemnify the landlord.

The court held that the negligence of the landlord was *not* on the portion of the leased premises within the exclusive control of the tenant. Rather, the court found that the failure to construct the handicapped restroom in the common area rendered the office of the physician a common area as patrons had no choice but to use those restrooms. The court held that the negligence of the landlord related to common areas such that the indemnification provision of the lease was void pursuant to the code.

Additionally, the Workers' Compensation Act limits the liability of an employer in suits related to injuries sustained by an employee.[24] Absent an express waiver or an agreement to assume an obligation for contribution or to indemnify, an employer cannot be liable to a third party.[25] An employer cannot be found liable to a third party based upon a theory of implied or quasi-contractual indemnity.[26]

3. INDEMNITY AGREEMENTS AS INSURED CONTRACTS

A Maryland federal court recently concluded that an insured's agreement to indemnify another constitutes an "insured contract" within the meaning of a liability insurance policy.[27] In fact, "[c]ourts should construe 'insured contract' provisions broadly, in favor of coverage."[28]

4. OPERATION OF AN AGREEMENT TO INDEMNIFY REFERRING TO OR REQUIRING INSURANCE

A promise to obtain insurance is different from a promise to indemnify.[29] Where a contract contains both an indemnity provision and an agreement to obtain insurance, the indemnitor has agreed to provide insurance coverage that is co-extensive of the agreement to indemnify.[30] This is consistent with Maryland's policy of freedom of contract.[31]

It has been suggested that a general contractor cannot require a subcontractor to obtain insurance to cover the general contractor's sole negligence.[32] Such a requirement would violate the statutory provision voiding agreements to indemnify for an indemnitee's sole negligence in the construction context.[33] Yet once the insurance policy has been issued and paid for, it is valid and will be enforced even if the wrong party paid the premiums.[34] The first principle of construction is to apply insurance policies as written when there is no ambiguity in the contract.[35] If a contractor procures insurance that is broader than is required under the contract, the policy is valid and the insurer would be obligated to the limits of coverage.[36]

The policy considerations that weigh against enforcing agreements to indemnify a party for its own negligence are inapplicable to insurance contracts.[37] Indeed, the primary purpose of insurance contracts is generally to identify a party against its own negligence.[38] Also, an insurer is rarely an unwary or uninformed promisor in need of protection.[39]

---

24. MD. CODE ANN., Labor and Employment §§ 9-101, *et. seq.*

25. Am. Radiator and Standard Sanitary Corp. v. Mark Eng'g Co., 230 Md. 584, 590 (1963).

26. *Id.*

27. Ryland Mortg. Co., Inc. v. Travelers Indem. Co. of Ill., 177 F. Supp. 2d 435, 441 (D. Md. 2001).

28. Utica Mut. Ins. Co. v. Miller, 130 Md. App. 373 (Md. Ct. Spec. App. 2000), *cert. denied*, 359 Md. 31 (2000) (citing Mid-Continent Cas. Co. v. Swift Energy Co., 206 F.3d 487, 492–93 (5th Cir. 2000)).

29. Heat & Power Corp. v. Air Prod's & Chem's, Inc., 320 Md. 584, 593–94 n.2 (1990) (citing *Bethlehem Steel Corp.*, 304 Md. at 183 (Rodowsky, J., dissenting)).

30. *Id.*

31. *Tingall*, 102 F. Supp. 2d at 304 (citations omitted).

32. *Heat & Power Corp.*, 320 Md. at 595.

33. *Id.*

34. *Id.*

35. *Mass Transit Admin.*, 349 Md. at 312.

36. *Heat & Power Corp.*, 320 Md. at 596.

37. *Id.*

38. *Id.*

39. *Id.*

Massachusetts

Julianna Malogolowkin
Hinckley, Allen, & Snyder LLP
Kurt Mullen and Sydney Pritchett
Nixon Peabody, LLP

1. GENERAL RULES OF CONTRACTUAL INDEMNITY

The Massachusetts Supreme Judicial Court held in *New York, N.H. & H.R. Co. v. Walworth Co.*, that contractual agreements to indemnify are enforceable and are subject to the same rules of construction applicable to contracts generally, and this principle.[1] "Massachusetts courts employ the general rules of contract interpretation to construe indemnification provisions. As with any contract, a written indemnification agreement is to be interpreted in light of its language, background and purpose."[2] This has particular implications when the contracting parties are commercial entities.[3]

> Where commercial entities have negotiated on a level playing field before entering their contractual arrangements, it is not necessary to explore the theoretical underpinnings of the indemnity doctrine . . . . Agreements voluntarily made . . . are not to be lightly set aside on the ground of public policy or because as events have turned it may be unfortunate for one party.[4]

The determination that an indemnity provision is valid and in accordance with public policy is a question of law for a court.[5] The fact that public policy bars certain exculpatory clauses, however, does not mean that indemnity agreements that implicate that public policy are per se invalid. For example, while a common carrier may not contractually exculpate itself from liability vis-à-vis its passengers, the carrier is not prohibited from obtaining indemnification from another commercial entity to whom it owes no duty as a passenger.[6] In the same vein, although it cannot seek tort-based indemnity, a tortfeasor can recover express contractual indemnity from an injured party's employer even though the employer is protected by the worker's compensation bar.[7] The tortfeasor can even go so far as to assign its rights to contractual indemnification to the injured employee, thus creating a situation where the employee will recover directly from his or her employer any amounts owed by the employer under the indemnity agreement with the tortfeasor.[8]

Decisions from the past twenty years show a departure from the general rule that required that indemnity agreements be construed strictly against the indemnitee:

> The rule that indemnity contracts are to be strictly construed against the indemnitee no longer [applies] in Massachusetts. The modern rule is that contracts of

1. New York, N.H. & H.R. Co. v. Walworth Co., 162 N.E.2d 789, 792 (Mass. 1959); *see also* Laiho v. CONRAIL, 4 F. Supp. 2d 45 (D. Mass. 1998).
2. Herson v. New Boston Garden Corp., 667 N.E.2d 907, 914 (Mass. App. Ct. 1996).
3. Kelly v. Dimeo, Inc., 581 N.E.2d 1316 (Mass. App. Ct. 1991).
4. *Id.* at 1318 (internal citations omitted).
5. Post v. Belmont Country Club, Inc., 60 Mass. App. Ct. 645, 647 (2004); *see also* Martino v. Mobil Oil Corp., 1987 U.S. Dist. LEXIS 1311 (D. Mass. Jan. 29, 1987).
6. *Martino*, 1987 U.S. Dist. LEXIS 1311.
7. *See* Whittle v. Pagani Bros. Constr. Co., 422 N.E.2d 779 (Mass. 1981); Connolly v. Pope Housing, Inc., 4 Mass. L. Rep. 267 (Mass. Super. Ct. 1995).
8. *See* Spellman v. Shawmut Woodworking & Supply, Inc., 840 N.E.2d 47 (Mass. 2006).

indemnity are to be fairly and reasonably construed in order to ascertain the intention of the parties and to effectuate the purpose sought to be accomplished. Courts are expected to give effect to the parties' intentions at the time of the agreement and to give them reasonable meaning.[9]

Similarly, the rule followed in most jurisdictions—which rejects indemnity for the indemnitee's own negligence absent express and unambiguous language to the contrary—has been abandoned in Massachusetts.[10] Since contracts of indemnity are to be fairly and reasonably construed in order to ascertain the intention of the parties, "something less than an express reference in the contract to losses from the indemnitee's negligence as indemnifiable will suffice to make them so if the intent otherwise sufficiently appears from language and circumstances."[11] "In Massachusetts, where there is nothing to require strict construction of the clause under general contract rules, 'contracts of indemnity are to be fairly and reasonably construed in order to ascertain the intention of the parties and to effectuate the purpose sought to be accomplished.'"[12]

Although there is earlier authority from the Massachusetts Supreme Judicial Court that adheres to the general rule that "a contract will not be construed as indemnifying one against his own negligence or that of his employees unless express language unequivocally so requires,"[13] this authority has been implicitly overruled. In *Shea v. Bay State Gas Co.*, the appeals court relied on the above-quoted passage from *Walworth* and held that an agreement that did not specifically provide for indemnification for the indemnitee's own negligence was not enforceable.[14] By reversing the appeals court, and by citing cases that did not require express language regarding the indemnitee's own negligence, the Supreme Judicial Court implicitly overruled and abandoned the rule from *Walworth*. Since *Shea* was decided in 1981, *Walworth* has been cited only once by a majority of the Supreme Judicial Court in *Seaco Ins. Co. v. Barbosa* and only for the proposition that "a person is liable for his own negligent acts, absent an express agreement to the contrary."[15] Although the lease agreement at issue in *Seaco* included an indemnity provision, the case did not directly address issues of contractual indemnity. And in one post-*Shea* appeals court decision, the court cited *Walworth* for certain principles, but then cited *Shea* for the proposition that it is not "necessary that an indemnity clause state expressly that it covers the indemnitee's negligence."[16]

Thus, the general rule requiring express language to indemnify one for his or her own negligence has been abandoned. The rule from *Shea*, that the scope of the indemnity agreement will be determined by ascertaining the intention of the parties, now applies.

9. MacGlashing v. Dunlop Equip. Co., 89 F.3d 932, 940 (1st Cir. 1996) (internal citations omitted). *See also* N. Am. Site Developers, Inc. v. MRP Site Dev., Inc., 827 N.E.2d 251, 255 (Mass. App. Ct. 2005) (The "rule that indemnity agreements are to be strictly construed against the indemnitee [is] not followed in Massachusetts.").

10. Shea v. Bay State Gas Co., 418 N.E.2d 597 (Mass. 1981). *See also* Post v. Belmont Country Club, 805 N.E.2d 63 (Mass. App. Ct. 2004) (explaining distinction between Massachusetts and other jurisdictions that provide for strictly construing indemnity provisions, deciding any ambiguity against the indemnitee, and requiring clear and certain terms to indemnify the indemnitee for its own negligence).

11. *Shea*, 418 N.E.2d at 600 (internal citations omitted). *See also* Speers v. H. P. Hood, Inc., 495 N.E.2d 880, 881 (Mass. App. Ct. 1986) ("[W]here the sense is reasonably clear, an indemnity provision may be read to cover situations of indemnitee's negligence although there is no explicit statement to that effect."); Callahan v. A. J. Welch Equip. Corp., 634 N.E.2d 134, 138 (Mass. App. Ct. 1994) ("The mere fact that an indemnity clause does not expressly provide for indemnity even where the indemnitee is negligent will not preclude the right to indemnity if the intent sufficiently appears in the language and circumstances attending its execution.").

12. *Post*, 805 N.E.2d at 69.

13. New York, N. H. & H. R. Co. v. Walworth Co., 162 N.E.2d 789, 792 (Mass. 1959).

14. Shea v. Bay State Gas Co., 418 N.E.2d 597 (Mass. 1981).

15. Seaco Ins. Co. v. Barbosa, 761 N.E.2d 946, 948 (Mass. 2002).

16. Aho v. Blanchette, 463 N.E.2d 1203, 1205 (Mass. App. Ct. 1984).

2. EXCEPTIONS TO GENERAL RULES OF CONTRACTUAL INDEMNITY

Massachusetts has enacted statutory prohibitions on certain indemnity agreements, specifically in the construction and landlord-tenant contexts.

Massachusetts General Laws ch. 149, § 29C provides:

> Any provision for or in connection with a contract for construction, reconstruction, installation, alteration, remodeling, repair, demolition or maintenance work, including without limitation, excavation, backfilling or grading, on any building or structure, whether underground or above ground, or on any real property, including without limitation any road, bridge, tunnel, sewer, water or other utility line, which requires a subcontractor to indemnify any party for injury to persons or damage to property not caused by the subcontractor or its employees, agents or subcontractors, shall be void.[17]

A contractual indemnification clause is, however, valid and enforceable against the subcontractor if the clause is limited to indemnification for injuries or damages that were caused by or resulted from the acts or omissions of the subcontractor, its employees, agents, or subcontractors.[18] A valid indemnification clause involving a subcontractor will be triggered even where the employee of the subcontractor who is negligent is the same employee who is injured,[19] and full indemnification from the subcontractor will be required even if the indemnified general contractor is partially negligent:

> We discern nothing in our case law or the language or history of [Mass. Gen. Laws ch. 149,] § 29C that prevents parties from agreeing to full indemnification in the event of concurrent negligence. If the Legislature had intended that indemnification provisions in construction contracts be interpreted to reflect the application of our comparative negligence statute, or to preclude indemnification when the injured claimant is an employee of the subcontractor, it could have said so.[20]

Thus, "§ 29C does not proscribe full indemnification when the conduct of the subcontractor is only a partial cause of the injury. Otherwise put, § 29C does not prohibit contractual indemnity arrangements whereby the subcontractor agrees to assume indemnity obligations for the entire liability when both the subcontractor and the general contractor or owner are causally negligent."[21]

To enforce any agreement by a subcontractor to indemnify another, the evidence must establish "a causal link between the liability incurred by the general contractor and something that the subcontractor, or its subcontractors, did or did not do to bring about the injury or damage, [or else] the general contractor may not be indemnified and a contractual provision purporting to do so is unenforceable."[22] For example, a subcontractor who agrees to indemnify the general contractor for the acts of a sub-subcontractor will be held to that indemnity agreement if the sub-subcontractor or its employees are negligent.[23]

To determine if an agreement to indemnify executed by a subcontractor is invalid, the courts do not look to the specific facts of the case, but instead look solely at the language of the agreement.[24] "In determining the validity of an indemnity provision under § 29C, it

17. Mass. Gen. Laws ch. 149, § 29C (2014).

18. *See* Collins v. Kiewit Constr. Co., 667 N.E.2d 904 (Mass. App. Ct. 1996).

19. *See id.*

20. *Id.* at 907 (internal citations).

21. Herson v. New Boston Garden Corp., 667 N.E.2d 907, 914 (Mass. App. Ct. 1996).

22. Erland Constr. Co. v. Park Steel Corp., 671 N.E.2d 953 (Mass. App. Ct. 1996).

23. *See id.*

24. *See Herson*, 667 N.E.2d 907.

is upon the language of the indemnity clause that we focus rather than upon a finding of the facts of the particular accident and an assessment of fault of the parties."[25] Thus, even where there may be evidence that the subcontractor was negligent, it will not be required to indemnify the general contractor if the indemnity agreement at issue violates the terms of § 29C.[26] If the indemnity agreement is not invalid on its face and contains a "savings clause" that provides for indemnity to "the fullest extent permitted by law," such a clause will be read to allow indemnity to the full extent permitted by § 29C.[27] Similarly, since the statute only speaks in terms of "indemnity," language in a contract that requires the subcontractor to defend claims that would otherwise be violative of § 29C are enforceable.[28]

A Massachusetts Superior Court judge has concluded that the public policy promoted by Massachusetts General Laws ch. 149, § 29C is enforceable even where the contract contains a choice of law provision.[29] If "a strong public policy of Massachusetts would be violated by enforcing a contract provision based upon the application of a foreign law, the Courts will strike the offending provision."[30] Thus, an indemnity agreement that includes a choice of law provision that fails to account for the provisions of ch. 149, § 29C will essentially be ignored.

As a matter of public policy, certain indemnification agreements in the landlord-tenant context are also prohibited by Massachusetts General Laws ch. 186, § 15:

> Any provision of a lease or other rental agreement relating to real property whereby a lessee or tenant enters into a covenant, agreement or contract, by the use of any words whatsoever, the effect of which is to indemnify the lessor or landlord or hold the lessor or landlord harmless, or preclude or exonerate the lessor or landlord from any or all liability to the lessee or tenant, or to any other person, for any injury, loss, damage or liability arising from any omission, fault, negligence or other misconduct of the lessor or landlord on or about the leased or rented premises or on or about any elevators, stairways, hallways or other appurtenance used in connection therewith, shall be deemed to be against public policy and void.[31]

The purpose of ch. 186, § 15 "is to preclude a landlord from shifting responsibility for its own negligence to its tenants."[32]

Unlike the prohibition on indemnification by subcontractors discussed above, courts addressing ch. 186, § 15 look at the actual facts of the case and determine whether the indemnity agreement, as applied to the particular facts, has the effect of indemnifying the lessor for its own negligence.[33] The effect, however, is that any agreement that is broadly worded such that a lessee will be forced to indemnify the lessor for injuries arising from "any" cause will be invalidated. This is because if the landlord is not negligent, there is no need for the indemnity agreement, and if the landlord is negligent, seeking indemnity would run afoul of the statute.[34]

---

25. *Id.* at 914.

26. *See* Harnois v. Quannapowitt Dev., 619 N.E.2d 351 (Mass. App. Ct. 1993) ("[A] contractual obligation to indemnify is void whenever it provides for indemnification by a subcontractor regardless of the fault of the indemnitee, or its employees, agents or subcontractors, and this is so even if the indemnitee could prove at trial that the injured employee of the subcontractor was negligent."). *But compare Callahan*, 634 N.E.2d 134, (comparing the indemnity agreement in *Harnois*, which would on its face require indemnity from the subcontractor for injuries not caused by the subcontractor, with an indemnity agreement (found to be valid) that only required indemnity in the event of the subcontractor's negligence).

27. Sheehan v. Modern Cont'l/Healy, 822 N.E.2d 305, 306 n.2 (Mass. App. Ct. 2005).

28. *Id.* (citing *Herson*, 667 N.E.2d 907).

29. Hayes v. May Dep't Stores Co., 1994 Mass. Super. LEXIS 123 (Mass. Super. Ct. Dec. 13, 1994).

30. *Id.* at *3.

31. Mass. Gen. Laws ch. 186, § 15 (2014).

32. Norfolk & Dedham Mut. Fire Ins. Co. v. Morrison, 456 Mass. 463, 468 (2010).

33. *See id. See also* Hudson v. Atiniz, 1 Mass. L. Rep. 332 (Mass. Super. Ct. 1993).

34. *See Knous*, 10 Mass. L. Rptr. 47; Blanchard v. Soc'y for the Pres. of New Eng. Antiquities, 15 Mass. L. Rep. 390, 2002 Mass. Super. LEXIS 437 (Mass. Super. Ct. 2002).

Further, the public policy goals of ch. 186, § 15 have been limited to nongovernmental entities/tenants.[35]

> [T]he statute voids indemnity agreements in leases because they are contrary to public policy; the statute is designed to protect lessees . . . . [T]he statute is inapplicable where the lessee is a governmental entity that freely chooses to enter a contract that normally would be void for public policy reasons where the voiding statute is designed to protect contracting parties in the same position as the governmental entity.[36]

The protection afforded by ch. 186, § 15, and the public policy behind the statute, is not limited to the indemnity context. In the case of a residential lease, "absent an express provision in a lease establishing a tenant's liability for loss from a negligently started fire, the landlord's insurance is deemed held for the mutual benefit of both parties."[37] This rule does not apply, however, to commercial leases.[38]

3. INDEMNITY AGREEMENTS AS INSURED CONTRACTS

An agreement to indemnify would generally fall within a liability policy exclusion for liability assumed in a contract.[39]

It has been recognized, however, that a contractual undertaking to indemnify constitutes an "insured contract" as that term is used in the commercial general liability (CGL) policy.[40] In *Garnet Construction Co. v. Acadia Insurance Co.*, a subcontractor sought a declaratory judgment against its CGL insurer in order to indemnify another subcontractor from liability for the injury of an employee. Although the trial court in *Garnet* did not find any enforceable indemnity agreement for which coverage could be afforded, the implication from the decision is that coverage may extend to indemnity agreements as "insured contracts."[41] *Garnet* was affirmed by the appeals court, which held that the applicability of the "insured contract" exception requires that the insured expressly agree to indemnify another, either in writing or orally, and that a claim for "implied" contractual indemnity did not fall within the exception for "insured contracts."[42]

4. OPERATION OF AN AGREEMENT TO INDEMNIFY REFERRING TO OR REQUIRING INSURANCE

Due to the abandonment of strict rules applicable to indemnity agreements, and the adoption of the modern rule of interpreting indemnity agreements to ascertain the intent of the parties without concern for express language regarding indemnification for the indemnitee's own negligence, agreements to obtain insurance are viewed as further evidence of the parties' intent.[43] "Often the presence of a requirement that the indemnifying party purchase insurance sheds light on the parties' intention to indemnify and defend against claims."[44] Since *Shea*, courts have repeatedly relied on agreements under which the indemnitor is to

35. *See Connolly*, 4 Mass L. Rep. 267.
36. *Id.* at *8.
37. Peterson v. Silva, 704 N.E.2d 1163, 1165 (Mass. 1999).
38. *See Seaco*, 761 N.E.2d 946.
39. *See* Aetna Casualty & Surety Co. v. Cotter, 522 N.E.2d 1013 (Mass. App. Ct. 1988).
40. *See* Garnet Constr. Co. v. Acadia Ins. Co., 15 Mass. L. Rep. 472 (Mass. Super. Ct. 2002).
41. *Id.*
42. *See* Garnet Constr. Co. v. Acadia Ins. Co., 814 N.E.2d 23 (Mass. App. Ct. 2004).
43. *See* Henkels & McCoy v. Boston & Me. Corp., 2000 Mass. Super. LEXIS 196 (Mass. Super. Ct. Feb. 25, 2000).
44. *Id.* at *9.

procure insurance as evidence to support a finding that a broadly worded indemnification agreement covers the indemnitee's own negligence.[45]

For example, in *Speers v. H.P. Hood, Inc.*, a case in which an independent contractor (BSG) agreed to indemnify a dairy plant owner (Hood) against injuries arising from the work under the contract, and simultaneously agreed to procure liability insurance that would cover the indemnity agreement, the appeals court stated:

> Here we have a common situation in which Speers would ordinarily have worker's compensation through his relation to his own employer, BSG. Hood, however, is exposed to possible common law liability at the suit of Speers. Quite naturally, Hood wants to shed this possible responsibility toward a worker not part of its force, and proceeds to shift it to the worker's own employer, the independent contractor temporarily on the premises to do a particular job. It is expected that BSG will obtain insurance to meet this contract-assumed risk.[46]

An agreement to obtain insurance is considered evidence that a parallel indemnity agreement is meant to cover the indemnitee's sole negligence, since the indemnitor can procure insurance that covers losses arising from the indemnitee's sole negligence.[47]

In addition, an agreement by a subcontractor to obtain insurance does not run afoul of the prohibitions of Massachusetts General Laws ch 149, § 29C addressed above.

Massachusetts General Laws ch 149, § 29C does not address an insurance policy as a form of indemnification, and it can only be assumed that if the legislature intended for insurance policies to be included it would have said so. Furthermore, the purpose of having the subcontractor's insurance name the general contractors as "additional insured" is the strong likelihood that the general contractor would be a party in a negligence action.[48]

Thus, where a subcontractor agrees to obtain liability insurance for the benefit of the general contractor, ch. 149, § 29C will not bar enforcement of that insurance agreement.[49]

The same exception applies to the statutory prohibition on indemnity agreements in lease contracts.[50] A contractual requirement that the lessee provide insurance coverage does not run afoul of ch. 186, § 15.[51] Thus, although an agreement to obtain insurance will effectively shield a lessor from liability, such an agreement is not technically an indemnification agreement. Therefore, § 15 should not be implicated and the agreement to obtain such insurance should be enforced.

Finally, although not directly addressed in relation to an indemnity agreement, "the policy underlying the use of waiver of subrogation clauses in construction contracts" has been recognized.[52] "A waiver of subrogation is useful in such projects because it avoids disruption and disputes among the parties to the project. It thus eliminates the need for lawsuits, and yet protects the contracting parties from loss by bringing all property damage under the all risks builder's property insurance."[53]

---

45. *See Speers*, 495 N.E.2d 880; Martino v. Mobil Oil Corp., 1987 U.S. Dist. LEXIS 1311 (D. Mass. Jan. 29, 1987); Cohen v. Steve's Franchise Co., 927 F.2d 26 (1st Cir. 1991).

46. *Speers*, 495 N.E.2d at 882, (internal citations omitted).

47. *Id.*

48. Cosica v. Constrs. Collaborative, Inc., 16 Mass. L. Rep. 628 (Mass. Super. Ct. 2003) (internal citations omitted).

49. *See id.*

50. *See* Bergstresser v. Cooke, 12 Mass. L. Rep. 466 (Mass. Super. Ct. 2000); *see also Morrison*, 924 N.E.2d at 269 ("Quite simply, the statute does not apply to insurance provisions, where the duty of indemnification resides, where it should—with the insurer.").

51. *Id.* at *23.

52. Haemonetics Corp. v. Brophy & Phillips Co., 501 N.E.2d 524 (Mass. App. Ct. 1986).

53. *Id.* at 526.

Michigan

Charles M. Denton
Barnes & Thornburg LLP*

1. GENERAL RULES OF CONTRACTUAL INDEMNITY

A contract may expressly provide for a right of indemnification under Michigan law.[1] General contract law governs the requisites and validity of contracts of indemnity.[2] An indemnity contract should be construed to ascertain and give effect to the intentions of the parties, and should be interpreted to give a reasonable meaning to all of the contract's provisions.[3] Courts determine intent by considering not only the language of the contract, but also the circumstances surrounding the contract, including the situation of the parties.[4] An express indemnity contract is construed strictly against its drafter, and the indemnitor's obligation to indemnify the indemnitee must be described clearly and unambiguously.[5]

2. EXCEPTIONS TO GENERAL RULES OF CONTRACTUAL INDEMNITY

Indemnity against the consequences of an act that is not a crime, civil wrong, or contrary to statute or public policy is not illegal.[6] Public policy does not prevent making a contract of indemnification against the consequences of one's own negligence, unless the contract exempts one from the consequences of willfully inflicted harm, or harm caused by gross or wanton negligence.[7] An indemnification provision in certain settings may not protect an indemnitee from its sole negligence.[8]

Although the Workers' Compensation Act limits an employee's right to recover against his or her employer, it does not preclude indemnification of a contractor by the employer.[9] Indemnity will not be enforced where the relationship between the contracting parties is essentially that of employer and employee, or where the party claiming to be exempt is charged with a public duty.[10]

By statute, indemnity agreements entered into in construction projects whereby the indemnitee is indemnified for its own sole negligence are unenforceable.[11] Such provisions

---

* Charles M. Denton, a partner with Barnes & Thornburg LLP, has been active with the ABA Section of Litigation for many years; he can be reached at (616) 742-3974 or cdenton@BTLaw.com. The assistance of Alexander Barnstead (Alex.Barnstead@btlaw.com) is greatly appreciated.

1. Hubbell, Roth & Clark, Inc. v. Jay Dee Contractors, Inc., 642 N.W.2d 700 (Mich. Ct. App. 2001). Michigan courts recognize a common law indemnity cause of action, sustainable by a party passively liable against an active tortfeasor. Botsford Continuing Care Corp. v. Intelistaf Healthcare, Inc., 807 N.W.2d 354, 361 (Mich. Ct. App. 2011).

2. Badiee v. Brighton Area Sch., 695 N.W.2d 521, 531 (Mich. Ct. App. 2005).

3. Zahn v. Kroger Co. of Michigan, 764 N.W.2d 207, 211 (Mich. 2009).

4. Ajax Paving Indus., Inc. v. Vanopdenbosch Const. Co., 797 N.W.2d 704, 707 (Mich. Ct. App. 2010).

5. Skinner v. D-M-E Corp., 335 N.W.2d 90, 92 (Mich. Ct. App. 1983) (citing Fireman's Fund American Ins. Co. v. General Electric Co., 253 N.W.2d 748 (Mich. Ct. App. 1977)).

6. McLouth Steel Corp. v. A.E. Anderson Constr. Corp., 210 N.W.2d 448 (Mich. Ct. App. 1973).

7. Klann v. Hess Cartage Co., 214 N.W.2d 63, 65 (Mich. Ct. App. 1973).

8. Fishbach-Natkin Co. v. Power Process Piping, Inc., 403 N.W.2d 569, 571–72 (Mich. Ct. App. 1987).

9. *McLouth Steel Corp.*, 210 N.W.2d at 450–52.

10. Blazic v. Ford Motor Co., 166 N.W.2d 636, 638 (Mich. Ct. App. 1968).

11. Mich. Comp. Laws § 691.991 (2005); *see generally* Miller-Davis Co. v. Ahrens Const., Inc., 848 N.W.2d 95, 102 (Mich.), *reh'g denied*, 845 N.W.2d 742 (Mich. 2014).

are not automatically void, but will only become so if the indemnitee seeks to enforce the provision in the face of its sole negligence.[12]

Local government units must be expressly given any of their powers, such as the power to hire third parties. However, that power does not imply that the local government unit has the power to enter into an indemnification agreement with the third party, and effectively act as an insurer.[13] The power to indemnify is not essential to the express power of hiring.[14] The power to enter into an indemnity agreement must be expressly given to the local government unit by the state constitution or state statutes, or it will be considered ultra vires.[15]

3. INDEMNITY AGREEMENTS AS INSURED CONTRACTS

An insurance policy may cover indemnity liability in contracts where the insured assumes a third party's tort liability, or "liability imposed by law in the absence of any contract or agreement."[16] This type of indemnity falls under the "insured contract" exception to the exclusion for contractual liability. But an obligation to indemnify a third party may be excluded from coverage if the third party is liable solely because of a contract.[17] As stated by a federal court in *Lebow Associates, Inc. v. Detroit Bank & Trust*:

> [a] provision in a liability policy specifically excluding from coverage liability contractually assumed by the insured is operative only in situations where the insured would not be liable to a third party except for the fact that he assumed liability under an express agreement. Conversely such a provision is inoperative when the liability of the insured assumed under an express contact with the third party is coextensive with the insured's liability imposed by law.[18]

4. OPERATION OF AN AGREEMENT TO INDEMNIFY REFERRING TO OR REQUIRING INSURANCE

If an insured agrees to indemnify an entity identified as an additional insured under a policy of insurance issued to the indemnitor, the insurer may be forced to pay any judgment against the insured, as well as its legal expenses defending the action against the additional insured.[19]

A contractual obligation to procure insurance does not extinguish a concurrent express contractual right to indemnification contained within the same contract.[20] If the parties intend to waive claims against each other, where insurance covers any loss, they can include a waiver clause within the contract.[21]

---

12. *Fishbach-Natkin Co.*, 403 N.W.2d at 571–72.
13. Huntington Leasing Co. v. Manistee Intermediate Sch. Dist., No. 250942, 2005 WL 991309, at *2 (Mich. Ct. App. Apr. 28, 2005).
14. *Id.*
15. *See generally* Michigan Mun. Liab. & Prop. Pool v. Muskegon Cnty. Bd. of Cnty. Rd. Comm'rs, 597 N.W.2d 187, 191–92 (Mich. Ct. App. 1999).
16. Dale Osburn, Inc. v. Auto Owners Ins. Co., 2003 Mich. App. LEXIS 2887, at *13–14 (Mich. Ct. App. Nov. 18, 2003) (unpublished).
17. *Id.* at *13–15.
18. Lebow Assocs., Inc. v. Detroit Bank & Trust, 439 F. Supp. 1288, 1291 (E.D. Mich. 1977).
19. *See generally Lebow Assocs.*, 439 F. Supp. 1288.
20. Wausau Underwriters Insurance Company v. Ajax Paving Industries, Inc., 671 N.W.2d 539, 544 (Mich. Ct. App. 2003).
21. *Id.*

Minnesota

Matthew Lawlyes
Wilson Law Group

1. GENERAL RULES OF CONTRACTUAL INDEMNITY

Contractual indemnity is permitted in Minnesota "[w]here there is an express contract between the parties containing an explicit undertaking to reimburse for liability of the character involved."[1] "A contract of indemnity should be construed to cover all losses, damages or liabilities which reasonably appear to have been within the contemplation of the parties, but not those losses or liabilities which are neither expressly within its terms nor of such a character that it can be reasonably inferred that the parties intended to include them."[2] Claims for indemnity do not accrue until the person entitled to the indemnity has sustained damage either by paying a loss or discharging a liability that should properly be the responsibility of another.[3]

The rules for establishing a contract for indemnity mirror those for other contracts, and consideration is a necessary component.[4] Likewise, the rules of construction for indemnity contracts follow those of general contract law.[5] These rules include construing a contract to give effect to the intention of the parties,[6] interpreting the language of a contract in accordance with its plain and ordinary meaning,[7] and considering the contract as a whole.[8]

"Agreements seeking to indemnify a party for losses resulting from that party's own negligent acts are not favored in the law and are not construed in favor of indemnification, unless such intention is expressed in clear and unequivocal terms."[9] Agreements for indemnity of another's negligence should attempt to encompass specific facts regarding what, where, and when the agreement is in effect.[10] The courts use a test that analyzes the facts in a temporal, geographical, or causal relationship to the work performed and the injury.[11] Indemnity agreements have been held inapplicable when the injury occurred after work that was not contemplated by the agreement.[12]

---

1. Ploog v. Ogilvie, 309 N.W.2d 49, 54 n.3 (Minn. 1981) (quoting Hendrickson v. Minn. Power & Light Co., 104 N.W.2d 843, 848 (Minn. 1960)), *superseded on other grounds*, Zamberletti v. Zamberletti, 1989 Minn. Ct. App. LEXIS 1190, at *4 (Minn. Ct. App. Nov. 7, 1989).

2. FMC Corp. v. Ne. Pump Co., 1985 U.S. Dist LEXIS 20314, at *7 (D. Minn. Apr. 29, 1985).

3. Leisure Dynamics, Inc. v. Falstaff Brewing Corp., 298 N.W.2d 33, 38 (Minn. 1980).

4. Elk River Concrete Prods. Co. v. American Casualty Co., 129 N.W.2d 309, 316 (Minn. 1964).

5. Chi. v. Famous Brands, Inc., 324 F.2d 137, 140 (8th Cir. 1963).

6. *See* Art Goebel, Inc. v. N. Suburban Agencies, Inc., 567 N.W.2d 511, 515 (Minn. 1997).

7. *See* Thommes v. Milwaukee Ins. Co., 641 N.W.2d 877, 880 (Minn. 2002).

8. *See* Chergosky v. Crosstown Bell, Inc., 463 N.W.2d 522, 525 (Minn. 1990).

9. Oster v. Medtronic, Inc., 428 N.W.2d 116, 118 (Minn. Ct. App. 1988).

10. *See* R.E.M. IV, Inc. v. Robert F. Ackermann & Assoc., Inc., 313 N.W.2d 431, 433–34 (Minn. 1981) (holding subcontractor was not required to indemnify general contractor for general contractor's own negligence where contractual indemnification provision of subcontract did not extend to damage that occurred after work covered by subcontract was completed).

11. Fossum v. Kraus-Anderson Constr. Co., 372 N.W.2d 415, 417 (Minn. Ct. App. 1985); *see generally* Anstine v. Lake Darling Ranch, 233 N.W.2d 723 (Minn. 1975) (defining the purpose and intent of an indemnity agreement).

12. *See generally Fossum*, 372 N.W.2d at 418.

2. EXCEPTIONS TO GENERAL RULES OF CONTRACTUAL INDEMNITY

Building and construction contracts of indemnity are given special attention in Minnesota, and the scope of allowable indemnity within such contracts is limited. Section 337.02 of the Minnesota Statutes provides:

> An indemnification agreement contained in, or executed in connection with, a building and construction contract is unenforceable except to the extent that: (1) the underlying injury or damage is attributable to the negligent or otherwise wrongful act or omission, including breach of a specific contractual duty, of the promisor or the promisor's independent contractors, agents, employees, or delegatees; or (2) an owner, a responsible party, or a governmental entity agrees to indemnify a contractor directly or through another contractor with respect to strict liability under environmental laws.

The statutory prohibition of Minnesota Statutes § 337.02 ensures that each party will be responsible for its own negligent acts or omissions.[13] This prohibition does not apply to the following:

> [A]n agreement by which a promisor that is a party to a building and construction contract indemnifies a person, firm, corporation, or public agency for whose account the construction is not being performed, but who, as an accommodation, permits the promisor or the promisor's independent contractors, agents, employees, or delegatees to enter upon or adjacent to its property for the purpose of performing the building and construction contract.[14]

Prior to 2013, Minnesota Statutes § 337.05, subdivision 1 carved out an exception to the general prohibition against indemnifying parties for their own negligence. That version of subdivision 1, stating "regardless of section 337.02, the promisee shall have indemnification from the promisor to the same extent as the specified insurance" eviscerated the general prohibition, authorizing contractors to impose upon subcontractors contractual requirements to procure insurance indemnifying the contractor for its own negligence.[15] On August 1, 2013, the Minnesota legislature amended § 337.05, subdivision 1, breaking subdivision 1 into three paragraphs. New paragraph (b) reinstates the prohibition against indemnification for one's negligence.

> A provision that requires a party to provide insurance coverage to one or more parties, including third parties, for the negligence or intentional acts or omissions of any of those parties, including third parties, is against public policy and is void and unenforceable.[16]

Subparagraph (b), in clear and unequivocal terms, does away with the exception to the rule. But what clarity subparagraph (b) gives, subparagraph (c) takes away. Subparagraph (c) reads, "[p]aragraph (b) does not affect the validity of a provision that requires a party to provide or obtain . . . project-specific insurance[.]"[17] At this time, it is not clear to what "project-specific insurance" refers. It is not a term regularly used within the industry and

---

13. Holmes v. Watson-Fosberg Co., 488 N.W.2d 473, 475 (Minn. 1992).

14. MINN. STAT. § 337.03 (2005).

15. *See* Van Vickle v. C.W. Scheurer & Sons, Inc., 556 N.W.2d 238, 241 (Minn. Ct. App. 1996), and MINN. STAT. § 337.05 (1984) (amended 2013).

16. MINN STAT. § 337.05(b) (2013).

17. *Id.*

until a time that the Minnesota courts take up the question, it will remain unclear if, and to what extent, the amended version of § 337.05 differs from its predecessor.

Every employer must carry worker's compensation insurance or seek a written exemption permitting self-insurance.[18] The Workers' Compensation Act prevents a general contractor from shifting his or her responsibilities under the Act via an indemnity agreement.[19] Allowing a general contractor to shift its worker's compensation expenses by means of an indemnification provision would contravene the public policy at the core of the Act, which requires employers to bear the burden of their employees' work-related injuries.[20]

Nonetheless, a party to an indemnity agreement can bring an action for indemnity against the employer of the injured party despite the immunity of the Workers' Compensation Act.[21]

3. INDEMNITY AGREEMENTS AS INSURED CONTRACTS

Minnesota courts have suggested that an insurance policy may cover indemnity liability in contracts where the insured assumes a third party's tort liability.[22] This type of indemnity falls under the "insured contract" exception to the exclusion for contractually assumed liability. A contractual obligation to pay defense costs, however, may not fall within the purview of an insured contract provision.[23]

4. OPERATION OF AN AGREEMENT TO INDEMNIFY REFERRING TO OR REQUIRING INSURANCE

By statute, indemnity provisions in building and construction contracts attempting to provide indemnity for one's own negligence are normally unenforceable.[24] There is, however, a significant statutory exception where there is insurance coverage for the benefit of others.[25]

For that exception to apply, the contract for indemnity must contain clear and unequivocal language that shifts liability for all such claims and for those that require the purchase of insurance to cover all of such claims.[26] When the meaning of an agreement is uncertain, all doubts and ambiguities must be resolved against the one who prepared the agreement.[27] Agreements to procure insurance have been construed more broadly than agreements to indemnify.[28]

If the risk of loss is directly related to and arising out of the work performed under the subcontract, the parties may place the risk of loss upon an insurer by requiring one of the parties to insure against that risk.[29] There is no indication that a contractual obligation to procure insurance extinguishes a concurrent express contractual right to indemnification contained within the same contract. If the parties intend to waive claims against each other, where insurance covers any loss, they must presumably include a waiver clause within the contract.

18. MINN. STAT. §176.181 (2005).

19. D.W. Hutt Consultants, Inc. v. Constr. Maint. Sys., Inc., 526 N.W.2d 62, 65 (Minn. Ct. App. 1995).

20. *Id.*

21. Carlson v. Smogard, 215 N.W.2d 615 (1974); *see also* MINN. STAT. § 176.061.

22. Soo Line R.R. Co. v. Brown's Crew Car, 2003 Minn. Ct. App. LEXIS 289, at *7–8 (Minn. Ct. App. Mar. 11, 2003).

23. *Id.* at *13–14 (citing Progressive Cas. Ins. Co. v. Brown's Crew Car, 27 F. Supp. 2d 1288, 1293 (D. Wyo. 1998)).

24. MINN. STAT. § 337.02.

25. MINN. STAT. § 337.05.

26. Katzner v. Kelleher Constr., 545 N.W.2d 378, 382 (Minn. 1996).

27. Salminen v. Frankson, 245 N.W.2d 839, 841 (Minn. 1976).

28. Lift-Stak & Stor, Inc. v. Lumbermens Mut. Cas. Co., 2000 Minn. Ct. App. LEXIS 1021, at *6 (Minn. Ct. App. Sept. 26, 2000).

29. *Holmes*, 488 N.W.2d at 475.

Mississippi

Michael Gwin
Watkins & Eager PLLC

1. GENERAL RULES OF CONTRACTUAL INDEMNITY

A contract for indemnification must meet the same requirements for validity as any other contract.[1] Accordingly, there must be an offer, acceptance, and valid consideration. In addition, the contract cannot violate public policy.[2] Indemnity agreements are construed under the normal rules of contract construction.[3] In this regard, "the cardinal rule of construction is to give effect to the mutual intentions of the parties."[4] "Parol evidence as to surrounding circumstances and intent may be brought in where the contract is ambiguous . . . ."[5] An indemnity contract, as any other contract, does not violate public policy "unless the contract is prohibited by the Constitution, a statute, or condemned by some decision by the courts construing the subject matter."[6]

A party may, by contract, obtain indemnity for its own negligence, subject to certain limitations and requirements. "[T]he indemnitee will be indemnified against his own negligence when the contract shows by clear and unequivocal language that this is the intention of the contracting parties."[7] Though the contractual indemnity language must be "clear and unequivocal," it need not be express: "[I]ndemnity agreements can be interpreted to provide indemnification from loss occasioned by the negligence of the indemnitee, even where no express language to that effect is found in the agreement."[8] Accordingly, broad, but not express, language of indemnification in a contract is "clear and unequivocal enough" to protect an indemnitee against the consequences of his own negligence.[9]

An indemnity provision cannot be procedurally unconscionable. Indicators of procedural unconscionability are lack of knowledge and lack of voluntariness.[10] The relative sophistication of the parties is one factor to be considered under a "lack of knowledge" inquiry.[11] Lack of voluntariness was proven against a sole-supplier electric utility company that presented its customers with a service agreement containing an indemnity provision on a "take it or leave it basis."[12] The court held that where "the contract is essentially a contract of adhesion, any indemnity clause is presumed unconscionable."[13]

1. Accu-Fab & Const. v. Ladner ex rel. Ladner, 970 So. 2d 1276, 1286 (Miss. Ct. App. 2000) (citing Anderton v. Business Aircraft, Inc., 650 So. 2d 473, 476 (Miss. 1995)).
2. *Id.*
3. Heritage Cablevision v. New Albany Elec. Power Sys., 646 So. 2d 1305, 1312 (Miss. 1994).
4. *Id.*
5. *Id.*
6. *Id.* (citing *Cappaert v. Junker*, 413 So. 2d 378, 380 (Miss. 1982)).
7. Blain v. Sam Finley, Inc., 226 So. 2d 742, 746 (Miss. 1969).
8. Mississippi Power Co. v. Roubicek, 462 F.2d 412, 416 (5th Cir. 1972) (applying Mississippi law).
9. Lorenzen v. S. Cent. Bell Tel. Co., 546 F. Supp. 694, 697 (S.D. Miss. 1982), *aff'd*, 701 F.2d 408 (5th Cir. 1983).
10. Entergy Mississippi, Inc. v. Burdette Gin Co., 726 So. 2d 1202, 1207 (Miss. 1998).
11. *Id.*
12. *Id.* at 1208.
13. *Id.*

2. EXCEPTIONS TO GENERAL RULES OF CONTRACTUAL INDEMNITY

Certain types of indemnity agreements are prohibited by public policy. For example, a public utility or common carrier cannot contract against liability for its own negligence as a matter of public policy.[14] On this basis, in *Entergy Mississippi, Inc. v. Burdette Gin Co.*, the Mississippi Supreme Court found an indemnity provision in the service contract between an electric power company and its customer to be void as against public policy.[15] The *Entergy* court distinguished prior cases upholding indemnity clauses in public utility contracts, noting those cases involved contracts between the utility and non-customers and, therefore, revolved around the negotiation of two private concerns.[16]

In another application of the "public policy" exception, one court held an indemnity contract unenforceable where the indemnitor was prevented by the indemnitee from properly warning of a hazardous condition caused by the indemnitee's negligence.[17]

Similarly, by Mississippi statute certain construction contracts that contain indemnity agreements may violate public policy.[18] The statute provides:

> With respect to all public or private contracts or agreements, for the construction, alteration, repair or maintenance of buildings, structures, highway bridges, viaducts, water, sewer or gas distribution systems, or other work dealing with construction, or for any moving, demolition or excavation connected therewith, every covenant, promise and/or agreement contained therein to indemnify or hold harmless another person from that person's own negligence is void as against public policy and wholly unenforceable.
>
> This section does not apply to construction bonds or insurance contracts or agreements.[19]

An indemnity agreement between a construction contractor and a surety company entered in conjunction with the surety's issuance of a performance bond is excepted by the last sentence of Mississippi Code Annotated § 31-5-41, even though the performance bond incorporated by reference the terms of the underlying construction contract between the owner and the contractor.[20]

The courts have generally placed a strict, not liberal, construction on what is a "construction contract" under § 31-5-41. "[A] contract must at least involve work to effect or assist in the construction or alteration or maintenance of a building or structure to be within the statute's reach."[21]

If an indemnity provision broadly indemnifies against the indemnitor's own negligence as well as the negligence of other parties, then the entire indemnity provision is void under § 31-5-41 and therefore "null" with "no legal force or binding effect."[22] Nevertheless, Mississippi law would not completely void an indemnity agreement if it contains a savings provision, for example, granting indemnity "to the maximum extent permitted by law."

14. Illinois Cent. R.R. v. Standard Oil Co., 292 F. Supp. 337, 339–40 (S.D. Miss. 1968).

15. Entergy Mississippi, Inc. v. Burdette Gin Co., 726 So. 2d 1202, 1206 (Miss. 1998).

16. *Id.*

17. Butler v. United States, 726 F.2d 1057, 1065–66 (5th Cir. 1984).

18. Miss. Code Ann. § 31-5-41 (1972). Ramsey v. Georgia-Pac. Corp., 597 F.2d 890, 892 (5th Cir. 1979).

19. Miss. Code Ann. § 31-5-41.

20. Fid. & Deposit Co. of Maryland v. Ralph McKnight & Son, Const., Inc., 28 So. 3d 1282 (Miss. 2010).

21. Eagle Pac. Ins. Co. v. Quintanilla, 923 So. 2d 266, 271 (Miss. Ct. App. 2006) (§ 31-5-41 not applicable to contract to supply labor to a construction project); Illinois Cent. Gulf R.R. v. Int'l Paper Co., 824 F.2d 403, 407 (5th Cir. 1987) (applying Mississippi law).

22. Travelers Prop. Cas. Co. of Am. v. Federated Rural Elec. Ins. Exch., No. 3:08cv83-DPJ-JCS, 2009 WL 2900027 at *3 (S.D. Miss. Sept. 3, 2009).

In this event, the indemnity provision would only be void to the extent it indemnified the indemnitor's own negligence.[23]

3. INDEMNITY AGREEMENTS AS INSURED CONTRACTS

Under Mississippi insurance law, an agreement to indemnify another can meet the definition of an "insured contract" within the language commonly used in liability policies as an exception to the exclusion for contractually assumed liability.[24]

There is, however, a question of the extent to which an indemnity provision void or unenforceable under Mississippi law can be an "insured contract" entitled to coverage. While one court has held that a contract void under Mississippi law cannot constitute an "insured contract" under a liability policy,[25] another court held it would "sharply distinguish coverage determinations (i.e. whether the contract is an insured contract) from indemnity determinations (i.e. whether the indemnity provision is valid)."[26]

4. OPERATION OF AN AGREEMENT TO INDEMNIFY REFERRING TO OR REQUIRING INSURANCE

Courts have found that an agreement to procure insurance for another is distinct from an agreement to indemnify.[27] When an agreement to procure insurance coverage is a separate obligation from the indemnity obligation, such a contractual obligation is separately enforceable, regardless of whether the indemnity obligation is void or unenforceable.[28] If an indemnitee is named as an additional insured, that indemnitee is entitled to coverage in accordance with the terms of the additional insured endorsement, despite the lack of enforceability of an indemnity agreement.[29]

Further, if an indemnitor and an indemnitee each have separate liability insurance coverage, certain cases recognize an "indemnity exception" to each policy's "other insurance" clause so that the loss is shifted to the insurer of the contractual indemnitor, despite the language of the respective "other insurance" clauses in each liability policy.[30] Stated differently by one court: "When a subcontractor agrees to indemnify a general contractor as to certain claims, subcontractors' insurance policy is considered the primary insurance policy concerning those claims."[31]

Mississippi indemnity law generally recognizes the "voluntary payment" doctrine under which a voluntary payment by one party cannot be recovered from another party

---

23. *Id.* ("Mississippi would allow a joint tortfeasor to recover indemnity under a construction contract, but not for its own negligence"); *Ramsey*, 597 F.2d at 894.

24. Leaf River Cellulose, L.L.C. v. Mid-Continent Cas., No. 2:11cv54-KS-MTP, 2012 WL 1906529 (S.D. Miss. May 25, 2012).

25. Certain London Mkt. Ins. v. IES v. Pennsylvania Nat'l Mut. Cas. Ins., 269 F. Supp. 2d 722, 724 (N.D. Miss. 2003), *aff'd*, 106 F. App'x 884 (5th Cir. 2004).

26. Pilot Travel Ctrs., L.L.C. v. Mid-Continent Cas., No. 3:15cv360-CWR-LRA, 2016 WL 1633060 (S.D. Miss. April 21, 2016) (citing Mid-Continent v. Swift Energy Co., 206 F.3d 487, 496 (5th Cir. 2000)); *see also* Roy Anderson Corp. v. Trans. Con. Ins. Co., 358 F. Supp. 2d 553, 562 (S.D. Miss. 2005) (distinguishing *Certain London, supra*). *See generally* Jeffrey Jackson, Miss. Ins. Law and Prac. § 16:27 (2017 ed.) ("Absent clear policy language, an insurer ordinarily cannot refuse to defend under an 'insured contract' on the basis that the underlying indemnity agreement violates section 31-5-41.").

27. Roy Anderson Corp. v. Trans-Cont'l Ins., 358 F. Supp. 2d 553, 566–68 (S.D. Miss. 2005).

28. *Id.*

29. *Id.*

30. Am. Indem. Lloyds v. Travelers Prop & Cas. Ins., 335 F.3d 429, 436–40 (5th Cir. 2003) (applying Texas law and citing Chubb Ins. Co. of Canada v. Mid-Continent Cas. Co., 982 F. Supp. 435, 438 (S.D. Miss. 1997) ("[I]t is the parties' rights and liabilities to each other which determine the insurance coverage; the insurance coverage does not define the parties' rights and liabilities one to the other.")).

31. Carl E. Woodward, L.L.C. v. Acceptance Ins. Co., No. 1:09cv781-HSO-RHW, 2012 WL 1574936, at *3 (S.D. Miss. May 3, 2012).

under indemnity principles.[32] Nevertheless, analyzing the applicability of the "voluntary payment" doctrine in the insurance context, courts have observed, "whether a payment was compelled or made voluntarily is a highly factual determination."[33] For example, where two co-primary insurance carriers disputed which should cover a claim, the carrier who defended and settled the claim could still seek reimbursement from the non-paying primary insurance carrier.[34] Similarly, in a dispute between a primary carrier and an umbrella carrier, the court found that a settlement payment made on behalf of the insured with whom the insurer had a contractual obligation to defend was not voluntary.[35]

32. Genesis Ins. v. Wausau Ins., 343 F.3d 733, 736 (5th Cir. 2008) ("[a] voluntary payment cannot be recovered back, and a voluntary payment within the meaning of this rule is a payment made without compulsion, fraud, mistake of fact, or agreement to repay a demand which the payor does not owe, and which is not enforceable against him. . . .").

33. *Id.* at 739.

34. State Farm Mut. Auto Ins. v. Allstate Ins., 255 So. 2d 667 (Miss. 1971).

35. Guidant Mut. Ins. v. Indem. Ins. Co. of N. Am., 13 So. 3d 1270, 1279 (Miss. 2009); *see also* Travelers Prop. Cas. v. Federated Rural Elec. Ins. Exch., No. 3:08cv83-DPJ-JCS, 2009 WL 2900027, at *6 (S.D. Miss. Sept. 3, 2009) (finding the excess carrier to not be a "stranger or intermeddler" where its duties were coterminous with indemnity obligations under a construction contract); Southern Ins. v. Affiliated FM Ins., 830 F.3d 337 (5th Cir. 2016) (holding that because the paying carrier "acted pursuant to its duty to pay" under its policy, it was not a "volunteer" and therefore could recover from the non-paying carrier).

Missouri

Kathryn Kasper
Hancock, Daniel & Johnson, P.C.

1. GENERAL RULES OF CONTRACTUAL INDEMNITY

It is the general rule that indemnity contracts will be construed to cover only such losses, damages, or liability reasonably intended by the parties.[1] Consequently, the interpretation of a contract is a question of law for a court to decide using an objective test.[2] When construing the meaning of contract language, words are viewed in light of the meaning that would ordinarily be understood by the layperson.[3] Further, language reasonably open to different constructions is typically considered ambiguous.[4] "[I]n a private contract, where the parties stand on a substantially equal footing, one may legally agree to indemnify the other against the results of the indemnitee's own negligence."[5] But a contract of indemnity "will not be construed so as to indemnify one against loss or damage resulting from his own negligent acts unless such intention is expressed in clear and unequivocal terms."[6] In the absence of such clear expression, or where doubt exists as to the parties' intention, Missouri courts will not construe a contract of indemnity to indemnify against the indemnitee's own negligence.[7] The rules applicable to the construction of contracts generally also apply to indemnification agreements.[8]

In the context of a subcontractor on a construction project agreeing to indemnify the contractor and others against any and all claims "only to the extent caused" in whole or in part by the negligence of the subcontractor,[9] the Missouri Supreme Court found that the phrase "to the extent caused" expressed an intention to limit the indemnitor's liability to the portion of fault attributed to the indemnitor:

> The preferred construction of the indemnification provision at issue, one that provides a reasonable meaning to each phrase of the provision, requires nothing more than that [the indemnitor] indemnify [the indemnitee] for [the indemnitor's] negligence even if [the indemnitee] participates in part in [the indemnitor's] negligent conduct. To hold otherwise would make the intended expression to limit liability to the acts of indemnitor meaningless.[10]

1. Kansas City Power & Light Co. v. Fed. Constr. Corp., 351 S.W.2d 741, 745 (Mo. 1961).
2. United Fire & Cas. Co. v. Gravette, 182 F.3d 649, 656 (8th Cir 1999).
3. *Id.*
4. *Id.*
5. *Kansas City Power & Light Co.*, 351 S.W.2d at 745.
6. *Id.*; Nusbaum v. City of Kansas City, 100 S.W.3d 101, 105 (Mo. 2003); Fed. Ins. Co. v. Gulf Ins. Co., 162 S.W.3d 160, 166 (Mo. Ct. App. 2005).
7. Parks v. Union Carbide Corp., 602 S.W.2d 188, 190 (Mo. 1980); Sw. Bell Tel. Co. v. J.A. Tobin Constr. Co., 536 S.W.2d 881, 885 (Mo. Ct. App. 1976).
8. Teter v. Morris, 650 S.W.2d 277, 282 (Mo. Ct. App. 1982); *see also* Burns & McDonnell Eng'g Co. v. Torson Constr. Co., 834 S.W.2d 755, 758 (Mo. Ct. App. 1992).
9. *Nusbaum*, 100 S.W.3d at 105–06.
10. *Id.* at 106–07 (citations omitted).

2. EXCEPTIONS TO GENERAL RULES OF CONTRACTUAL INDEMNITY

A Missouri statute precludes indemnity related to certain construction contracts. The statute provides: "[I]n any contract or agreement for public or private construction work, a party's covenant, promise or agreement to indemnify or hold harmless another person from that person's own negligence or wrongdoing is void as against public policy and wholly unenforceable."[11] But the statute also contains nine exceptions:

(1) A party's covenant, promise or agreement to indemnify or hold harmless another person from the party's own negligence or wrongdoing or the negligence or wrongdoing of the party's subcontractors and suppliers of any tier;
(2) A party's promise to cause another person or entity to be covered as an insured or additional insured in an insurance contract;
(3) A contract or agreement between state agencies or political subdivisions or between such governmental agencies;
(4) A contract or agreement between a private person and such governmental entities for the use or operation of public property or a public facility;
(5) A contract or agreement with the owner of the public property for the construction, use, maintenance, or operation of a private facility when it is located on such public property;
(6) A permit, authorization or contract with such governmental entities for the movement of property on the public highways, roads, or streets of this state or any political subdivision;
(7) Construction bonds, or insurance contracts or agreements;
(8) An agreement containing a party's promise to indemnify, defend, or hold harmless another person, if the agreement also requires the party to obtain specified limits of insurance to insure the indemnity obligation and the party had the opportunity to recover the cost of the required insurance in its contract price; provided, however, that in such case the party's liability under the indemnity obligation shall be limited to the coverage and limits of the required insurance; or
(9) Railroads regulated by the Federal Railroad Administration.[12]

For purposes of the statute, "construction work" includes, but is not limited to, "the construction, alteration, maintenance or repair of any building, structure, highway, bridge, viaduct, or pipeline, or demolition, moving or excavation connected therewith," and includes "the furnishing of surveying, design, engineering, planning or management services, or labor, materials or equipment, in connection with such work."[13] The statute applies only to those contracts or agreements entered into after August 28, 1999.[14]

3. INDEMNITY AGREEMENTS AS INSURED CONTRACTS

Missouri courts have not addressed whether and under what circumstances an agreement to indemnify constitutes an "insured contract" in the context of the typical exception to the general liability policy exclusion for contractually assumed liability. Various cases suggest that the indemnity of a third party by the insured is an "insured contract."[15] Based upon the

11. Mo. Rev. Stat. § 434.100(1) (2006).
12. *Id.* at § 434.100(2).
13. *Id.* at § 434.100(3).
14. *Id.* at § 434.100(4).
15. Kramer v. Ins. Co. of N. Am., 54 S.W.3d 613, 615–16 (Mo. Ct. App. 2001) (recognizing "insured contracts" as exceptions to exclusions in insurance policies); *See also* Cincinnati Ins. Co. v. Venetian Terrazzo, Inc., 198 F. Supp. 2d 1074, 1078 (E.D. Mo. 2001) (discussing defendant's argument that policy exclusion did not apply because of "insured contract" provision, but deciding the case on different grounds); *See also United Fire & Cas. Co.*, 182 F.3d 649, 656 (8th Cir 1999) (survivors in a wrongful death case alleged they were entitled to indemnity under the "insured contract" exception in the insured's commercial automobile policy).

policy of finding the broadest possible coverage, a Missouri court would likely recognize the "insured contract" exception to a policy exclusion and find an agreement to indemnify for tort liability to constitute an "insured contract."

4. OPERATION OF AN AGREEMENT TO INDEMNIFY REFERRING TO OR REQUIRING INSURANCE

Parties to a contract may allocate the risk of loss by agreeing that one party shall maintain insurance in order to save harmless the other party from liability.[16] Even in a construction setting, a party may include, or promise to include, another party as an insured or an additional insured under an insurance contract.[17]

The courts have not addressed the extent of an insurer's obligation to an indemnitee in light of the underlying agreement of the insured to indemnify the additional insured. As noted above, Missouri applies the general rule that insurance contracts are interpreted strictly against the insurer and in favor of the insured. Consequently, it is doubtful that an insurer would prevail on an argument that its duty to indemnify an additional insured under a policy of liability insurance could be limited by the named insured's underlying indemnity agreement, where no such limitation was placed on the coverage at the time the policy was written.

16. Mo. Rev. Stat. § 434.100(2).
17. *Id.*

Montana

Erin D. Doran and Laura Hanson
Meagher & Geer, PLLP

1. GENERAL RULES OF CONTRACTUAL INDEMNITY

Indemnity is defined in Montana as a "contract by which one engages to save another from a legal consequence of the conduct of one of the parties or some other person."[1] Montana courts have "long recognized the legality of indemnity clauses and that they should be liberally construed in favor of the party intended to be indemnified."[2] A party may contract for indemnification against its own negligence, whether sole or concurrent.[3] For an indemnification agreement for damages caused by negligent acts of the indemnitee to be enforceable, however, the contractual indemnity provision must be expressed in clear and unequivocal terms.[4]

Thus, in *Ryan Mercantile Co. v. Great Northern Railroad Co.*, the court found that an indemnity agreement using phrases such as "any and all personal injuries," "of every name and nature which may in any manner arise," and "whether due or not due to the negligence of [indemnitee]" demonstrated the parties' intent that the lessee would cover any claim made against the lessor for damages, even if the lessor's sole negligence caused the damages. Additionally, the court held that this language was broad enough to cover all claims no matter where on the premises mentioned in the lease such claim arose.[5]

Similarly, in a case involving a contract for seismic exploration testing, the Montana Supreme Court examined the effect of contractor's agreement to indemnify "against all claims, liabilities, demands, causes of action and judgments" resulting "in whole or in part" from "the negligent acts or omissions or willful misconduct" of the contractor or its employees. The court concluded that the agreement provided indemnity for allegations of concurrent negligence but would not apply to the indemnitee's sole negligence.[6]

Most recently, the Montana Supreme Court examined an indemnity provision in a subcontract related to a state highway paving project.[7] The provision provided that the subcontractor would indemnify the general contractor from "liability on account of any act or omission of the Subcontractor, or any of his officers, agents, employees or servant[s]."[8] Based on this language, the subcontractor was required to provide indemnity regardless of whether he was negligent.[9] Thus, the indemnity clause required only a "direct causal relationship between the act or omission [by the Subcontractor]" and the alleged loss.[10]

1. MONT. CODE ANN. § 28-11-301.
2. *See* Lesofski v. Ravalli Cty. Elec. Coop., 439 P.2d 370, 371–72 (Mont. 1968).
3. Ryan Mercantile Co. v. Great N. Ry. Co., 294 F.2d 629, 633 (9th Cir. 1961).
4. *Id.*; *see also* Slater v. Central Plumbing & Heating Co., 912 P.2d 780, 782 (Mont. 1996) (finding that the subcontractor did not have to indemnify general contractor for his own negligent acts as the contract was not clear and unambiguous); Amazi v. Atlantic Richfield Co., 816 P.2d 431, 433 (Mont. 1991) ("In order for a contract to indemnify a party against its own negligence, such indemnification must be expressed in 'clear and unequivocal terms.'"); Sweet v. Colburn School Supply, 639 P.2d 521, 523 (Mont. 1982); *Lesofski*, 439 P.2d at 372.
5. *Ryan Mercantile Co.*, 294 F.2d at 633.
6. *Amazi*, 816 P.2d at 433.
7. A.M. Welles, Inc. v. Montana Materials, Inc., 342 P.3d 987, 990 (Mont. 2015).
8. *Id.* at 989.
9. *Id.* at 990.
10. *Id.*

2. EXCEPTIONS TO GENERAL RULES OF CONTRACTUAL INDEMNITY

In 2003, Montana enacted legislation barring indemnification for a party's own negligence in the construction context.[11] Montana Code Annotated § 28-2-2111 states:

> [A] construction contract provision that requires one party to the contract to indemnify, hold harmless, insure or defend the other party to the contract . . . for liability, damages, losses, or costs that are caused by the negligence, recklessness, or intentional misconduct of the other party . . . is void as against the public policy of this state.[12]

The statute does allow indemnity provisions that act to indemnify a party for all negligence other than his or her own.[13] No Montana decisions have analyzed this statute.

Montana also prohibits indemnification for known unlawful conduct. The Montana Code states that an agreement to indemnify a person against an intentional wrongful act is void.[14] The courts have noted, however, that modern insurance contracts typically provide coverage for a host of tortious activities. Thus, "the need to reduce financial risks and promote economic stability in modern society has rendered this statute applicable only to conduct defined as criminal."[15]

A longstanding statute in Montana also provides that, "[a]ll contracts which have for their object, directly or indirectly, to exempt anyone from responsibility for his own fraud, for willful injury to the person or property of another, or for violation of law, whether willful or negligent, are against the policy of the law."[16] Most cases have been careful to point out that this statutory provision[17] applies to exculpatory clauses, not to indemnity clauses. Contracts for indemnity purporting to relieve one from the results of his or her failure to exercise ordinary care are not ordinarily contrary to public policy.[18] The *Ryan Mercantile* court, in addressing the predecessor statute to Montana Code Annotated § 28-2-702, reasoned: "Neither law nor public policy prevents the ordinary contractor from buying from a third party indemnity from the pecuniary result of his own negligence. That is legitimate as insurance."[19] As such, the *Ryan Mercantile* court concluded that the agreement between the parties that the lessee would hold the lessor harmless from any judgment, was not contrary to public policy under the statute.[20]

On the other hand, in 2001, the Montana Supreme Court held that Montana Code Annotated § 28-2-702 precluded a defendant from being indemnified for his or her own negligence. But it is not clear that the underlying indemnity agreement would have been sufficient under the clear and unambiguous standard needed to uphold an indemnification for the sole or concurrent negligence of the indemnitee.[21] Another recent decision held that under § 28-2-702, an indemnity provision is void if it acts like an exculpatory claim. In *Fox v. Plum Creek Timber Co.*, a lessee sued his landlord for injuries he suffered while logging the land.[22] The lease required the lessee to indemnify the landlord for all claims. The court

11. Mont. Code Ann. § 28-2-2111.

12. *Id.*

13. *Id.*

14. Mont. Code Ann. § 28-11-302 (agreements to indemnify another "against an act thereafter to be done is void if the act be known by such person, at the time of doing it, to be unlawful").

15. First Bank (N.A.)-Billings v. Transamerica Ins. Co., 679 P.2d 1217, 1220 (Mont. 1984).

16. Mont. Code Ann. § 28-2-702 (originally enacted in 1895).

17. *Id.*

18. *Id.*

19. *Ryan Mercantile*, 294 F.2d at 635.

20. *Id.* at 636.

21. Langemo v. Montana Rail Link, Inc., 38 P.3d 782, 786 (Mont. 2001).

22. Fox v. Plum Creek Timber Co., No. CV 12-2-M-DLC-JCL, 2012 WL 6933199, at *2 (D. Mont. Nov. 19, 2012), *report and recommendation adopted*, No. CV 12-2-M-DLC-JCL, 2013 WL 308891 (D. Mont. Jan. 25, 2013).

rejected the landlord's claim that the lease had the obligation to defend and indemnify it against the lessee's own claims based on § 28-2-702 because allowing for indemnification would have, in effect, exculpated the landlord from liability.

Montana's worker's compensation statutes also prohibit contractual indemnity claims against an employer for injuries to an employee for which a third party has paid. An indemnitee cannot rely on a contractual indemnity agreement to circumvent the employer's immunity under the Workers' Compensation Act:

> For all employments covered under the Workers' Compensation Act or for which an election has been made for coverage under this chapter, the provisions of this chapter are exclusive. Except as provided in part 5 of this chapter for uninsured employers and except as otherwise provided in the Workers' Compensation Act, an employer is not subject to any liability whatever for the death of or personal injury to an employee covered by the Workers' Compensation Act or for any claims for contribution or indemnity asserted by a third person from whom damages are sought on account of such injuries or death.[23]

This statute has been applied to bar a claim for contractual indemnity against an employer who had paid worker's compensation benefits to the injured party.[24] However, a Montana federal court held that under Montana law a subcontractor's insurer was required to provide insurance coverage to a general contractor for claims asserted by the subcontractor's employee, even though the employee could not assert claims directly against the subcontractor.[25]

3. INDEMNITY AGREEMENTS AS INSURED CONTRACTS

A Montana federal court recently addressed when an agreement to indemnify another for the indemnitee's tort liability falls within the "insured contract" exception to the standard commercial general liability (CGL) policy exclusion for contractually assumed liability.[26] The court held that an indemnity provision in a construction contract in which the subcontractor agrees to indemnify the general contractor for claims arising out of the subcontractor's work is an "insured contract."[27]

4. OPERATION OF AN AGREEMENT TO INDEMNIFY REFERRING TO OR REQUIRING INSURANCE

In *Anaconda Co. v. General Accident Fire & Life Assurance Corp.*, the owner required his general contractor to name him as an additional insured on his liability policy, insuring against "risks of any kind relating to the construction" at the owner's smelter facilities.[28] A subcontractor's employee was later injured when the owner's employee dropped a plank some thirty feet, striking and injuring the subcontractor's employee.[29] The injured employee filed suit against the owner, alleging that the negligence of the owner's employee caused his injury.[30] The owner made a formal demand to the general contractor's insurer, requesting

---

23. Mont. Code Ann. § 39-71-411.

24. Raisler v. Burlington N. Ry., 717 P.2d 535 (Mont. 1985).

25. Liberty Mut. Ins. Co. v. Cont'l Res., Inc., No. CV 10-35-BLG-RFC-CSO, 2011 WL 2982221, at *1 (D. Mont. Apr. 25, 2011), *report and recommendation adopted*, No. CV 10-35-BLG-RFC-CSO, 2011 WL 3024326 (D. Mont. July 21, 2011), *aff'd*, 501 F. App'x 626 (9th Cir. 2012).

26. WBI Energy Transmission, Inc. v. Colony Ins. Co., 56 F. Supp. 3d 1194, 1203 (D. Mont. 2014).

27. *Id.*

28. Anaconda Co. v. General Accident Fire and Life Assurance Corp., 616 P.2d 363 (Mont. 1980).

29. *Id.* at 363–66.

30. *Id.*

a defense, and the insurance company denied coverage.[31] In the ensuing case to determine whether the insurer owed a duty to defend the owner, the Montana Supreme Court overturned a lower court's entry of summary judgment in favor of the owner. Despite the seemingly broad language of coverage, the court determined that questions of fact remained as to whether the owner's employees were performing work within the scope of the underlying contract when they caused the injury, even though it was undisputed that the injured party was injured in the course of performing the underlying contract. In doing so, the court read into the agreement an unstated provision that the "injuring" party had to be acting within the scope of the contract: "Were we to focus merely on the activities of the injured workman and not the activities of the named insureds, we would render application of [the contract] overly broad and make [the insurer] the insurer of all [of the owner's] activities at the Smelter that resulted in injuries to anyone working pursuant to the contract, regardless of control and benefit. This Court will place no such burden on anyone."[32]

In determining if an indemnitee is entitled to seek insurance coverage under a policy issued to the indemnitor, Montana courts have generally found that coverage is determined by the language of the policy and not the language of the indemnity provision. In *United National Insurance Co. v. St. Paul Fire & Marine Ins. Co.*, the court examined whether the general contractor was entitled to coverage as an additional insured under its subcontractor's insurance policy, even though it was not entitled to direct indemnity under its contract with its subcontractor.[33] To the court, the claims against the general contractor fell within the scope of the additional insured coverage provided by the subcontractor's policy.

31. *Id.*
32. *Id.* at 366.
33. United Nat'l Ins. Co. v. St. Paul Fire & Marine Ins. Co., 214 P.3d 1260, 1268 (Mont. 2009).

Nebraska

Anthony Alt
Meagher & Geer, PLLP

1. GENERAL RULES OF CONTRACTUAL INDEMNITY

Generally, Nebraska law defines a contract of indemnity as "the obligation or duty resting on one person to make good any loss or damage another has incurred or may incur by acting at his request or for his benefit."[1] "'An indemnitee may be indemnified against his own negligence if the contract contains express language to that effect or contains clear and unequivocal language that that is the intention of the parties.'"[2] Otherwise, the parties are presumed to intend that the indemnitee shall not be indemnified for a loss caused by his or her own negligence.[3]

"The general rules governing construction and interpretation of contracts other than indemnity contracts apply in construing indemnity contracts and in determining rights and liabilities of the parties thereunder."[4] "An indemnity contract should be construed so as to ascertain and give effect to the intention of the parties to it, if that can be done consistent with legal principles."[5] "In construing an indemnity contract, the terms and language used must be given fair and reasonable interpretation, the contract read in its entirety, and consideration given not only to the contract's language but also to the situation of the parties and circumstances surrounding them at the time of making the contract."[6]

Notice of suit or tender of defense is not ordinarily a condition precedent to recovery on an indemnity contract for a liability incurred or determined in a prior action against the indemnitee.[7] "In the absence of notice or tender of defense, the amount to be indemnified is a question of fact rather than being conclusively established by the prior judgment."[8] Any failure to notify the indemnitor does not preclude recovery against the indemnitor on the indemnity contract, but leaves the indemnitee with the burden of proving the amount for which it is entitled to be indemnified.[9]

A cause of action for indemnity pursuant to the terms of an indemnity contract does not accrue, and the statute of limitations does not begin to run, until the loss occurs, i.e., moneys are paid by the indemnitee, triggering the indemnity obligation.[10]

Nebraska law allows a third party to be indemnified by an employer for the third party's loss incurred by payment to the employer's injured employee.[11] If an injured employee files a claim against a third party for damages, the Nebraska Workers' Compensation Act exclusivity provision for employers bars the third party's right to seek payment from the

1. Lyhane v. Durtschi, 13 N.W.2d 130, 134 (Neb. 1944).

2. Omaha Pub. Power Dist. v. Natkin & Co., 227 N.W.2d 864, 867 (Neb. 1975) (quoting Peter Kiewit Sons Co. v. O'Keefe Elevator Co., Inc., 213 N.W.2d 731, 732 (Neb. 1974)); *accord* Anderson v. Nashua Corp., 560 N.W.2d 446, 449 (Neb. 1997).

3. *Peter Kiewit Sons Co.*, 213 N.W.2d at 733.

4. *Id.* at 732; *accord* Union Pac. R.R. Co. v. Kaiser Agric. Chem. Co., 425 N.W.2d 872, 879 (Neb. 1988).

5. *Peter Kiewit Sons Co.*, 213 N.W.2d at 732.

6. Currency Servs., Inc. of Minn. v. Passer, 133 N.W.2d 19, 21 (Neb. 1965).

7. Warner v. Reagan Buick, Inc., 483 N.W.2d 764, 771 (Neb. 1992).

8. Ins. Co. of N. Am. v. Hawkins, 246 N.W.2d 878, 881 (Neb. 1976).

9. *Id.*

10. Dutton-Lainson Co. v. Cont'l Ins. Co., 716 N.W.2d 87, 100 (Neb. 2006); City of Wood River v. Geer-Melkus Constr. Co., 444 N.W.2d 305, 311 (Neb. 1989); Lyhane v. Durtschi, 13 N.W.2d 130, 135 (Neb. 1944).

11. Union Pac. R.R. Co. v. Kaiser Agric. Chem. Co., 425 N.W.2d 872, 879 (Neb. 1988); Harsh Int'l v. Monfort Indus., 662 N.W.2d 574, 580 (Neb. 2003).

employer, unless there is an express contract of indemnity that creates a contractual duty of reimbursement to the third party, thereby circumventing the immunity afforded by the Workers' Compensation Act.[12]

2. EXCEPTIONS TO GENERAL RULES OF CONTRACTUAL INDEMNITY

The Nebraska legislature has enacted a statute that prohibits indemnification provisions in construction-related contracts for a party's own negligence. Pursuant to Nebraska Revised Statutes § 25-21,187(1):

> In the event that a public or private contract or agreement for the construction, alteration, repair, or maintenance of a building, structure, highway bridge, viaduct, water, sewer, or gas distribution system, or other work dealing with construction or for any moving, demolition, or excavation connected with such construction contains a covenant, promise, agreement, or combination thereof to indemnify or hold harmless another person from such person's own negligence, then such covenant, promise, agreement, or combination thereof shall be void as against public policy and wholly unenforceable. This subsection shall not apply to construction bonds or insurance contracts or agreements.

Parties seeking to invoke the protection of this section will need to raise it; a failure to raise it may be deemed a waiver.[13] This section will not operate to invalidate a provision in a contract that requires one party to provide liability insurance for the sole negligence of the other party.[14] Additionally, if there is an indemnification provision in a construction contract that includes indemnification for one's own negligence and includes obligations for indemnification in other circumstances, only the portion prohibited by § 25-21,187 is stricken from the indemnification clause and the language remaining may be interpreted to impose liability on the indemnitor.[15]

3. INDEMNITY AGREEMENTS AS INSURED CONTRACTS

Nebraska law implicitly recognizes that the exclusion found in most insurance policies against coverage for liability assumed by the insured under any contract or agreement may bar coverage for agreements to indemnify another, depending upon the language of the exclusion.[16] There are exceptions to the exclusion, such as for an "insured contract," often defined under policies as "that part of any other contract or agreement pertaining to your business . . . under which you assume the tort liability of another party to pay for 'bodily injury' or 'property damage' to a third person or organization."[17] Generally, "[p]arties to an insurance contract may contract for any lawful coverage, and an insurer may limit its liability and impose restrictions and conditions upon its obligations under the contract if the restrictions and conditions are not inconsistent with public policy or statute."[18]

---

12. *Union Pac. R.R. Co.*, 425 N.W.2d at 879 (Neb. 1988); *Harsh Int'l*, 662 N.W.2d at 580.

13. Day v. Toman, 266 F.3d 831, 835 (8th Cir. 2001).

14. *See* Anderson v. Nashua Corp., 560 N.W.2d 446, 449 (Neb. 1997).

15. Hiway 20 Terminal, Inc. v. Tri-County Agri-Supply, Inc., 443 N.W.2d 872, 875–76 (Neb. 1989).

16. *See* Royal Indem. Co. v. Aetna Cas. & Sur. Co., 229 N.W.2d 183, 188 (Neb. 1975) (noting in a case involving an indemnification provision that "[a]lthough it is possible that the case might have quite simply been disposed of on the grounds that a clause in the insurance policy of Empire Insurance Company provided that the policy did not apply 'to liability assumed by the insured under any contract or agreement,' nevertheless, the court proceeded to point out that even if that clause were ignored, the result would still be the same").

17. *Day*, 266 F.3d at 835–36.

18. Mefferd v. Sieler & Co., 676 N.W.2d 22, 25 (Neb. 2004).

4. OPERATION OF AN AGREEMENT TO INDEMNIFY REFERRING TO OR REQUIRING INSURANCE

An indemnitee may require another to insure losses incurred by reason of the indemnitee's negligence "if the contract contains express language to that effect or contains clear and unequivocal language establishing that that is the intention of the parties."[19] This is essentially the same standard applied to analyze the validity of an indemnification agreement requiring indemnity for the indemnitee's own negligence.[20] The express language of Nebraska Revised Statutes § 25-21,187(1) provides that the prohibition on indemnity for one's own negligence does "not apply to construction bonds or insurance contracts or agreements." Therefore, Nebraska Revised Statutes § 25-21,187(1) does not prohibit an agreement requiring one party to procure insurance for the other party's negligence.[21]

19. *Anderson*, 560 N.W.2d at 449; Federated Serv. Inc. Co. v. Alliance Constr., LLC, 805 N.W.2d 468, 475–76 (Neb. 2011).

20. *See, e.g.*, Omaha Pub. Power Dist. v. Natkin & Co., 227 N.W.2d 864, 867 (Neb. 1975); *Peter Kiewit Sons Co.*, 213 N.W.2d at 732.

21. *Anderson*, 560 N.W.2d at 449.

Nevada

Howard Russell
Weinberg, Wheeler, Hudgins, Gunn & Dial, LLC

1. GENERAL RULES OF CONTRACTUAL INDEMNITY

Express agreements to indemnify are enforceable in Nevada, but they are strictly construed.[1] Ambiguous indemnity contracts will be interpreted against the indemnitee, particularly when the indemnitee was the drafter of the agreement.[2] "When the duty to indemnify arises from contractual language, it generally is not subject to equitable considerations; rather it is enforced in accordance with the terms of the contracting parties agreement."[3] An agreement in which indemnity extends to the indemnitee for his or her own negligence is enforceable, but the provision "must clearly and unequivocally express the indemnitor's assumption of liability for the negligent acts of the indemnitee."[4] Any such agreement will similarly be strictly construed.[5] The requirement to "clearly and unequivocally" set forth the indemnitor's liability is satisfied only by an express statement that the indemnitor is agreeing to indemnify the indemnitee for the indemnitee's own negligence. A broad "hold harmless" clause generally does not satisfy this requirement.[6]

Further, the obligation to indemnify for another's own negligence may require a finding that the indemnitor's negligence actually caused the loss. For example, if the indemnity obligation is triggered "to the extent [the loss is] caused" by the indemnitor's negligence, a factual finding must first be made that the indemnitor's negligence caused the loss before a duty to defend is even triggered.[7] Such language "must be strictly construed as limiting an indemnitor's liability to cover the indemnitee's losses only to the extent the injuries were caused by the indemnitor."[8]

2. EXCEPTIONS TO GENERAL RULES OF CONTRACTUAL INDEMNITY

Unlike in other states, no statute prohibits indemnity agreements in the construction context; however, such agreements are subject to the same rules of interpretation set forth above. In analyzing indemnity agreements in the construction context, the Nevada Supreme Court has noted that such clauses are enforceable, even in favor of the indemnitee's own negligence, so long as the indemnity obligation is clear and unequivocal.[9] "[S]ince Nevada has not adopted an anti-indemnity statute, parties have great freedom in allocating indemnification responsibilities between one another."[10]

1. Calloway v. City of Reno, 939 P.2d 1020, 1028 (Nev. 1997). The *Calloway* decision has since been withdrawn and replaced by 993 P.2d 1259 (Nev. 2000). However, the republished decision did not address the indemnification issues mentioned above. Accordingly, the earlier decision remains good law as for the propositions set forth above.

2. *Id.*

3. United Rentals Hwy. Techs. v. Wells Cargo, 289 P.3d 221, 226 (2012) (internal quotations omitted). *See also* Reyburn Lawn v. Plaster Dev. Co., 255 P.3d 268, 274 (2011).

4. *Calloway*, 939 P.2d 1020.

5. *United Rentals*, 289 P.3d at 226.

6. *Calloway*, 939 P.2d 1020.

7. *United Rentals*, 289 P.3d at 227.

8. *Id.*

9. *See Reyburn Lawn*, 255 P.3d 268.

10. *Id.*

3. INDEMNITY AGREEMENTS AS INSURED CONTRACTS

The Nevada federal district court has recognized that an agreement to indemnify constitutes an "insured contract" within the meaning of the exception of a liability insurance policy to the form exclusion for contractually assumed liability.[11]

4. OPERATION OF AN AGREEMENT TO INDEMNIFY REFERRING TO OR REQUIRING INSURANCE

The Nevada Supreme Court has rejected the argument that an agreement to procure insurance is a *de facto* agreement to indemnify one for his or her own negligence. While noting that some courts have held that "when an indemnity agreement contains both hold harmless and insurance provisions, the parties clearly intend that [the indemnitee] will be indemnified against the consequences of its own negligence," the Nevada Supreme Court construed a contractual obligation to procure insurance as not expanding the scope of the contractual indemnity obligations. The *United Rentals* court held that an agreement to hold the indemnitee harmless and to name the indemnitee as an insured on certain liability insurance policies does not expand a party's contractual duty to indemnify beyond the contractual indemnity language.[12]

---

11. USF Ins. Co. v. Smith's Food & Drug Center, Inc., 921 F. Supp. 2d 1082 (D. Nev. 2013).
12. *United Rentals*, 289 P.3d at 228 n.5.

New Hampshire

Julianna Malogolowkin
Hinckley, Allen, & Snyder LLP
Kurt Mullen and Sydney Pritchett
Nixon Peabody, LLP

1. GENERAL RULES OF CONTRACTUAL INDEMNITY

Contracts of indemnification that purport to indemnify a party against his or her own wrongful acts are looked upon with disfavor in New Hampshire.[1] Indemnity agreements, whether express or implied, are strictly construed.[2] Put another way, indemnity agreements are to be rarely implied.[3] New Hampshire courts will not imply an indemnity agreement where the indemnitor's liability has not been extinguished.[4]

While indemnification agreements that seek to relieve a party from the consequences of his or her own future negligence are strictly construed, these contracts are generally not prohibited or void on public policy grounds.[5] Such agreements will be enforced where the indemnitor clearly and unequivocally agrees by the terms of the contractual agreement to indemnify the indemnitee against his or her own negligence.[6] "The indemnity provision, however, need not state explicitly the parties' intent to provide indemnity for the negligence of another." Express language is not necessary "where the parties' intention to afford protection for another's negligence is clearly evident."[7]

An agreement to indemnify for "any and all claims and demands, actions and causes of action, damages, costs, loss of service, expenses and compensation, including, but no [sic] limited to any and all claims for personal injury and/or death and property damages which may, in any way, arise from or out of the operations of the [indemnitor] pursuant to the terms of this Agreement," was broad enough to reach the indemnitee's own negligence where it arose in connection with the indemnitor's operations under the contract.[8]

An indemnitee can maintain an action for indemnity against the employer of an injured party despite the worker's compensation bar, as the contractual right to indemnity is an independent obligation owed to the indemnitee.[9]

New Hampshire courts have held that insurance policy language may permit a commercial tenant to seek indemnification or contribution under a landlord's insurance policy as additional insureds.[10] The New Hampshire Supreme Court also has upheld the ability of a landlord's insurer to seek indemnification for a tort claim from a commercial tenant under the tenant's lease agreement.[11]

1. *See* Merimac Sch. Dist. v. Nat'l Sch. Bus. Serv., Inc., 661 A.2d 1197 (N.H. 1995).
2. Gray v. Leisure Life Indus., 77 A.3d 1117 (N.H. 2013).
3. *Id.* at 1121.
4. *Id.*
5. *Id.*
6. *Id.* at 1199.
7. *Id.* (internal punctuation omitted).
8. *Id.*
9. Wentworth Hotel v. F. A. Gray, Inc., 272 A.2d 583 (N.H. 1970).
10. Great Am. Dining v. Philadelphia Indem. Ins. Co., 62 A.3d 843 (N.H. 2013).
11. One Beacon Ins. v. M&M Pizza, 8 A.3d 18 (N.H. 2010).

2. EXCEPTIONS TO GENERAL RULES OF CONTRACTUAL INDEMNITY

New Hampshire expressly prohibits indemnity of design professionals.[12] In this regard,

> Any agreement or provision whereby an architect, engineer, surveyor or his agents or employees is sought to be held harmless or indemnified for damages and claims arising out of circumstances giving rise to legal liability by reason of negligence on the part of any said persons shall be against public policy, void and wholly unenforceable.[13]

This statutory prohibition of exculpatory agreements for negligence claims, however, does not prevent parties to a contract from negotiating the extent of their contractual rights and liabilities.[14]

3. INDEMNITY AGREEMENTS AS INSURED CONTRACTS

An insured's contractual agreement to indemnify another, in relation to its business, constitutes an "incidental contract" within the meaning of a policy covering "any contract or agreement relating to the conduct of the named insured's business."[15]

4. OPERATION OF AN AGREEMENT TO INDEMNIFY REFERRING TO OR REQUIRING INSURANCE

In *Chadwick v. CSI, Ltd.*, the New Hampshire Supreme Court addressed the effect of an agreement to purchase insurance in the context of a "waiver of subrogation" executed in conjunction with an agreement to indemnify.[16] Although exculpatory agreements are generally unenforceable in New Hampshire, a "waiver of subrogation," by which parties agree to waive claims against each other and look to insurance for their losses, is permissible.

> [Waivers of subrogation] exist in the contract as part of a larger comprehensive approach to indemnifying the parties involved in the construction project, allocating the risks involved, and spreading the costs of different types of insurance. These paragraphs do not present the same concerns as naked exculpatory provisions . . . . [T]he insurance provisions of the standard AIA contract are not designed to unilaterally relieve one party from the effects of its future negligence, thereby foreclosing another party's avenue of recovery. Instead, they work to ensure that injuries or damage incurred during the construction project are covered by the appropriate types and limits of insurance, and that the costs of that coverage are appropriately allocated among the parties.[17]

Even if a parallel indemnity agreement exists, such that the parties indicate an intention that one would assume the risk of loss, a waiver of subrogation clause may preclude a claim between the contracting parties. In *Chadwick*, the waiver of subrogation clause provided that it was effective even though one party may owe an indemnity obligation,[18] and as such, a waiver of subrogation clause that by its terms trumps any parallel indemnity obligation will control.

12. N.H. Rev. Stat. Ann. § 338-A:1.
13. *Id.*
14. Dartmouth College v. N. Branch Constr. Inc., 2014 N.H. Super. LEXIS 4 (N.H. Mar. 24, 2014).
15. White Mountain Cable Constr. Corp. v. Transamerica Ins. Co., 631 A.2d 907 (N.H. 1993).
16. Chadwick v. CSI, Ltd., 629 A.2d 820 (N.H. 1993).
17. *Id.* at 826.
18. *Id.*

New Jersey

Sherilyn Pastor
McCarter & English, LLP

1. GENERAL RULES OF CONTRACTUAL INDEMNITY

New Jersey courts generally recognize the enforceability of express indemnification agreements contained within commercial contracts.[1] Parties in a commercial setting are "free to negotiate the allocation of tort liability regardless of fault."[2] Generally, agreements to indemnify another for the indemnitee's own negligence, either partial or sole, are not enforceable unless an intent to indemnify is unequivocally spelled out in the contract.[3] There is no general "public policy impediment to an indemnitor undertaking to indemnify the indemnitee with respect to the indemnitee's own negligence."[4] An "indemnification agreement may be worded so broadly and clearly as to provide for absolute indemnification of [the indemnitee], even though [the indemnitee]'s negligence—whether it be sole or concurring, active or passive—caused the injury."[5]

Indemnification agreements allocating tort liability are interpreted in accordance with the general rules governing construction of contracts, but when an indemnity clause is ambiguous, it is strictly construed against the indemnitee.[6] Thus, "a contract will not be construed to indemnify the indemnitee against losses resulting from its own negligence unless such an intention is expressed in unequivocal terms."[7] To bring a negligent indemnitee within the scope of an indemnification agreement, the agreement must specifically reference the negligence resulting from the fault of the indemnitee.[8]

Although agreements indemnifying the indemnitee for its own negligent acts are "perhaps antithetical to the policy of compelling tortfeasors to bear responsibility for conduct heedless of the risks to others," the practical result of such agreements, whether through traditional insurance or otherwise, is the rightful allocation of financial responsibility as part of the general bargaining process.[9]

2. EXCEPTIONS TO GENERAL RULES OF CONTRACTUAL INDEMNITY

There is a statutory prohibition on indemnification agreements related to the construction, repair, maintenance, or service of buildings, highways, and railroads.[10] While the statute originally barred all indemnification agreements within its scope, a 1983 amendment narrowed the prohibition to apply only to contracts that indemnify for the indemnitee's "sole negligence." The statute states in relevant part:

1. Mantilla v. NC Mall Assocs., 770 A.2d 1144, 1148–49 (N.J. 2001).

2. Stier v. Shop Rite of Manalapan, 492 A.2d 1055, 1059 (N.J. Sup. Ct. App. Div. 1985); Gulf Oil Corp. v. ACF Indus., Inc., 534 A.2d 1025, 1028 (N.J. Sup. Ct. App. Div. 1987).

3. *Mantilla*, 770 A.2d at 1148; Ramos v. Browning Ferris Indus., Inc., 510 A.2d 1152, 1159 (N.J. 1986).

4. Leitao v. Damon G. Douglas Co., 693 A.2d 1209, 1211 (N.J. Sup. Ct. App. Div. 1997).

5. *Stier*, 492 A.2d at 1059; Romnell v. United States Steel Corp., 168 A.2d 437, 443 (N.J. Sup. Ct. App. Div. 1961).

6. *Ramos*, 510 A.2d at 1159; *Mantilla*, 770 A.2d at 1148–49.

7. *Ramos*, 510 A.2d at 1159.

8. Azurak v. Corporate Prop. Investors, 814 A.2d 600, 601 (N.J. 2003).

9. *Leitao*, 693 A.2d at 1211–12; *see also* Jamison v. Ellwood Consol. Water Co., 420 F.2d 787, 789 (3d Cir. 1970).

10. N.J. Stat. Ann. § 2A:40A-1.

> A covenant, promise, agreement or understanding in, or in connection with or collateral to a contract, agreement or purchase order, relative to the construction, alteration, repair, maintenance, servicing, or security of a building, structure, highway, railroad, appurtenance and appliance . . . purporting to indemnify or hold harmless the promisee against liability for damages arising out of bodily injury to persons or damage to property caused by or resulting from the sole negligence of the promisee, his agents, or employees, is against public policy and is void and unenforceable, provided that this section shall not affect the validity of any insurance contract . . . or agreement issued by an authorized insurer.[11]

One purpose of the amendment was to allow indemnification in the case of contributory negligence.[12] Consequently, there is no public policy bar for a party to a construction contract to indemnify another for the indemnitee's own negligence, so long as the indemnitee is not solely at fault.[13] This principle "derives from the judicial recognition that ordinarily the financial responsibility for the risk of injury during the course of a construction project is shifted in any event by the primary parties to their insurance carriers."[14] The impact of the indemnity agreement is to allow the parties to allocate between themselves the total acquired insurance protection for the project.[15] "The parties ought to be free to determine how the insurance burdens will be distributed between them and who will pay for a specific coverage for a specific risk."[16]

The prohibition for indemnification of a third party's "sole negligence" is inapplicable to agreements "made directly with a railroad relative to construction, alteration, repair, maintenance or access upon, under or across the right of way of an operating railroad."[17] Another exception exists for "contract[s], agreement[s], understanding[s] or purchase order[s] to which the State of New Jersey or any of its departments, agencies, or authorities is a party."[18]

Agreements attempting to indemnify architects, engineers, or surveyors for losses resulting from their sole negligence are against public policy and are statutorily void and unenforceable.[19] The statute provides in relevant part:

> A covenant, promise, agreement . . . whereby an architect, engineer, surveyor or his agents . . . shall be indemnified or held harmless for damages . . . caused by or resulting from the sole negligence of an architect, engineer, surveyor or his agents . . . arising either out of (1) the preparation or approval . . . of maps, drawings, opinions, reports, surveys, change orders, designs or specifications, or (2) the giving of or the failure to give directions or instructions . . . provided such giving or failure to give is the cause of the damage claim, loss or expense, is against public policy and is void and unenforceable.[20]

This statute does not apply to limitation of liability clauses, as distinguished from agreements to indemnify.[21]

---

11. *Id.*
12. Statement to Assembly Bill No. 590–L. 1983, c. 107; *see* Secallus v. Muscarelle, 586 A.2d 305, 306–07 (N.J. Super. Ct. App. Div. 1991).
13. *Leitao*, 693 A.2d at 1211; Carvalho v. Toll Bros. & Devs., 675 A.2d 209, 215 (N.J. 1996); Bradford v. Kupper Assoc., 662 A.2d 1004, 1019 (N.J. Super. Ct. App. Div. 1995).
14. Doloughty v. Blancher Constr. Co., 352 A.2d 613, 616 (N.J. 1976), *overruled on other grounds by Azurak*, 814 A.2d at 601.
15. *Id.*
16. *Leitao*, 693 A.2d at 1211 (internal quotation marks omitted).
17. N.J. Stat. Ann. § 2A:40A-3.
18. *Id.*
19. N.J. Stat. Ann. § 2A:40A-2.
20. *Id.*
21. Marbro, Inc. v. Borough of Tinton Falls, 688 A.2d 159, 164 (N.J. Super. Ct. Law Div. 1996).

3. INDEMNITY AGREEMENTS AS INSURED CONTRACTS

New Jersey law recognizes that an indemnification agreement can constitute an "insured contract," such that the standard exclusion in a liability insurance policy for contractually assumed liability does not apply to an insured's agreement to indemnify another.[22] Courts have recognized that "[i]t is not unusual for liability insurance policies to exclude from coverage liability assumed by an insured under a contract generally one in which the insured agrees to indemnify to save harmless a third party (that is, if the party would not otherwise be liable under the law)."[23] Nevertheless, the general rule with respect to exclusionary provisions is that they do not preclude coverage, even if liability is assumed by contract, where the insured would have been liable regardless of his or her contractual undertaking.[24] Put another way, the contractual liability assumed is excluded from coverage only if the obligation would not have been independently imposed upon the insured by law.[25]

4. OPERATION OF AN AGREEMENT TO INDEMNIFY REFERRING TO OR REQUIRING INSURANCE

Mutual agreements to shift the risk of loss or damage to insurance do not violate New Jersey public policy.[26] The distribution of risk in this manner entails no elements of injustice and does not conflict with the public interest.[27] The rule is stated as follows:

> [P]rovisions in leases and other commercial agreements . . . whether couched in language of *indemnity or exculpation* or imposing obligations with respect to obtaining insurance, are to be viewed realistically as normal, common-sense efforts by businessmen to allocate between them the cost or expense of risks of property damage. They contemplate that such risks will be covered by insurance, and the only practical feature of such bargains ordinarily is the decision as to who is to bear the cost of insurance.[28]

Under that rule, mutual agreements to allocate risks to insurers are construed to provide "mutual exculpation" to the bargaining parties and to "accord with the understanding of reasonable businessmen."[29] The bargaining parties are deemed to have agreed to look solely to their insurance and to have relieved each other from liability.[30] At least one New Jersey court has held that courts should "approach a contract of *indemnity* in the same manner as any other contract which distributes various insurance burdens between and among the parties."[31]

New Jersey courts do not find that insurers' agreements to indemnify insureds from negligent conduct somehow run afoul of general public policy prohibitions on indemnification agreements. The general approach taken by the courts seems to imply that indemnity agreements will not be subject to general public policy prohibitions if they provide that the indemnitor will obtain liability insurance sufficient to cover the potential risk involved.

---

22. Conduit & Found. Corp. v. Hartford Cas. Ins. Co., 746 A.2d 1053, 1055 n.3 (N.J. Super. Ct. App. Div. 2000); Metta v. Fitchburg Mut. Ins. Co., 2008 N.J. Super. Unpub. LEXIS 2227, at *4–6 (N.J. Super. Ct. App. Div. June 28, 2008).

23. Karadis Bros. Painting Co. v. Penn. Nat'l Mut. Cas. Ins. Co., 292 A.2d 42, 45 (N.J. Super. Ct. Ch. Div. 1972).

24. *Id.*

25. *Id.*

26. Continental Ins. Co. v. Boraie, 672 A.2d 274, 277 (N.J. Sup. Ct. Law Div. 1995); Mayfair Fabrics v. Henley, 234 A.2d 503, 508 (N.J. Sup. Ct. Law Div. 1967).

27. *Mayfair Fabrics*, 234 A.2d at 508.

28. *Id.* at 507 (emphasis added); *see also Continental*, 672 A.2d at 277; Buscaglia v. Owens-Corning Fiberglass, 172 A.2d 703, 707 (N.J. Sup. Ct. App. Div. 1961), *aff'd*, 178 A.2d 208 (N.J. 1962).

29. *Mayfair Fabrics*, 234 A.2d at 507, 508; Mortgage Corp. of N.J. v. Manhattan Sav. Bank, 177 A.2d 326, 331 (N.J. Sup. Ct. Law Div. 1962).

30. *Mayfair Fabrics*, 234 A.2d at 507.

31. Cozzi v. Owens-Corning Fiber Glass Corp., 164 A.2d 69, 74 (N.J. Super. Ct. App. Div. 1960) (emphasis added).

New Mexico

Howard Russell
Weinberg, Wheeler, Hudgins, Gunn & Dial, LLC

1. GENERAL RULES OF CONTRACTUAL INDEMNITY

Express contracts of indemnity are enforceable under New Mexico law.[1] "Enforcing express contracts of indemnity is no more than enforcing the loss distribution agreed to by the contracting parties."[2] Accordingly, there exists strong public policy to enforce indemnity contracts, "unless they clearly contravene some positive law or rule of public morals."[3]

New Mexico does not require an express reference to the indemnitee's negligence as a condition precedent to his or her being held harmless for his or her own negligence.[4] Rather, broad indemnification provisions that hold the indemnitee harmless for "all actions, suits, demands, damages, losses or expenses" have been held sufficient to provide indemnification for losses caused by the actions of the indemnitee.[5] But the scope of the provision must be clearly drafted. Applying New Mexico law, the Tenth Circuit has held that the language of an indemnification provision must clearly and unequivocally set forth the intention of the parties to provide indemnification to the indemnitee for his or her own negligence.[6] Broad clauses, such as that mentioned above, must clearly manifest an intent to cover all damages in order to be deemed to contain the unequivocal terms needed to enforce the indemnification.[7]

Although there must be a clear and unequivocal intent to indemnify the indemnitee for its own negligence, the scope of indemnity and intent of the parties may be a question of fact.[8] The absence of specific language limiting the indemnity to the indemnitor's own negligence can lead to competing interpretations on whether the agreement reaches the indemnitee's own negligence.[9] Further, the extent to which the parties agree that the indemnitee will be named an additional insured may be relevant to determining whether the indemnity extends to the indemnitee's own negligence.[10]

2. EXCEPTIONS TO GENERAL RULES OF CONTRACTUAL INDEMNITY

New Mexico limits by statute the availability of contractual indemnity in construction contracts. New Mexico Statutes Annotated § 56-7-1(A) provides that indemnity provisions in construction contracts purporting to hold the indemnitee harmless from injury or damages caused or resulting "in whole or in part" from the indemnitee's own acts or omissions are against public policy and unenforceable.[11] Further, § 56-7-1(E)'s prohibition on an

1. City of Artesia v. Carter, 610 P.2d 198 (N.M. Ct. App. 1980).
2. *Id.* at 201.
3. *Id.* (finding that the worker's compensation statute does not bar an indemnity claim by a third party against an employer when that claim is based on an express claim of indemnity).
4. Eichel v. Goode, Inc., 680 P.2d 627 (N.M. 1984).
5. *Id.* at 631.
6. Tyler v. Dowell, Inc., 274 F.2d 890, 895 (10th Cir. 1960).
7. Metro. Paving Co. v. Gordon Herkenhoff & Assocs., Inc., 341 P.2d 460, 463 (N.M. 1959).
8. Krieger v. The Wilson Corp., 139 N.M. 274, 131 P.3d 661 (2005).
9. *Id.* at 280, 667.
10. *Id.*
11. N.M. Stat. Ann. § 56-7-1(A).

agreement to "indemnify" or "hold harmless" includes naming the indemnified party as an additional insured in the indemnitor's insurance coverage.[12]

The statute articulates the circumstances under which indemnity provisions and insurance clauses in a construction contract will be held valid. First, clauses that indemnify the indemnitee for losses caused by or arising from the acts or omissions of the indemnitor will be enforceable.[13] Second, § 56-7-1(B)(2) clarifies that provisions requiring a contractor to purchase a "project-specific insurance policy" are valid.[14]

Previous New Mexico case law, based upon the broad "in whole or in part" language of § 56-7-1(A), invalidated expansive indemnification clauses.[15] This proposition was based on the holding in *Sierra v. Garcia*, a 1987 New Mexico Supreme Court decision.[16] However, recent decisions have called into question *Sierra*'s holding. In *Sierra*, the court found that the indemnification provision did not need to mention the negligence of the indemnitee to be found unenforceable. Rather, if the scope of an indemnity is broad enough to include the acts or omissions of the indemnitee, it will be invalidated. Moreover, once an indemnification provision is found to be in violation of the New Mexico statute, courts will not redact the offending portions and enforce the remaining indemnity obligations. Instead, the entire indemnity clause is voided.[17]

In *Holguin v. Fulco Oil Services L.L.C.*,[18] the New Mexico Court of Appeals explained that the *Sierra* court's decision needed to be reexamined, as the *Sierra* court was interpreting the 1971 version of the statute and not the 2003 version of the statute.[19] The 1971 version of the statute did not include the language now contained in § 56-7-1(B).[20] The court concluded that § 56-7-1(A), i.e., declaring a provision that requires indemnification for the indemnitee's own negligence to be void and unenforceable, referred to that particular provision within the indemnity clause, and not the entire indemnity clause.[21] The court further declared that to hold otherwise would render meaningless the language in § 56-7-1(B), which permits indemnity clauses in construction contracts for indemnification against the indemnitor's own negligence.[22] Harmonizing § 56-7-1(A) and § 56-7-1(B), the *Holguin* court ruled the indemnity clauses at issue could be enforced to the extent that those clauses required the indemnifying party to indemnify the indemnitee for the indemnitor's negligence, but not for the negligence of the indemnitee.[23]

New Mexico has a similar anti-indemnity statute pertaining to contracts related to "any well for oil, gas, or water, or mine for any mineral."[24] In this context, any agreement purporting to indemnify the indemnitee for damages "arising from the sole or concurrent negligence of the indemnitee" is void and unenforceable.[25] New Mexico courts have interpreted this provision to mean "that the indemnitee cannot contract away liability for his own percentage of negligence."[26]

Like the statutory prohibition on certain construction-related indemnity agreements found in § 56-7-1, the statute invalidating certain indemnity agreements in the mining

12. N.M. Stat. Ann. § 56-7-1(F).
13. N.M. Stat. Ann. § 56-7-1(B)(1).
14. N.M. Stat. Ann. § 56-7-1(B)(2).
15. *See* Sierra v. Garcia, 746 P.2d 1105 (N.M. 1987) (finding an indemnification provision that indemnified the contractor and owner from damages and losses "however caused resulting directly or indirectly from or connected with the performance of this subcontract" to run afoul of N.M. Stat. Ann. § 56-7-1(A)); *see also Metro. Paving Co.*, 341 P.2d at 463.
16. *Sierra*, 746 P.2d at 1105.
17. *Id.*
18. Holguin v. Fulco Oil Services L.L.C., 245 P.3d 42 (N.M. Ct. App. 2010).
19. *Id.* at 50.
20. *Id.*
21. *Id.*
22. *Id.*
23. *Id.* at 51.
24. N.M. Stat. Ann. § 56-7-2(A).
25. *Id.*; *see also* Guitard v. Gulf Oil Co., 670 P.2d 969 (N.M. Ct. App. 1983).
26. *Guitard*, 670 P.2d at 972.

context also directly addresses insurance contracts. Specifically, New Mexico Statutes Annotated § 56-7-2(C) provides:

> A provision in an insurance contract indemnity agreement naming a person as an additional insured or a provision in an insurance contract or any other contract requiring a waiver of rights of subrogation or otherwise having the effect of imposing a duty of indemnification on the primary insured party that would, if it were a direct or collateral agreement described in Subsections A and B of this section, be void, is against public policy and void.

The New Mexico legislature has acted to prevent additional insured loopholes to its anti-indemnification statutes. These statutory provisions comport with decisions of the New Mexico Supreme Court, holding that allowing an indemnitor to provide insurance to cover an indemnitee for the indemnitee's own negligence equally violates New Mexico public policy to promote safety.[27]

3. INDEMNITY AGREEMENTS AS INSURED CONTRACTS

The court of appeals has recognized that an indemnity agreement can constitute an "insured contract" as defined by the standard commercial general liability (CGL) policy.[28] Further, an indemnitee may be entitled to bring an action directly against an insurer.[29] While the extent of coverage for an "insured contract" will depend on the scope of the indemnity, the court of appeals held in *Krieger* that these can be questions of fact, and permit an indemnitee claiming the benefit of the indemnitor's coverage for an "insured contract" to seek coverage directly from the insurer.[30]

4. OPERATION OF AN AGREEMENT TO INDEMNIFY REFERRING TO OR REQUIRING INSURANCE

Nothing in New Mexico case law indicates that indemnification agreements requiring the indemnitor to procure insurance to cover his or her indemnification obligations impact the enforceability of the indemnity clause. However, an indemnification agreement that is otherwise invalid is not suddenly enforceable simply because the obligation is insured.[31] The plain language of New Mexico Statutes Annotated §§ 56-7-1 and 56-7-2 precludes that outcome.[32]

27. First, the public policy behind § 56-7-2(A), is to promote safety. The indemnitee, usually the operator of the well or mine, will not be allowed to delegate to subcontractors his or her duty to see that the well or mine is safe. Our interpretation furthers the public policy behind the statute, which is to promote safety. Both the operator and the subcontractor will have incentive to monitor the safety of the operation knowing that they will be responsible for their respective percentage of negligence. Amoco Prod. Co. v. Action Well Service, Inc., 755 P.2d 52, 55 (N.M. 1988).

28. *Krieger*, 139 N.M. at 287, 131 P.3d at 674.

29. *Id.*

30. *Id.*

31. *Amoco Prod.*, 755 P.2d at 55.

32. *See* N.M. STAT. ANN. §§ 56-7-1(E), 56-7-2(C) (invalidating the practice of using insurance to avoid the anti-indemnification policies of the state).

New York

Nicole B. Weinstein
Beveridge & Diamond, P.C.

1. GENERAL RULES OF CONTRACTUAL INDEMNITY

Contractual agreements to indemnify are enforceable in New York.[1] However, a duty to indemnify exists only if there is manifestation of a clear and "'unmistakable intention' to indemnify."[2] If the parties' intent is unclear, or there is a reasonable basis for a difference of opinion, "the court is required to consider extrinsic evidence of intent."[3]

If the intent is clear, however, "an indemnification agreement will be enforced even if it provides indemnity for one's own or a third party's negligence."[4] Such intent may be "implied from the language and purposes of the entire agreement, and the surrounding facts and circumstances"; it need not expressly refer to the indemnitee's negligence.[5] Sufficiently clear indemnification clauses are generally enforceable, even if the indemnitee is actively negligent.[6]

For example, an agreement to indemnify for "any and all loss . . . occasioned directly or indirectly by the act of negligence of the [indemnitor] or . . . otherwise" expresses a clear intent to indemnify another for the indemnitee's negligence.[7] Likewise, an agreement providing for indemnification "whether [the] damages or injuries be attributable to negligence of the Contractor or his employees or otherwise" extends to the indemnitee's own negligence.[8]

On the other hand, New York courts disfavor catch-all phrases that attempt to seek broadly sweeping indemnification. For example, a phrase indemnifying for "other obligations and liabilities arising in the ordinary course of business" fails to establish an unmistakable intent to assume an obligation to indemnify.[9] Similarly, words of limitation following the terms of an indemnification provision may diminish otherwise "unmistakable intent" to indemnify for the indemnitee's own negligence.[10]

1. Bradley v. Earl B. Feiden, Inc., 864 N.E.2d 600, 605 (N.Y. 2007); *see also* Levine v. Shell Oil Co., 269 N.E.2d 799, 801–02 (N.Y. 1971); Kurek v. Port Chester Hous. Auth., 223 N.E.2d 25, 27 (N.Y. 1966).

2. Heimbach v. Metro. Transp. Auth., 553 N.E.2d 242, 246 (N.Y. 1990) (articulating the standard one must satisfy in order to have a valid and enforceable indemnity agreement) (citing Hooper Assocs. v. AGS Computers, 548 N.E.2d 903, 905 (N.Y. 1989); *Levine*, 269 N.E.2d at 802); Bank of Am. Corp. v. Lemgruber, 385 F. Supp. 2d 200, 226 (S.D.N.Y. 2005) (same).

3. Commander Oil Corp. v. Advance Food Serv. Equip., 991 F.2d 49, 51 (2d Cir. 1993) (citing Slatt v. Slatt, 477 N.E.2d 1099, 1100 (N.Y. 1985)).

4. *Bradley*, 864 N.E.2d at 605–06. *See also* N.Y. Jur. 2d (2010) § 91.

5. Margolin v. N.Y. Life Ins. Co., 297 N.E.2d 80, 82–83 (N.Y. 1973).

6. *Kurek*, 223 N.E.2d at 27–28 (finding enforceable an agreement to hold harmless the indemnitee "against all claims and demands . . . of whatsoever kind or nature").

7. *Levine*, 269 N.E.2d at 802 (collecting cases that upheld indemnification language) (citations and internal quotation marks omitted); Gibbs-Alfano v. Burton, 281 F.3d 12, 19 (2d Cir. 2002) ("[W]here there is all-encompassing language in an indemnification agreement, the New York Court of Appeals has divined the 'unmistakable intent of the parties' to indemnify against the indemnitee's negligent acts." (citations and internal quotation marks omitted)).

8. Jordan v. City of New York, 162 N.Y.S.2d 145, 149–50 (N.Y. App. Div. 1957), *aff'd*, 5 N.Y.2d 723 (1958). *See also* N.Y. Jur. 2d (2010) §§ 92–93 (discussing examples of effective and ineffective indemnification language).

9. Haynes v. Kleinewefers & Lembo Corp., 921 F.2d 453, 457–58 (2d Cir. 1990) (finding no indemnification obligation beyond certain enumerated liabilities in a purchase and sale agreement containing catch-all for "other obligations and liabilities arising in the ordinary course of . . . business"). *See also* N.Y. Jur. 2d (2010) § 78 (discussing strict construction); *but see id.* § 79 (noting that broad indemnity clauses can still be given effect where sufficiently clear and unambiguous).

10. *Heimbach*, 553 N.E.2d at 244, 246.

2. EXCEPTIONS TO GENERAL RULES OF CONTRACTUAL INDEMNITY

Under New York statute, it is against public policy for a construction agreement to contain an indemnification clause requiring the promisor to indemnify the promisee for bodily injury or property damage liability caused by the promisee's negligence.[11] If an indemnification agreement contemplates such indemnification, the agreement is unenforceable under the statute.[12] The statute provides in pertinent part:

> A covenant, promise, agreement or understanding in, or in connection with . . . a contract or agreement relative to the construction, alteration, repair or maintenance of a building . . . purporting to indemnify or hold harmless the promisee against liability for damage arising out of bodily injury to persons or damage to property contributed to, caused by or resulting from the negligence of the promisee, his agents or employees, or indemnitee, whether such negligence be in whole or in part, is against public policy and is void and unenforceable. . . . This subdivision shall not preclude a promisee requiring indemnification for damages . . . caused by or resulting from the negligence of a party other than the promisee, whether or not the promisor is partially negligent.[13]

The statute "prevent[s] a prevalent practice in the construction industry of requiring subcontractors to assume liability by contract for the negligence of others."[14] (The New York legislature concluded that practice was unfair to subcontractors and driving up "the cost of construction by limiting the number of contractors able to obtain the necessary hold harmless insurance.")[15]

Consistent with the statutory language and underlying rationale, an indemnification agreement between a general contractor and subcontractor can be enforced if the language is limited to the subcontractor's (or other third party's) negligence.[16] A broadly written indemnification that could cover the general contractor's negligence, on the other hand, may only be enforced if the general contractor has been found "free from negligence, and liability is merely imputed or vicarious."[17]

Statutes restricting indemnification for negligence similarly have been enacted for other industries, such as catering, building services, architect designs, and places of public recreation.[18]

Additionally, a party may not be indemnified for intentional criminal conduct or intentional tortious conduct, although "one whose intentional act causes an unintended injury may be . . . indemnified."[19] Indemnification for punitive or exemplary damages is not permissible.[20] An exception has also been found for indemnification of a tortfeasor for a settlement that has not been approved by a court when made with an infant suffering personal

---

11. N.Y. Gen. Oblig. Law § 5-322.1; Itri Brick & Concrete Corp. v. Aetna Cas. & Sur. Co., 680 N.E.2d 1200, 1204–05, 89 N.Y.2d 786, 794–95 (1997) ("[T]he statute applies to the indemnification agreements in their entirety where, as here, the general contractor/promisee is actually found to have been negligent."); Potter v. M.A. Bongiovanni, Inc., 707 N.Y.S.2d 689, 690 (N.Y. App. Div. 2000).

12. N.Y. Gen. Oblig. Law § 5322.1. *Itri Brick & Concrete*, 89 N.Y.2d at 795 (noting that the indemnity contract would be enforceable where the contractor was free from negligence).

13. N.Y. Gen. Oblig. Law § 5322.1 [1].

14. *Itri Brick & Concrete*, 89 N.Y.2d at 794.

15. *Id.*

16. *Id.* at 795.

17. *Potter*, 707 N.Y.S.2d at 690 (citations omitted); *see also* Brown v. Two Exch. Plaza Partners, 556 N.E.2d 430, 434 (N.Y. 1990); Cabrera v. Bd. of Educ. of City of N.Y., 823 N.Y.S.2d 419, 421 (N.Y. App. Div. 2006).

18. *See* N.Y. Gen. Oblig. Law §§ 5321 through 5-326.

19. Pub. Serv. Mut. Ins. Co. v. Goldfarb, 425 N.E.2d 810, 814 (N.Y. 1981).

20. *Id.* at 400 (explaining that although it is not against public policy to indemnify compensatory damages for gross negligence, recklessness, or wantonness, any associated punitive or exemplary damage would be barred).

injuries.[21] Other exceptions to the general rule allowing indemnification have been found for acts of bad faith; fraud; willful, reckless, or grossly negligent misconduct; and self-dealing.[22]

3. INDEMNITY AGREEMENTS AS INSURED CONTRACTS

New York courts have recognized that an insured's agreement to indemnify another constitutes an "insured contract" within the meaning of an exception to the exclusion for contractually assumed liability found in standard form general liability insurance policies.[23] However, the insured bears the burden of proving the exception applies.[24]

4. OPERATION OF AN AGREEMENT TO INDEMNIFY REFERRING TO OR REQUIRING INSURANCE

If an agreement contains an insurance procurement requirement but the required insurance is not obtained, New York courts generally have found a breaching promisor (i.e., the party that agreed to procure insurance) liable for the damages that would have been within the covered limits had the required insurance policy been procured.[25] The promisee (i.e., the party that would have been added as an insured had the insurance been procured) is not, however, entitled to indemnification for damages resulting from breach of an insurance procurement provision if an indemnification agreement would not have been enforceable in the first instance.[26] On the other hand, the insurer generally cannot invoke a statute prohibiting indemnification as a defense to coverage, absent intentional injuries.[27]

---

21. Valdimer v. Mount Vernon Hebrew Camps, Inc., 172 N.E.2d 283, 284–86 (N.Y. 1961).

22. Kalisch-Jarcho, Inc. v. City of N.Y., 448 N.E.2d 413 (N.Y. 1983) ("[A]n exculpatory clause is unenforceable when, in contravention of acceptable notions of morality, the misconduct for which it would grant immunity smacks of intentional wrongdoing. This can be explicit, as when it is fraudulent, malicious or prompted by the sinister intention of one acting in bad faith. Or, when, as in gross negligence, it betokens a reckless indifference to the rights of others, it may be implicit.") (citations omitted); *In re Joan & David Halpern Inc.*, 248 B.R. 43, 45–46 (S.D.N.Y. 2000) (discussing exceptions to indemnification of trustees of *inter vivos* trusts).

23. *See, e.g.*, Hunt v. Ciminelli-Cowper Co., 939 N.Y.S.2d 781, 784–85 (2012) (finding an indemnification agreement constitutes an "insured contract" under a commercial general liability policy); Maksymowicz v. N.Y.C. Bd. of Educ., 647 N.Y.S.2d 780 (N.Y. App. Div. 1996) ("The ruling here contains an 'insured contract' clause, under which the exclusion for employee injuries 'does not apply to liability assumed by the insured under an 'insured contract,' defined as 'that part of any other contract or agreement pertaining to your business under which you assume the tort liability of another to pay damages because of 'bodily injury'. . . to a third person. Clearly, the asbestos removal contract is an 'insured contract' included within the coverage of the policy.") (holding based on anti-subrogation rule); Hailey v. N.Y. State Elec. & Gas Corp., 626 N.Y.S.2d 912, 912 (N.Y. App. Div. 1995) (noting that the "effect of [a contractual liability] exclusion and the exception thereto is to deny coverage for claims for contribution and common-law indemnification while covering the insured for claims or contractual indemnification").

24. Travelers Ins. Co. v. Nory Const. Co., 708 N.Y.S.2d 252, 255 (Sup. Ct. 2000) (discussing the insured contract exception and noting that "[w]here, as here, coverage depends upon application of an exception to a policy exclusion, the insured bears the burden of establishing the applicability of the exception" (citations omitted)).

25. *See* Encarnacion v. Manhattan Powell L.P., 685 N.Y.S.2d 227, 228 (N.Y. App. Div. 1999) (holding that where the procurement provision was breached, the promisee "is liable for the resulting damages, including the amount of damages awarded to or paid to the injured party in the main action, within the limits of the policy that was to have been procured, as well as the costs incurred in defense of the main action" (citing Kinney v. G.W. Lisk Co., 556 N.E.2d 1090, 1092 (N.Y. 1990))).

26. *See* Port Parties, Ltd. v. Merch. Mart Props., Inc., 959 N.Y.S.2d 37, 39 (N.Y. App. Div. 2013) (holding that where an indemnification provision would violate General Obligations Law § 5-323, that awarding damages for a failure to procure insurance would violate the statute).

27. *See, e.g.*, St. Paul Fire & Marine Ins. Co. v. Universal Builders Supply, 409 F.3d 73, 86–87 (2d Cir. 2005) (insurance procurement requirement enforceable even for gross negligence); Great N. Ins. Co. v. Interior Constr. Corp., 857 N.E.2d 60, 63 (N.Y. 2006) (insurance procurement requirement permissible even where a standard indemnification provision would violate General Obligations Law § 5-321).

Legislation has been proposed that would amend § 5-322.1 of the General Obligations Law to prohibit the use of procurement provisions to circumvent the New York public policy against indemnification for one's own negligence in construction contracts. *See, e.g.*, N.Y. S. Res. 5239, 239 Leg. Sess. § 1 (2017) ("[A] provision in a construction contract that requires the purchase of additional insured coverage, or any coverage endorsement, or provision within an insurance policy providing additional insured coverage, is void and unenforceable to the extent that it requires coverage, the scope of which is prohibited under this subdivision.").

If insurance has been procured under an agreement, New York courts have held that "the extent of coverage (including a given policy's priority vis-à-vis other policies) is controlled by the relevant policy terms, not by the terms of the underlying trade contract that required the named insured to purchase coverage."[28] As a result, an insurance policy naming the indemnitee as an "additional insured" and providing coverage in an amount or type greater than what was promised under the indemnification agreement may entitle the indemnitee to coverage beyond the scope of the original indemnity agreement, absent a provision in the policy specifically referencing the underlying agreement.[29]

New York courts have also used an agreement to procure insurance as evidence of the scope of a given indemnity. For example, in *Covert v. Binghamton*, the court reviewed parallel indemnity and insurance agreements, under which the general contractor-indemnitor was to provide insurance for its own work and provide insurance covering the city-indemnitee.[30] The court stated:

> Given the broad contractual indemnification clause, [the contractor] would be required to indemnify the City for any liability for injuries incurred by the City. The inclusion of the clause requiring [the contractor] to obtain insurance coverage for its contractual liability for injuries clearly indicates the intent of the parties that, in the event of the City's being held liable for a personal injury caused by anyone's negligence, the loss should be charged to [the contractor] and be borne by the insurance carrier which insured either [the contractor's] contractual liability or the City's liability.[31]

Thus, the indemnity agreement was used as a basis to define the scope of coverage for the insurance purchased pursuant to the contract. Although not decided in the context of an insurance dispute, the court recognized an interplay between the indemnity and insurance provisions.[32]

28. Bovis Lend Lease LMB, Inc. v. Great Am. Ins. Co., 855 N.Y.S.2d 459, 464 (N.Y. App. Div. 2008).

29. *See id.* at 145–46 (assessing a priority of coverage dispute and noting that "the Court of Appeals looked to the subcontract because the insurance policy itself expressly provided that the terms of the subcontract would determine whether the additional insured coverage afforded was primary or excess" (citations omitted)).

30. Covert v. Binghamton, 459 N.Y.S.2d 721 (Sup. Ct. 1983).

31. *Id.* at 1078.

32. *Id.* at 1078–79.

North Carolina

Kathryn Kasper
Hancock, Daniel & Johnson, P.C.

1. GENERAL RULES OF CONTRACTUAL INDEMNITY

Contractual agreements to indemnify are enforceable in North Carolina.[1] When interpreting a contract of indemnity, the general rules of contract construction apply.[2] This includes giving effect to the intention of the parties.[3] If the language of the agreement is clear and unambiguous, the court must interpret it as written.[4]

While an indemnity contract purporting to relieve the indemnitee from liability for its own negligence or the negligence of its employees is not favored by the law and will be strictly construed, such an indemnity provision is not against public policy if the contract is private and the interest of the public is not involved, and if there is no gross inequality in bargaining power.[5] Although the issue of contractual indemnification for an intentional tort has not been ruled upon by the courts, one court indicated that although its ruling did not reach that question, a contractual provision that was construed to relieve another defendant from liability for its intentional torts would be void as against public policy.[6]

2. EXCEPTIONS TO GENERAL RULES OF CONTRACTUAL INDEMNITY

There are several exceptions to the general rules regarding indemnity.

Under North Carolina General Statutes § 22B-1, construction indemnity provisions cannot hold one party responsible for the negligence of another:[7] "A promise or agreement entered into in connection with construction/physical labor that purports to indemnify a promisee against liability for damages arising out of bodily injury to persons or damage to property proximately caused by or resulting from negligence of the promisee, in whole or in part, the promisee's independent contractors, agents, employees, or indemnities, is void and not enforceable."[8] In other words, a construction agreement may indemnify a party from damages arising from the other party's negligence; it cannot indemnify a party from its own negligence.

The indemnity provisions to which this statute applies are those construction indemnity provisions that attempt to hold one party responsible for the negligence of another and this rule does not affect insurance contracts or any agreement issued by an insurer.[9]

1. *See* Kaleel Builders, Inc. v. Ashby, 587 S.E.2d 470, 474 (N.C. Ct. App. 2003).
2. Kirkpatrick & Assoc. v. Wickes Corp., 280 S.E.2d 632, 634 (N.C. Ct. App. 1981).
3. Dixie Container Corp. v. Dale, 273 N. C. 624, 160 S.E.2d 708 (1968).
4. *Kirkpatrick*, 280 S.E.2d at 634.
5. *See* New River Crushed Stone, Inc. v. Austin Powder Co., 210 S.E.2d 285, 287 (N.C. Ct. App. 1974).
6. *See* Lewis v. Dunn Leasing Corp., 244 S.E.2d 706, 709 (N.C. Ct. App. 1978).
7. N.C. Gen. Stat. § 22B-1. The term "construction" is defined as "design, planning, construction, alteration, repair or maintenance of a building, structure, highway, road, appurtenance or appliance, including moving, demolition and excavating connected therewith."
8. *Id.* (A contract in which one party agrees to indemnify a second party or its independent contractors, agents, employees, or indemnities against liability for damages resulting from the sole negligence of the first party, its agents, or employees is not affected by N.C. Gen. Stat. § 22B-1.)
9. *See* Bridgestone/Firestone, Inc. v. Ogden Plant Maint. Co. of N.C., 548 S.E.2d 807 (N.C. Ct. App. 2001).

By exempting insurance contracts from § 22B-1, the legislature intended to prevent insurance policies that name the buyer of construction services as an insured from being invalidated.[10]

3. INDEMNITY AGREEMENTS AS INSURED CONTRACTS

The agreement to indemnify another is an "insured contract" within the meaning of the exception to the form commercial general liability insurance policy exclusion for contractual liability, applicable where the insured agrees to assume the tort liability of another.[11] Giving effect to the plain language of this exception to the contractual liability exclusion, it has been held that the assumption of tort liability speaks to the liability of the indemnitee, not to the tort liability of the insured/indemnitor.[12]

4. OPERATION OF AN AGREEMENT TO INDEMNIFY REFERRING TO OR REQUIRING INSURANCE

Unlike the rule in many states, an agreement to obtain insurance to cover liability for an agreement to indemnify will not make an indemnity that is prohibited by North Carolina General Statutes § 22B-1 into one that is enforceable, even on a limited basis.[13] In fact, the carrier of the insured-indemnitor may properly deny a defense to the insured on the basis that the liability for which the insured seeks coverage arises from a void contractual obligation,[14] even if the agreement may not yet have been adjudicated at the point in time the request for a defense is made.[15]

10. *See* Miller Brewing Co. v. Morgan Mech. Contractors, Inc., 368 S.E.2d 438 (N.C. Ct. App. 1988).

11. *See* Pa. Nat'l Mut. Cas. Ins. Co. v. Assoc. Scaffolders and Equip. Co., Inc., 579 S.E.2d 404 (N.C. Ct. App. 2003).

12. Harleysville Mut. Ins. Co. v. Reliance Nat'l Ins. Co., 256 F. Supp. 2d 413 (M.D.N.C. 2002).

13. *Pa. Nat'l Mut. Cas. Ins. Co.*, 579 S.E.2d at 404 (N.C. Ct. App. 2003).

14. *Id.*

15. *Id.*

North Dakota

Matthew Lawlyes
Wilson Law Group

1. GENERAL RULES OF CONTRACTUAL INDEMNITY

Indemnity agreements are construed using the ordinary rules of contract interpretation.[1] The parties' intent is gleaned from the entirety of the contract rather than from isolated provisions in it.[2] If their intent as to the scope of indemnification is not expressed, North Dakota courts apply statutory rules of interpretation for contracts of indemnity.[3] For instance, the indemnitee may recover only upon becoming liable.[4] Also, the indemnitor, upon request, must defend actions or proceedings brought against the indemnitee for matters within the scope of the indemnification.[5] These statutory rules, however, do not take priority over the parties' expressed intent.[6]

Parties may contractually indemnify others in any desired fashion that does not contravene public policy.[7] Permissible indemnification includes indemnification for the indemnitee's sole negligence, so long as the parties' intent to so indemnify is "very clearly" expressed by the language of the agreement.[8] To the courts, a clear intention exists where the agreement provides for the purchase of insurance and additional insured status for the indemnitee.[9] So long as insurance is required in a specified amount and the indemnitee is named as an additional insured in the policy, other wording creating indemnification for the indemnitee's sole negligence is unnecessary.[10] This is because "there could be no purpose for the insurance provision other than to protect [the indemnitee] from the consequences of its own negligent acts."[11]

An indemnification provision that protects the indemnitee from stated categories of damage by "any person or persons" pertains only to claims of third parties; it does not indemnify as to claims between the contracting entities.[12]

Applied principles of indemnity law permit contracting parties to circumvent the exclusive remedy provision of the worker's compensation law.[13] North Dakota law permits parties to contract around the Workforce Safety and Insurance Law (worker's compensation),

1. *See* Vanderhoof v. Gravel Prods., Inc., 404 N.W.2d 485, 491 (N.D. 1987).

2. *See id. See also* Spagnolia v. Monasky, 660 N.W. 2d 223, 228 (N.D. 2003); N.D. CENT. CODE § 9-07-06 (2006).

3. N.D. CENT. CODE § 22-02-07.

4. N.D. CENT. CODE § 22-02-07(1). *See also* Specialized Contracting, Inc. v. St. Paul Fire & Marine Ins. Co., 825 N.W.2d 872 (N.D. 2012).

5. N.D. CENT. CODE § 22-02-07(4).

6. *Specialized Contracting, Inc.*, 825 N.W.2d at 881–82 (holding that contractual language indemnifying against "liability" and not "any and all claims" does not impart a duty to defend upon the indemnitor and it is not appropriate to apply § 22-02-07(4) simply because the contract failed to state that the indemnitor had no duty to defend if the intent of the parties can be determined).

7. *See Vanderhoof*, 404 N.W.2d at 491. *See also* N.D. CENT. CODE § 9-08-02; Barnsness v. Gen. Diesel & Equip. Co., 422 N.W.2d 819 (N.D. 1988).

8. Rupp v. Am. Crystal Sugar Co., 465 N.W.2d 614, 616 (N.D. 1991) (quoting Bridston v. Dover Corp., 352 N.W.2d 194, 196 (N.D. 1984)).

9. *See Rupp*, 465 N.W.2d at 617.

10. *See id.*

11. *Bridston*, 352 N.W.2d at 197.

12. Olander Contracting Co. v. Gail Wachter Invs., 643 N.W.2d 29, 36 (N.D. 2002), *rev'd on other grounds*, 6663 N.W.2d 204 (N.D. 2003).

13. *See Barnsness*, 422 N.W.2d at 824.

and an employer who agrees to indemnify another can be sued under that indemnity, even though it would be otherwise immune from suit under the worker's compensation law.[14]

2. EXCEPTIONS TO GENERAL RULES OF CONTRACTUAL INDEMNITY

The exceptions to the general rule of freedom of contract appears in North Dakota's indemnity statute, North Dakota Century Code §§ 22-02-01 through 22-02-10. Under the indemnity statute, a party cannot be indemnified for various items as set out in these sections, such as unlawful acts.

In addition, a North Dakota law, Century Code § 9-08-02.1, has limited indemnity agreements in the construction context. That section states:

> Any provision in a construction contract which would make the contractor liable for the errors or omissions of the owner or his agents in the plans and specifications of such contract is against public policy and void.[15]

Although this prohibition is expressly stated in North Dakota's statutes, no appellate court has applied it in striking as unenforceable an indemnity provision.

3. INDEMNITY AGREEMENTS AS INSURED CONTRACTS

North Dakota courts have not determined whether an agreement to indemnify another constitutes an insured contract in the context of the exception to the exclusion for contractually assumed liability in the form general liability policy. However, the North Dakota Supreme Court's interpretation of the exclusion itself—which requires the "assumption of liability" by the insured to be operative—suggests that an agreement to indemnify for another's tort liability is an insured contract.[16]

4. OPERATION OF AN AGREEMENT TO INDEMNIFY REFERRING TO OR REQUIRING INSURANCE

Several reported cases cite to indemnity agreements requiring insurance, and as discussed in Section 1 above, these often involve the extension of "additional insured" status to the indemnitee, whereby the promisor agrees in the indemnification provision to obtain a specified amount of insurance and include the indemnitee as an additional insured under the policy.[17] None of the reported cases expressly decide the scope of coverage afforded the indemnitee-additional insured in light of the underlying indemnity.

---

14. *See id.*

15. *Id.*

16. ACUITY v. Burd & Smith Constr., Inc., 2006 N.D. 187, 2006 N.D. LEXIS 191 (N.D. Aug. 24, 2006); Fisher v. Amer. Family Mut. Ins. Co., 1998 N.D. 109, 579 N.W.2d 599 (N.D. 1998).

17. *See Rupp*, 465 N.W.2d at 616; *Bridston*, 352 N.W.2d at 196.

Ohio

Jodi Spencer Johnson
Brouse McDowell LPA

1. GENERAL RULES OF CONTRACTUAL INDEMNITY

The scope of a contractual agreement to indemnify is determined by the intent of the parties as expressed in the contract.[1] Under Ohio law, "contracts of indemnity purporting to relieve one from the results of his failure to exercise ordinary care shall be strictly construed, and will not be held to provide such indemnification unless so expressed in clear and unequivocal terms."[2]

A contract of indemnity will not be construed to indemnify against the negligence of the indemnitee unless the contract clearly expresses the intention of the parties to indemnify for the indemnitee's own negligence "beyond doubt and by express stipulation."[3] Such agreements cannot be inferred or implied in the contract, and there is a general presumption against indemnifying a party for its own negligent acts.[4]

While an indemnity agreement will typically be strictly construed, a commercial agreement does not necessarily need to expressly mention indemnity to be enforced. "[W]hile clauses limiting the liability of the drafter are ordinarily to be strictly construed, we need not do so when such burden of indemnification was assented to in a context of free and understanding negotiation."[5] Agreements between sophisticated parties are not necessarily narrowly construed (as opposed to contracts of adhesion), and the contract need not include the word "negligence" if it otherwise uses words such as "for any and all harms however caused."[6]

An agreement that covers "any injury, loss or damage to any person or property on the premises for any event, including, but not limited to, fire, flood, mildew, theft, or any other cause" would "clearly and unambiguously encompass[] an act of negligence" on the part of the indemnitee.[7] In contrast, if the language of the agreement only includes some losses (i.e., the bailee's use of the property), then the agreement will not reach the indemnitee's own negligence.[8]

An employer can waive its immunity from actions by third parties for indemnification arising out of the injuries of employees, if there is an express agreement on the part of the employer giving rise to the third party's right of indemnification.[9]

1. Worth v. Aetna Cas. & Sur. Co., 513 N.E.2d 253, 256 (Ohio 1987), *rev'd in part on other grounds*, Worth v. Aetna Cas. & Sur. Co., 540 N.E.2d 249 (Ohio 1989); Cleveland Window Glass Door v. Nat'l Sur. Co., 161 N.E. 280, 281 (Ohio 1928); *see also* Portsmouth Ins. Agency v. Med. Mut. of Ohio, 934 N.E.2d 940, 944 (Ohio 2009).

2. Kay v. Pennsylvania R. Co., 103 N.E.2d 751, 752–53 (Ohio 1952) (quoting George H. Dingledy Lumber Co. v. Erie R. Co., 131 N.E. 723 (1921)).

3. *Id.*

4. *Id.*

5. Glaspell v. Ohio Edison Co., 505 N.E.2d 264 (Ohio 1987).

6. *Id.*

7. Krach v. Kotoch Family Ltd. P'ship, 1996 Ohio App. LEXIS 1219 (Ohio Ct. App., Mar. 29, 1996).

8. Burkette v. Chrysler Indus., Inc., 547 N.E.2d 1223 (Ohio Ct. App. 1988).

9. Williams v. Ashland Chem. Co., 368 N.E.2d 304 (Ohio Ct. App. 1976).

2. EXCEPTIONS TO GENERAL RULES OF CONTRACTUAL INDEMNITY

While agreements to indemnify another are generally enforceable in Ohio, certain types of indemnity agreements are prohibited by public policy.[10] Ohio Revised Code Annotated § 4123.82(A) provides:

> All contracts and agreements are void which undertake to indemnify or insure an employer against loss or liability for the payment of compensation to workers or their dependents for death, injury, or occupational disease occasioned in the course of the worker's employment, or which provide that the insurer shall pay a compensation, or which indemnify the employer against damages when the injury, disease, or death arises from the failure to comply with any lawful requirement for the protection of the lives, health, and safety of the employees, or when the same is occasioned by the willful act of the employer or any of his officers or agents, or by which it is agreed that the insurer shall pay any such damages.

The purpose of § 4123.82(A) is to prevent competition with the state insurance fund, and "to prevent liability insurance companies from underwriting workman's compensation insurance in cases where employers were authorized by the Industrial Commission to pay compensation under Ohio Rev. Code § 4123.25."[11]

Ohio Revised Code Annotated § 2305.31 similarly renders void certain indemnity provisions in construction agreements. The provision governs agreements to indemnify relating to the construction, repair, or maintenance of buildings, and reads in relevant part:

> A covenant, promise, agreement, or understanding in, or connection with or collateral to, a contract or agreement relative to the design, planning, construction, alteration, repair, or maintenance of a building, structure, highway, road, appurtenance, and appliance, including moving, demolition, and excavating connected therewith, pursuant to which contract or agreement the promisee, or its independent contractors, agents, or employees has hired the promisor to perform work, purporting to indemnify the promisee, its independent contractors, agents, employees or indemnities against liability for damages arising out of bodily injury to persons or damaged property initiated or proximately caused by or resulting from the negligence of the promisee, its independent contractors, agents, employees, or indemnities is against public policy and void. Nothing in this section shall prohibit any person from purchasing insurance from an insurance company authorized to do business in the State of Ohio for his own protection or from purchasing a construction bond.[12]

This provision thus bars the use of indemnity agreements in construction-related contracts wherein the indemnitor provides indemnification to the indemnitee for its own acts of negligence regardless of whether such negligence is sole or concurrent.[13] The public policy objective underlying § 2305.31 is to encourage employers to provide employees with safe conditions at the workplace.[14] This statutory prohibition does not preclude the

10. *Glaspell*, 29 Ohio St. 3d at 44; Ohio Rev. Code § 2305.31.

11 Ohio Rev. Code Ann. § 4123.25; LoGuidice v. Harris, 128 N.E.2d 842, 845–46 (Ohio Ct. App. 1954) (agreement between attorney and client/claimant under the Workers' Compensation Act that purported to indemnify an employer against loss pursuant to a consent judgment finding the client eligible to participate in the insurance fund, held to be void in accordance with § 4123.82).

12. Ohio Rev. Code Ann. § 2305.31.

13. Buckeye Union Ins. Co. v. Zavarella Bros. Constr. Co., 699 N.E.2d 127, 129 (Ohio Ct. App. 1997); Kendall v. U.S. Dismantling Co., 485 N.E.2d 1047 (Ohio 1985).

14. Lamb v. Armco, Inc., 518 N.E.2d 53, 55–56 (Ohio Ct. App. 1986).

purchase of a commercial liability insurance policy for public works construction projects, as these policies are not considered indemnity agreements within the scope of § 2305.31.[15]

3. INDEMNITY AGREEMENTS AS INSURED CONTRACTS

It has been expressly recognized that an agreement to indemnify another for the other's tort liability meets the definition in a liability insurance policy excepting from the exclusion for contractually assumed liability of an "insured contract."[16] The "other" for which the insured assumes liability does not need to be a party to a contract with the insured.[17]

4. OPERATION OF AN AGREEMENT TO INDEMNIFY REFERRING TO OR REQUIRING INSURANCE

While Ohio Revised Code Annotated § 2305.31 prohibits indemnity agreements indemnifying an indemnitee for its own negligence, a contract may require one party to obtain insurance coverage for the other party as an additional insured.[18] The Ohio Court of Appeals has rendered conflicting decisions with regard to whether or not the additional insured agreement will extend coverage to the indemnitee for its own negligent acts.

For example, in *Buckeye Union Insurance Co. v. Zavarella Brothers Construction Co.*, a subcontractor agreed to name the contractor as an additional insured under a commercial liability insurance policy.[19] After one of the subcontractor's employees was injured, the contractor's insurer defended the worker's compensation claim, and settled with the employee. The contractor subsequently sought indemnification from the subcontractor's insurer. The main issue before the court was "whether an agreement by a construction subcontractor to name its general contractor as an additional insured on the subcontractor's general commercial insurance policy constitutes an indemnity agreement prohibited by Ohio Rev. Code Ann. § 2305.31."[20] The court held that the additional insured agreement was inapplicable because Ohio Revised Code Annotated § 2305.31 prohibited coverage for the contractor's own negligent acts. The court found that the "additional insured agreement as a whole did not violate public policy, but that the express language of the policy did not afford coverage under the circumstances."[21]

In a contrasting decision, the Ohio Court of Appeals in *Stickovich v. City of Cleveland* found that compulsory public liability insurance did not contravene the public policy objectives of Ohio Revised Code Annotated § 2305.31. In that case, a contractor responsible for constructing a bridge for the city of Cleveland named the municipality as an additional insured on its liability insurance contract.[22] During construction, a crane, operated at the direction of the contractor by an unlicensed operator who had been drinking alcohol, touched an electric power line injuring two employees of an independent subcontractor.[23]

The insurer, Commercial Union, argued that its liability insurance coverage was void and against public policy, and that the trial court erred in finding "that the additional insured clause in the contractor's general commercial liability insurance policy provided

15. Stickovich v. City of Cleveland, 757 N.E.2d 50, 61 (Ohio Ct. App. 2001); *but see* Cleveland v. Vandra Bros. Constr., 948 N.E.2d 1027, 1030.

16. Legge Assocs. v. Dayton Power & Light Co., 1997 U.S. App. LEXIS 8702 (6th Cir., Apr. 22, 1997) (applying Ohio law).

17. *Id.*

18. *Buckeye Union*, 699 N.E.2d at 134.

19. *Id.* at 128.

20. *Id.*

21. *Id.*

22. *Stickovich*, 757 N.E.2d at 58; Brzeczek v. Standard Oil Co., 447 N.E.2d 760, 763 (Ohio Ct. App. 1982) (finding that § 2305.31 did not prohibit a contractor from purchasing insurance for the employer's protection against its own negligence).

23. *Stickovich*, 757 N.E.2d at 53.

coverage for the additional insured's own negligence."[24] Commercial Union contended that providing coverage for the additional insured's own negligence contravened public policy and violated Ohio Revised Code Annotated § 2305.31.[25]

The Ohio Court of Appeals disagreed, finding that "[s]ection 2305.31 does not invalidate commercial liability insurance coverage for construction projects,"[26] and that "a commercial liability insurance policy is not a construction indemnity agreement within the scope of Section 2305.31."[27] The court distinguished between indemnity agreements and liability insurance contracts, finding:

> [As] a matter of common understanding, usage, and legal definition, an insurance contract denotes a policy issued by an authorized and licensed insurance company whose primary business it is to assume specific risk of loss of the members of the public at large in consideration of the payment of a premium. There are, however, other risk-shifting agreements which are not insurance contracts. These include the customary private indemnity agreement where affording the indemnity is not the primary business of the indemnitor and is not the subject of governmental regulation but is merely ancillary to a furtherance of some other independent transactional relationship between the indemnitor and the indemnitee. The indemnitee is, thus, not the essence of the agreement creating the transactional relationship but is only one of its negotiated terms.[28]

Because the risk in a liability insurance contract is shifted to the commercial liability insurer rather than the contractor/promisor, the court held that these types of agreements are distinguishable from indemnity agreements and are not prohibited by § 2305.31.[29]

24. *Id.* at 59.
25. *Id.*
26. *Id.* at 60.
27. *Id.* at 61.
28. *Stickovich*, 757 N.E.2d at 61 (citing Britton v. Smythe Cramer Co., 743 N.E.2d 960, 972–73 (Ohio Ct. App. 2000)).
29. *Id.*

Oklahoma

Gregory E. Van Houten
Haynes and Boone, LLP

1. GENERAL RULES OF CONTRACTUAL INDEMNITY

An indemnity contract is interpreted under Oklahoma law according to the general rules of contract interpretation.[1] The parties' intent must be ascertained based upon the whole contract, and that intent will be given effect if it can be done within the bounds of the law.[2] An Oklahoma statutory scheme—codified as Oklahoma Statute tit. 15, § 427—enumerates specific rules of interpretation that apply to all indemnity agreements absent express intent providing otherwise.[3]

"Agreements to indemnify a party against its own negligence or liability are strictly construed."[4] For such an indemnity agreement to be enforceable, the agreement must satisfy three conditions: "(1) the parties must express their intent to exculpate in unequivocally clear language; (2) the agreement must result from an arm's-length transaction between parties of equal bargaining power; and (3) the exculpation must not violate public policy."[5] However, as discussed below in section 2, such agreements in the construction context are barred by statute.

---

1. Wallace v. Sherwood Constr. Co., Inc., 877 P.2d 632, 634 (Okla. Civ. App. 1994) (citing Luke v. American Surety Co. of N.Y., 114 P.2d 950 (Okla. 1941)); *see also* Okla. Stat. tit. 15, § 427 (2005).

2. *Wallace*, 877 P.2d at 634; *see also* Okla. Stat. tit. 15, § 152 (2005) ("A contract must be so interpreted as to give effect to the mutual intention of the parties, as it existed at the time of contracting, so far as the same is ascertainable and lawful."); *Id.* § 157 (2005) ("The whole of a contract is to be taken together, so as to give effect to every part . . . .").

3. The statute provides:

> In the interpretation of a contract of indemnity, the following rules are to be applied, unless a contrary intention appears:
>
> 1. Upon an indemnity against liability, expressly, or in other equivalent terms, the person indemnified is entitled to recover upon becoming liable.
> 2. Upon an indemnity against claims or demands, or damages or costs, expressly, or in other equivalent terms, the person indemnified is not entitled to recover without payment thereof.
> 3. An indemnity against claims or demands, or liability, expressly or in other equivalent terms, embraces the costs of defense against such claims, demands or liability incurred in good faith, and in the exercise of reasonable discretion.
> 4. The person indemnifying is bound, on request of the person indemnified, to defend actions or proceedings brought against the latter in respect to the matters embraced by the indemnity; but the person indemnified has the right to conduct such defense, if he chooses to do so.
> 5. If, after request, the person indemnifying neglects to defend the person indemnified, a recovery against the latter, suffered by him in good faith, is conclusive in his favor against the former.
> 6. If the person indemnifying, whether he is a principal or a surety in the agreement, has not reasonable notice of the action of proceedings against the person indemnified, or is not allowed to control its defense, judgment against the latter is only presumptive evidence against the former.
> 7. A stipulation that a judgment against the person indemnified shall be conclusive upon the person indemnifying is applicable if he had a good defense upon the merits, which, by want of ordinary care, he failed to establish in the action.
>
> Okla. Stat. tit. 15, § 427 (2005).

4. Noble Steel, Inc. v. Williams Bros. Concrete Constr. Co., 49 P.3d 766, 770 (Okla. Civ. App. 2002) (citing Transp. Constructors v. Grand River Dam Auth., 905 F.2d 1413, 1420 (10th Cir. 1990)).

5. *Id.*

2. EXCEPTIONS TO GENERAL RULES OF CONTRACTUAL INDEMNITY

Oklahoma law expressly prohibits indemnification for known unlawful acts.[6]

In addition, construction agreements cannot require a party to indemnify another for the other's own negligence. Indeed, tit. 15, § 221 provides:

> [A]ny provision in a construction agreement that requires an entity or that entity's surety or insurer to indemnify, insure, defend or hold harmless another entity against liability for damage arising out of death or bodily injury to persons, or damage to property, which arises out of the negligence or fault of the indemnitee, its agents, representatives, subcontractors, or suppliers, is void and unenforceable as against public policy.[7]

The first case to discuss this statute was *Tyson Foods, Inc. v. Routh Enterprises, Inc.*[8] In that case, Tyson Foods alleged that under its contract for services with a contractor, that contractor was required to procure insurance and indemnify Tyson Foods.[9] But the contractor's insurer, Emcasco Insurance Company (EMC), argued that Tyson Foods' claims against EMC were barred by the provision discussed above.[10] The U.S. District Court for the Eastern District of Oklahoma recognized that "[m]ost anti-indemnification statutes allow the reallocation of risk to an indemnitor's insurer, so that while an indemnification agreement may be voided by statute, a separate promise to procure insurance designed to shift the same risk is enforceable and unaffected by statutory bars."[11] The court held that the Oklahoma statute, however, does not draw such a distinction.[12] Instead, to the court, the Oklahoma statute provides that "a construction agreement that requires an entity or that entity's insurer to indemnify, *insure, defend* or hold harmless another entity against liability . . . which arises out of the negligence or fault of the indemnitee . . . is void and unenforceable

---

6. OKLA. STAT. tit. 15, § 422 (2005) ("An agreement to indemnify a person against an act thereafter to be done is void if the act be known by such person at the time of doing it to be unlawful."); *see also* Webb v. W. Carter Cty. Water & Sewage Corp., 575 P.2d 124, 126 (Okla. Civ. App. 1977) (citing OKLA. STAT. tit. 15, § 422).

7. OKLA. STAT. tit. 15 § 221(B) (2006). A "[c]onstruction agreement" is a contract or subcontract for construction, alteration, renovation, repair, or maintenance of any building, building site, structure, highway, street, highway bridge, viaduct, water or sewer system, or other works dealing with construction, or for any moving, demolition, excavation, materials, or labor connected with such construction. *Id.* § 221(A).

Section 221(B), which is quoted above in the accompanying text, is subject to two important exceptions. First, it does not apply to "any provision in a construction agreement that requires an entity or that entity's surety or insurer to indemnify another entity against liability for damage arising out of death or bodily injury to persons, or damage to property, but such indemnification shall not exceed any amounts that are greater than that represented by the degree or percentage of negligence or fault attributable to the indemnitor, its agents, representatives, subcontractors, or suppliers." *Id.* § 221(C); *see also* BITCO Gen. Ins. Corp. v. Commerce & Indus. Ins. Co., No. CIV-15-206-M, 2017 WL 835197, at *3 (W.D. Okla. Mar. 2, 2017) (determining that § 221(C) "is specifically limited to indemnity and does not include the duty to defend"). And second, it does not apply to "construction bonds nor to contract clauses which require an entity to purchase a project-specific insurance policy, including owners' and contractors' protective liability insurance, project management protective liability insurance, or builder's risk insurance." *Id.* § 221(D); *see also* BITCO Gen. Ins. Corp. v. Wynn Constr. Co., No. CIV-17-462-M, 2017 WL 3470584, at *2 (W.D. Okla. Aug. 11, 2017) (finding that § 221(D) exception did not apply because "the insurance policies at issue [were] not project-specific insurance policies").

8. Tyson Foods, Inc. v. Routh Enterprises, Inc., 2015 WL 457945 (E.D. Okla. Feb. 3, 2015); *see also* JP Energy Mktg., LLC v. Commerce & Indus. Ins. Co., 412 P.3d 121, 129 (Okla. Civ. App. 2017) (noting that "this is the first appellate court to examine the statute").

9. *Id.* at *2.

10. *Id.*

11. *Id.* (citing 3 BRUNER & O'CONNOR ON CONSTRUCTION LAW, § 10:91 (2014)).

12. *Id.*

as against public policy."[13] Accordingly, the Oklahoma anti-indemnification statute barred Tyson Foods' claims against EMC.[14]

3. INDEMNITY AGREEMENTS AS INSURED CONTRACTS

Despite the general contractual exclusion for "liability assumed under any contract or agreement," Oklahoma recognizes coverage for "insured contracts."[15] In *Federal Insurance Co. v. Tri-State Insurance Co.*,[16] a district court found that the agreement to indemnify contained in the parties' agreement was an "insured contract," and that coverage therefore existed based upon an exception to the exclusion for contractually assumed liability. The Tenth Circuit, however, found absent coverage based upon a separate, unrelated exclusion.[17]

4. OPERATION OF AN AGREEMENT TO INDEMNIFY REFERRING TO OR REQUIRING INSURANCE

The recent *Tyson Foods* case found that based on the plain language of Oklahoma's anti-indemnification statute, agreements to procure insurance in the construction context are prohibited by the statute.[18]

Oklahoma courts have not addressed the interface between an agreement to procure insurance and an indemnity agreement outside of the construction context. In *Federated Rural Electric Insurance Co. v. Williams*,[19] the Oklahoma Court of Appeals enforced an indemnity agreement and an agreement to procure insurance; however, the court did not address any limitations or expansions of the general rules of indemnity based upon the agreement to purchase insurance.[20]

---

13. *Id.* (emphasis in original).

14. *Id.* The court also held that the exception in subsection C (*see supra* note 7) did not apply because the words "insure" and "defend," which appear in subsection B (*see supra* note 7), are not repeated in subsection C. *Id.*

15. *See* Fed. Ins. Co. v. Tri-State Ins. Co., 157 F.3d 800, 805 (10th Cir. 1998).

16. *Id.*

17. *Id.*

18. *Tyson Foods*, 2015 WL 457945, at *2.

19. Federated Rural Elec. Ins. Co. v. Williams, 2002 Okla. Civ. App. LEXIS 65, at *15 (Okla. Civ. App. Apr. 26, 2002).

20. *Id.*

Oregon

Kathryn Kasper
Hancock, Daniel & Johnson, P.C.

1. GENERAL RULES OF CONTRACTUAL INDEMNITY

Contractual agreements for indemnification, including agreements covering an indemnitee's own negligence, are generally enforceable in Oregon, as long as the intent of the parties is clear and explicit.[1] Normal rules of contract interpretation apply to the review of indemnity agreements:[2] Like other contracts, they are interpreted to give weight to the plain meaning of the language employed.[3] If the language is ambiguous, "it must be interpreted in light of the surrounding circumstances and the situation of the parties so as to effectuate the parties' intent."[4] Ambiguities are generally construed against the drafter.[5]

As a general rule, indemnity agreements purporting to reach an indemnitee's own negligence are not favored.[6] However, courts have enforced agreements where a party is immunized "from the consequences of his or her own negligence" under certain circumstances.[7] "If contractual language clearly and explicitly provides that a party will be indemnified for a particular loss, even if caused by that party's negligence, the inquiry ends, and the provision is enforced."[8] Conversely, if the terms of the agreement are ambiguous and the parties' intent is unknown, courts look beyond the language of the agreement to determine whether to enforce it.[9]

The first Oregon decision to address an agreement to indemnify an indemnitee for its own negligence was *Southern Pacific Company v. Layman*.[10] In *Layman*, the Oregon Supreme Court held that an indemnity agreement between a railroad and a farmer who built a private road over the railroad's right of way was unenforceable due to the "harshness" of the agreement.[11] The agreement required the farmer to indemnify the railroad "against any and all loss, damage, injury, cost and expense of every kind and nature, from any cause whatsoever."[12] Approximately twenty years after the agreement was executed, a harvesting machine owned by a third party "was struck and practically demolished" by one of the railroad's trains.[13] It was undisputed that the railroad's negligence caused the accident.[14] The railroad was sued by the third party and tendered its defense to the farmer, who declined. The railroad sued the farmer, claiming a right to indemnification. But the court refused to enforce the agreement in this context because "[i]t could result in subjecting a farmer to a ruinous liability arising out of the negligence of the plaintiff in the operation of its trains, an

1. *See generally* S. Pac. Co. v. Morrison-Knudsen Co., 338 P.2d 665 (Or. 1959); S. Pac. Co. v. Layman, 145 P.2d 295 (Or. 1943).
2. Cook v. S. Pac. Transp. Co., 623 P.2d 1125, 1128 (Or. Ct. App. 1981).
3. *Id.*
4. *Id.*
5. *Id.*
6. *See* Estey v. Mackenzie Eng'g Inc., 927 P.2d 86 (Or. 1996).
7. *Id.* at 88.
8. Blanchfill v. Better Builds, Inc., 982 P.2d 53, 57 (Or. Ct. App. 1999); *see also Morrison-Knudsen Co.*, 338 P.2d at 665; *Layman*, 145 P.2d at 295.
9. *Blanchfill*, 982 P.2d at 57.
10. *See Layman*, 145 P.2d at 295.
11. *Id.*
12. *Id.* at 296.
13. *Id.*
14. *Id.*

operation over which it had no control."[15] The court did not believe "that for the mere privilege of passing over the plaintiff's tracks the defendant intended to assume such a risk, or that the railway intended to impose it."[16] Even though the language of the agreement was "broad and general enough to include loss caused solely by the plaintiff's negligence," to the court, the harsh reality of allocating all risk to the farmer made indemnification under the circumstances unintended.[17]

Layman (and its progeny) laid the groundwork for Oregon's "rule against harshness."[18] The courts use this rule when the parties' intent is unclear to determine how risk is allocated and whether enforcing the agreement circumvents the parties' original intent.[19] In general, under the rule, courts focus "not only the language of the contract, but also on the possibility of a harsh and inequitable result that would fall on one party by immunizing the other party from the consequences for his or her own negligence."[20]

2. EXCEPTIONS TO GENERAL RULES OF CONTRACTUAL INDEMNITY

By statute, Oregon bars agreements to indemnify another for its own negligence in the construction context.[21] The applicable statute provides:

> [A]ny provision in a construction agreement that requires a person or that person's surety or insurer to indemnify another against liability for damage arising out of death or bodily injury to persons or damage to property caused in whole or in part by the negligence of the indemnitee is void.[22]

However, the statute does not prohibit agreements to indemnify another for the indemnitor's own negligence:[23]

> This section does not affect any provision in a construction agreement that requires a person or that person's surety or insurer to indemnify another against liability for damage arising out of death or bodily injury to persons or damage to property to the extent that the death or bodily injury to persons or damage to property arises out of the fault of the indemnitor, or the fault of the indemnitor's agents, representatives or subcontractors.

The plain meaning of the statute is therefore clear: In the construction context, an indemnitor can indemnify an indemnitee for the indemnitor's negligence but not for the indemnitee's.[24] If an indemnity clause requires the indemnitor to indemnify the indemnitee both for claims based on its own fault and for claims based on the indemnitee's fault, the

---

15. *Id.*

16. *Id.*

17. *Id.* at 297.

18. *See Cook*, 623 P.2d at 1130; *see also Morrison-Knudsen Co.*, 338 P.2d at 673 (enforcing an indemnity clause similar to the clause at issue in *Layman* after finding that the privilege conferred on the parties fell "far short of being a 'mere privilege' with a 'comparatively small risk'").

19. *Cook*, 623 P.2d at 1130.

20. *Estey*, 927 P.2d at 88; *see also* Steele v. Mt. Hood Meadows Or., Ltd., 974 P.2d 794 (Or. Ct. App. 1999) (relying on *Layman*, the court refused to enforce an indemnification agreement printed on a skier's lift ticket requiring the skier to indemnify the ski resort for all personal injury claims because the agreement was unclear as to whether the parties intended the agreement to apply to the ski resort's negligence, nor was it likely that the skier would give a claim arising from such negligence).

21. *See* Or. Rev. Stat. § 30.140.

22. *Id.* at § 30.140(1).

23. *Id.* at § 30.140(2).

24. *Id.*; *see also* Hays v. Centennial Floors, Inc., 893 P.2d 564 (Or. Ct. App. 1995).

clause is enforceable with respect to indemnification for the indemnitor's own negligence only.[25]

Indemnity agreements subjecting an employer to liability beyond that prescribed under the worker's compensation statute are also void.[26] The applicable statute provides:

> (1)(a) The liability of every employer who satisfies the duty required by ORS 656.017 (1) is exclusive and in place of all other liability arising out of injuries, diseases, symptom complexes or similar conditions arising out of and in the course of employment that are sustained by subject workers, the workers' beneficiaries and anyone otherwise entitled to recover damages from the employer on account of such conditions or claims resulting therefrom, specifically including claims for contribution or indemnity asserted by third persons from whom damages are sought on account of such conditions, except as specifically provided otherwise in this chapter.
>
> (b) This subsection shall not apply to claims for indemnity or contribution asserted by a railroad, as defined in ORS 824.020, or by a corporation, individual or association of individuals which is subject to regulation pursuant to ORS chapter 757 or 759.
>
> (c) Except as provided in paragraph (b) of this subsection, all agreements or warranties contrary to the provisions of paragraph (a) of this subsection entered into after July 19, 1977, are void.[27]

Put differently, the worker's compensation statute provides the exclusive liability by an employee against an employer, thereby rendering void indemnification agreements creating liability of an employer proscribed under the statute.[28]

Indemnity agreements executed by parents of a minor with a personal injury claim are also invalid.[29] In *Ohio Casualty Insurance Co. v. Mallison*, parents of an unborn child were involved in an automobile accident with the insured.[30] After the minor's birth and before discovering the minor's injuries, the parents settled with the insured and executed a release.[31] The release contained an indemnity provision requiring the parents to hold the insured and its insurer harmless for any injuries suffered by the minor.[32] After discovering the minor's injuries, the parents sued the insured on the minor's behalf,[33] resulting in monetary judgment for the minor, which the insurance company paid.[34] The insurer subsequently attempted to enforce the release's indemnity provision against the parents to recover the amount of the judgment.[35] The Oregon Supreme Court, in finding that a parent's "interest in personal gain at the settlement table may well influence him to sacrifice the best interests of the child," invalidated the agreement as contrary to public policy.[36]

---

25. Montara Owners Ass'n v. La Noue Dev., LLC, 317 P.3d 257, 272 (Or. Ct. App. 2013), *aff'd*, 353 P.3d 563 (Or. 2015).
26. *See* Or. Rev. Stat. § 656.018 (2006).
27. *Id.*
28. *Id.*; *see also* Roberts v. Gray's Crane & Rigging, Inc., 697 P.2d 985 (Or. Ct. App. 1985) (indemnity agreement was void as lessee's duty to provide worker's compensation coverage was its exclusive liability to its workers).
29. *See generally* Ohio Cas. Ins. Co. v. Mallison, 354 P.2d 800 (Or. 1960).
30. *Id.* at 801.
31. *Id.*
32. *Id.*
33. *Id.*
34. *Id.*
35. *Id.*
36. *Id.* at 806.

3. INDEMNITY AGREEMENTS AS INSURED CONTRACTS

Oregon courts have not specifically addressed whether an agreement to indemnify is an "insured contract" within the meaning of the general liability policy.[37]

4. OPERATION OF AN AGREEMENT TO INDEMNIFY REFERRING TO OR REQUIRING INSURANCE

If an indemnity agreement explicitly states that the indemnitor will not indemnify the indemnitee for the indemnitee's own negligence and if (per the parties' agreement between the parties) the indemnitee is listed as an additional insured on the indemnitor's insurance policy, it will not preclude the indemnitee from obtaining the benefit of the indemnitor's insurance policy.[38] Based on the language of the insurance policy, an "additional insured" may be entitled to the same coverage as a named insured, including coverage for its own negligence, if the insurance policy fails to describe different coverage for additional insureds.[39] Such coverage exists even though the indemnity agreement explicitly states that the named insured will not indemnify the additional insured for the additional insured's negligence.[40]

Additionally, in the worker's compensation context, an agreement to procure liability insurance is not the same as an agreement to indemnify.[41] Thus, a breach of contract claim against an employer for its failure to procure liability insurance would not be precluded by the exclusivity provision of the Workers' Compensation Act, Oregon Revised Statutes § 656.018, although a claim to enforce an indemnity agreement against the employer would be.[42]

In *Montgomery Elevator Co. v. Tuality Community Hospital*, the Oregon Court of Appeals held that a breach of contract claim brought against a hospital for its failure to procure insurance was not precluded under Oregon's Workers' Compensation Act because (1) the statute only applied to compensable damages, and (2) an agreement to procure insurance is not an indemnity agreement.[43] The hospital had contracted with the plaintiff to provide elevator repairs and maintenance.[44] Per the maintenance agreement, the hospital agreed to procure comprehensive liability insurance "protecting plaintiff from personal injury and property damage claims from all persons, including defendant's employees"[45]—insurance which the hospital failed to obtain.[46] A hospital employee was subsequently injured while

---

37. However, in Holman Erection Co., Inc. v. Nw. Steel Constr. Co., 920 P.2d 1125 (Or. Ct. App. 1996), an "insured contract" in an indemnity agreement context is briefly discussed. In *Holman*, a subcontractor entered into an indemnity agreement with a contractor and an agreement to procure insurance on the contractor's behalf. The subcontractor's employee was injured and sued the contractor, who tendered the defense to the subcontractor and its insurer. The tender was denied, and the contractor sued the subcontractor for indemnification and breach of contract. The court found that the insurer of the subcontractor had no duty to defend the lawsuit on the basis that: (1) the subcontractor, under the terms of the insurance policy, could not be held liable for the employee's injuries, despite the indemnity agreement, pursuant to the exclusivity rule of the Workers' Compensation Act, Oregon Revised Statutes § 656.018; and (2) breach of contract claims are not covered under the general liability policy. Although the general liability policy contained an "insured contract" provision, the court implied that it did not apply because it only pertained to injuries suffered by third parties (and not the employees of the indemnitor). As such, the court made no reference as to the general application of "insured contracts" in Oregon jurisprudence. Similarly, in Am. Int'l Spec. Lines Ins. Co. v. Kindercare Learning Ctr., Inc., 2011 U.S. Dist. LEXIS 28212 (D. Or. Mar. 18, 2011), the court found that the indemnity provision at issue was unenforceable and therefore could not be considered an insured contract. It also did not address any Oregon case law on the topic.

38. *See* Hartford Accident and Indem. Co. v. U.S. Natural Resources, Inc., 897 F. Supp. 466, 471 (D. Or. 1995).

39. *Id.*

40. *See generally id.*

41. *See* Montgomery Elevator Co. v. Tuality Cmty. Hosp., Inc., 790 P.2d 1148 (Or. Ct. App. 1990).

42. *Id.*

43. *Id.* at 1149–50.

44. *Id.* at 1148.

45. *Id.*

46. *Id.*

using the hospital's elevator.[47] After settling with the injured employee, the plaintiff sued the hospital for breach of contract as a result of its failure to procure insurance that would have covered the claim.[48] In response, the hospital denied responsibility, asserting that "agreements to purchase insurance are identical to indemnity agreements," and therefore precluded under the Workers' Compensation Act, Oregon Revised Statutes § 656.018.[49] The court of appeals disagreed.[50]

First, the exclusivity rule of Oregon Revised Statutes § 656.018 only applied to compensable injuries and not breach of contract claims.[51] The agreement to procure insurance "was intended to protect the non-employer from liability for tort claims rather than to relieve the employer from its responsibility to provide worker's compensation coverage."[52] As such, the breach of contract claim did not come within the statutory proscription of Oregon Revised Statutes § 656.018 because it did not arise out of compensable injuries.[53] The court therefore held that the agreement to procure insurance was not precluded under § 656.018, even though the indemnity provision contained in the maintenance agreement pursuant to which the company was to be indemnified by the hospital from all losses and liabilities was void under the same statute.[54]

Second, agreements to procure insurance and agreements to indemnify are significantly different.[55] "Under an indemnity contract, payment by the insured is a prerequisite to the insurer's duty of reimbursement; under an insurance contract, the insurer's obligation attaches as soon as liability is established, and payment by the insured is immaterial."[56] Had the hospital purchased insurance, its obligation to the plaintiff would have been met, and "the insurer would have been responsible for any claim that occurred."[57] Conversely, under an indemnification agreement, the hospital, not its insurer, would have to assume all responsibility for the plaintiff and its injuries.[58] As such, the hospital was deemed to have breached its contract to procure insurance for the plaintiff and was therefore ordered to reimburse the plaintiff for its loss.[59]

In the construction context, an agreement requiring a party to procure liability insurance coverage naming the other as an additional insured is void under Oregon Revised Statutes § 30.140.[60] In *Walsh Construction Co. v. Mutual of Enumclaw*, the court of appeals interpreted § 30.140 to prohibit "not only 'direct' indemnity arrangements between parties to construction agreements but also 'additional insurance' arrangements by which one party is obligated to procure insurance for losses arising in whole or in part from the other's fault."[61] In that case, a general contractor entered into a construction agreement with a subcontractor, requiring the subcontractor to procure liability insurance naming the general contractor as an additional insured.[62] The subcontractor obtained the required insurance.[63] The subcontractor's employee was subsequently injured and sued the general contractor.[64] The general contractor tendered the defense to the subcontractor's insurer, which denied

47. *Id.*
48. *Id.*
49. *Id.* at 1148–49.
50. *Id.* at 1149.
51. *Id.* at 1149–50.
52. *Id.* at 1149.
53. *Id.*
54. *Id.* at 1148 n.1.
55. *Id.*
56. *Id.* at 1150.
57. *Id.*
58. *Id.*
59. *Id.*
60. Walsh Constr. Co. v. Mut. of Enumclaw, 76 P.3d 164 (Or. Ct. App. 2003), *aff'd*, 104 P.3d 1146 (Or. 2005).
61. *Id.* at 168.
62. *Id.* at 165.
63. *Id.*
64. *Id.*

the claim, asserting that the agreement to procure insurance naming the general contractor as an additional insured violated § 30.140 (which places a statutory bar on agreements to indemnify another for its own negligence in the construction context).[65] After settling with the employee, the general contractor initiated a breach of contract claim against the insurer "premised under its status as an 'additional insured'" under the subcontractor's policy.[66] The general contractor relied on the court's holding in *Tuality* that an agreement to procure insurance is different than an agreement to indemnify.[67] The court, in distinguishing its holding in *Tuality*, held that § 30.140 was designed to prevent a party with leverage in the construction context from shifting exposure for its own malfeasance to one of a lesser financial position, such as a subcontractor.[68] Thus, requirements to procure insurance in the construction context are void as the courts view such mandates as another form of shifting risk, an action strictly precluded under § 30.140.[69]

65. *Id.*
66. *Id.*
67. *Id.* at 166.
68. *Id.* at 168–69.
69. *Id.*

Pennsylvania

Joann Lytle and Sherilyn Pastor
McCarter & English, LLP

1. GENERAL RULES OF CONTRACTUAL INDEMNITY

Agreements of indemnity for loss or damage are enforceable in Pennsylvania[1] but are not favored and are consequently construed strictly against those seeking their protection.[2] Although the extent of liability under an indemnity agreement is determined by the parties' intent, given application of the rule of strict construction, indemnification provisions are an exception to the general rule of contract interpretation in which words and phrases are given their plain and ordinary meaning.[3] Accordingly, because an agreement to indemnify for another's negligence is so unusual and extraordinary, there is no presumption that the indemnitor intended to assume such a responsibility unless it is expressed in unequivocal terms,[4] commonly referred to as the "Perry-Ruzzi Rule."[5] A generally worded indemnification clause will not be construed to indemnify the indemnitee for liability resulting from the indemnitee's own negligence[6] "unless an agreement to do so is expressed in unequivocal terms."[7] "No inference from words of general import can establish such indemnification."[8] An unambiguous agreement to indemnify another for the indemnitee's own negligence is enforceable, however, and does not run afoul of public policy.[9]

Consequently, a construction agreement providing indemnity to the owner for "all loss, cost or expense . . . arising from accidents" to laborers did not create indemnity for the owner's own negligence.[10] However, where a seller agreed to indemnify a buyer "from any and all claims . . . whether the same results from negligence of Buyer or Buyer's employees or otherwise," the intent to indemnify for the buyer's own negligence was found to exist.[11]

In considering contractual indemnity provisions, the Pennsylvania courts have applied concepts applicable to common law indemnity, in one case interpreting an indemnity agreement to extend to the indemnitee's passive negligence, as distinguished from its active

1. Schroeder v. Gulf Refining Co., 300 Pa. 405, 411, 150 A. 665 (1930).

2. Coatman v. Lower Allen Leisure Enter., 42 Pa. D. & C.3d 19, 24–25 (1985).

3. *See* Deskiewicz v. Zenith Radio Corp., 561 A.2d 33, 35 (Pa. Super. Ct. 1989); Fulmer v. Duquesne Light Co., 543 A.2d 1100, 1104 (Pa. Super. Ct. 1988).

4. Perry v. Payne, 66 A. 553, 557 (Pa. 1907); Greer v. City of Philadelphia, 795 A.2d 376, 378–79 (Pa. 2002); *see also* Ocean Spray Cranberries, Inc. v. Refrigerated Distributors, Inc., 2006 Phila. Ct. Com. Pl. LEXIS 229, at *13 (Pa. Ct. Com. Pl. 2006) (analyzing application of Perry-Ruzzi rule in indemnification actions involving personal injury versus property damage, upholding long-standing rule that provisions to indemnify for another party's negligence are to be narrowly construed requiring a clear and unequivocal agreement before a party may transfer its liability to another party), *rev'd on other grounds*, 936 A.2d 81 (Pa. Super. Ct. 2007); Burlington Coat Factory of Pennsylvania, LLC v. Grace Const. Mgmt. Co., LLC, 2015 PA Super 227 (Oct. 29, 2015) ("Since Appellants drafted a contract with two conflicting indemnity provisions, we will enforce only the narrower of the two and exclude indemnity for the indemnitee's own negligence.").

5. *Ocean Spray Cranberries, Inc.*, 2006 Phila. Ct. Com. Pl. LEXIS 229, at *20.

6. *Deskiewicz*, 561 A.2d at 35.

7. Hershey Foods Corp. v. General Elec. Serv. Co., 619 A.2d 285, 288 (Pa. Super. Ct. 1992) (quoting Perry v. Payne, 66 A. 553 (1907)).

8. *Hershey Foods*, 619 A.2d at 288 (citing Ruzzi v. Butler Petroleum Co., 588 A.2d 1 (Pa. 1991)).

9. *See* Woodburn v. Consolidation Coal Co., 590 A.2d 1273, 1277 (Pa. Super. Ct. 1991); *Deskiewicz*, 561 A.2d 33; DiPietro v. City of Philadelphia, 496 A.2d 407, 410 (Pa. Super. Ct. 1985).

10. *Perry*, 66 A. at 254.

11. Westinghouse Elec. Co. v. Murphy, Inc., 228 A.2d 656, 657 (Pa. 1967).

negligence.[12] In a later case, however, the court found notions of primary and secondary liability to be inapplicable to written contracts of indemnity.[13]

2. EXCEPTIONS TO GENERAL RULES OF CONTRACTUAL INDEMNITY

While an agreement to indemnify may be enforceable where the foregoing standard is met, indemnification tantamount to exculpation from liability for violation of a statute intended to protect human life is void on grounds of public policy.[14] This rule serves two purposes: It avoids a loss of incentive on the part of a party to use reasonable care to avoid its own negligence, and it maintains an insurer's interest in loss prevention and inspection since the insurer also remains on the risk.[15]

Similarly, an indemnification provision in which one charged with a public duty is indemnified by the victim for the indemnitor's wrongdoing is unenforceable on grounds of public policy.[16] As between joint tortfeasors, indemnification by one against another is enforceable even where a public safety statute is implicated, however, so long as the indemnification is not for the sole negligence of the indemnitee.[17]

An agreement by a partner in a registered limited liability partnership to indemnify another partner arising from negligent or wrongful acts committed by the other partner is enforceable,[18] but not for willful misconduct or recklessness of the indemnitee.[19] A contract involving an architect, engineer, surveyor, or their agents in which the architect shall be indemnified or held harmless is void as against public policy and wholly unenforceable.[20]

3. INDEMNITY AGREEMENTS AS INSURED CONTRACTS

Pennsylvania courts have interpreted an insured's agreement to indemnify another as an assumption of tort liability so as to place the indemnification within the policy exception for an "insured contract" and outside the exclusion for contractually assumed liability.[21] Where the insured merely assumes a contractual obligation that does not amount to an assumption of liability in tort, however, the agreement to indemnify is not an "insured contract" and the policy exclusion applies.[22]

4. OPERATION OF AN AGREEMENT TO INDEMNIFY REFERRING TO OR REQUIRING INSURANCE

To the extent an insured purchases a policy of insurance to cover its underlying indemnity agreements with another party, the indemnified party receives no greater rights (unless named as an "additional insured") than it could against the named insured directly.[23] Where the underlying indemnity agreement limits the circumstances in which the named insured will be liable to the third party, coverage under an insurance policy referring to that

12. Urban Redevelopment Auth. of Pittsburgh v. Norelco Corp., 422 A.2d 563, 569 (Pa. Super. 1980).
13. *Fulmer*, 543 A.2d at 1101–02.
14. Warren City Lines, Inc. v. United Refining Co., 287 A.2d 149, 151 (Pa. Super. Ct. 1971).
15. *Id.* at 151–52.
16. DeFrancesco v. Western Pa. Water Co., 478 A.2d 1295, 1306 (Pa. Super. Ct. 1984).
17. *Fulmer*, 543 A.2d at 1104.
18. 15 Pa. Cons. Stat. § 8204(b)(iii) (2004).
19. 15 Pa. Cons. Stat. § 8510(b) (2005).
20. 68 Pa. Stat. § 491 (2005).
21. Brooks v. Colton, 760 A.2d 393, 395–97 (Pa. 2000); Tremco, Inc. v. Mfrs. Ass'n Ins. Co., 832 A.2d 1120, 1122 (Pa. Super. Ct. 2003).
22. Hertz Corp. v. Smith, 657 A.2d 1316, 1319 (Pa. 1995).
23. Lincoln Ins. Co. v. ITO Corp. of Ameriport, 18 Pa. D. & C.3d 607, 610–11 (1980).

indemnity agreement may be limited in the same way.[24] If an underlying indemnity provision only covers the indemnitor's negligence, then the insurance policy secured to cover that indemnity agreement may not extend to losses outside the indemnitor's negligence, i.e., the indemnitee's strict liability.[25]

Additionally, the rule that agreements to indemnify for one's own negligence be strictly construed applies to agreements to obtain insurance.[26] Whether an express agreement to indemnify for one's own negligence or an agreement to obtain insurance that will cover losses for one's own negligence is at issue, the "same principles are applicable because to hold otherwise would be to put the indemnitor at the mercy of the indemnitee's negligent conduct."[27]

Where an indemnified party is named as an "additional insured" on a policy with its indemnitor, the language of that policy, rather than the underlying indemnity agreement, controls.[28] Even where an indemnitor (named insured) may be able to avoid liability for direct indemnity, that fact is irrelevant to the determination of the indemnitee's rights as an additional insured.[29] The underlying indemnity agreement does not control "the legal relationship between [an additional insured] and [the insurer]."[30] Rather, the insurance agreement naming the indemnitee as "additional insured" "provides independent rights" to the indemnitee.[31] If the insurer wishes to restrict coverage to the limits expressed in the underlying indemnity agreement or otherwise, it must state that in the policy.[32]

24. *Id.*
25. *Id.*
26. DiPietro v. City of Philadelphia, 496 A.2d 407, 410 (Pa. Super. Ct. 1985).
27. *Id.*
28. Township of Springfield v. Ersek, 660 A.2d 672, 675–76 (Pa. Commw. Ct. 1995).
29. *Id.*
30. *Id.* at 675.
31. *Township of Springfield*, 660 A.2d at 676.
32. *Id.*

Rhode Island

J. Tyler Butts
Robinson & Cole LLP

1. GENERAL RULES OF CONTRACTUAL INDEMNITY

In Rhode Island, the right of indemnity may be created expressly or implied by a contract.[1] The right to indemnity is statutorily preserved.[2] While a party may contract to indemnify another for the other party's own negligence, a contract will not be construed to indemnify the indemnitee against its own negligence unless the parties' intention to do so is clearly and unequivocally expressed in the contract.[3]

Contractual indemnity provisions are interpreted using basic contract principles.[4] In interpreting these provisions, a court "should review the agreement in its entirety, construe provisions with reference to one another where possible, and read the contract as 'a rational business instrument which will effectuate the apparent intention of the parties.'"[5] Indemnity provisions are strictly construed against the party alleging the right to indemnification,[6] and courts will look for clear and unambiguous language in the contract evidencing the parties' intent to indemnify.[7]

Express contractual indemnity provisions may circumvent the exclusive remedy immunity of worker's compensation when an employer is sued by a third party to whom the employer owes contractual indemnification when that third party is sued by the employee.[8]

2. EXCEPTIONS TO GENERAL RULES OF CONTRACTUAL INDEMNITY

Indemnity agreements in construction contracts in which a party seeks indemnification from another for the consequences of its own or its agent's negligence are against public policy and void.[9] Rhode Island General Law § 6-34-1(a)[10] provides:

1. Helgerson v. Mammoth Mart, Inc., 335 A.2d 339, 341 (R.I. 1975) (explaining an action for indemnity may also arise as an equitable remedy to compel the party primarily liable to hold the one secondarily liable harmless); Silva v. Home Indem. Co., 416 A.2d 664, 666 (R.I. 1980) (citing *Helgerson*).

2. R.I. Gen. Laws § 10-6-9 (2004) ("This chapter [entitled Contribution Among Joint Tortfeasors] does not impair any right of indemnity under existing law."). The statute preserves a right of action for indemnity that is already in existence, and does not create a statutory right of indemnity. Wilson v. Krasnoff, 560 A.2d 335, 341 (R.I. 1989).

3. Corrente v. Conforti & Eisele Co., 468 A.2d 920, 922 (R.I. 1983); Rhode Island Hosp. Trust Nat'l Bank v. Dudley Serv. Corp., 605 A.2d 1325, 1327 (R.I. 1992) ("We have previously upheld exculpatory-indemnification clauses that negate liability for an individual's own negligence if the clause is sufficiently specific.").

4. Cosimini v. Atkinson-Kiewit Joint Venture, 877 F. Supp. 68, 72 (D.R.I. 1995).

5. *Id.* (quoting Taunton Mun. Lighting Plant v. Quincy Oil Inc., 503 F. Supp. 235, 237 (D. Mass. 1980), *aff'd,* 669 F.2d 710 (1st Cir. 1982)).

6. Muldowney v. Weatherking Prods., Inc., 509 A.2d 441, 443 (R.I. 1986); Sansone v. Morton Mach. Works, Inc., 957 A.2d 386, 393 (R.I. 2008).

7. *Rhode Island Hosp. Trust Nat'l Bank*, 605 A.2d at 1327; *Sansone*, 957 A.2d at 393.

8. Cosentino v. A.F. Lusi Constr. Co., 485 A.2d 105, 108 (R.I. 1984) (An "action for contract indemnification from [an] employer is not an action based upon the employee's injury but rather is an action for reimbursement based upon an expressed contractual obligation .... This obligation is independent of any statutory duty the employer may owe an employee.").

9. *Cosentino*, 485 A.2d at 107.

10. This statutory provision was enacted in 1976 and does not apply to indemnity agreements that pre-date the enactment. *See* Vaccaro v. E.W. Burman, Inc., 484 A.2d 880, 881 (R.I. 1984).

> A covenant, promise, agreement, or understanding in, or in connection with or collateral to, a contract or agreement relative to the design, planning, construction, alteration, repair, or maintenance of a building, structure, highway, road, appurtenance, and appliance, including moving, demolition, and excavating connected with a building, structure, highway, road, appurtenance, or appliance, pursuant to which contract or agreement the promisee or the promisee's independent contractors, agents, or employees has hired the promisor to perform work, purporting to indemnify the promisee, the promisee's independent contractors, agents, employees, or indemnitees against liability for damages arising out of bodily injury to persons or damage to property proximately caused by or resulting from the negligence of the promisee, the promisee's independent contractors, agents, employees, or indemnitees, is against public policy and is void; provided that that this section shall not affect the validity of any insurance contract, worker's compensation agreement, or an agreement issued by an insurer.

The legislature did not prohibit the use of all indemnification contracts in the construction industry.[11] A general contractor may seek indemnification from a subcontractor for claims resulting from the negligence of the subcontractor or its employees.[12]

Unless the circumstances indicate bad faith or deliberate overreaching on the part of the promisee, an otherwise void indemnity provision will be modified and enforced by the courts.[13] For example, in *Cosimini v. Atkinson-Kiewit Joint Venture*,[14] an injured employee brought suit against the general contractor after the subcontractor/employer paid the employee worker's compensation benefits. The subcontractor and contractor had entered into a contract containing an indemnity agreement and a corresponding insurance procurement clause. The indemnity agreement required the subcontractor to indemnify the contractor even if the contractor was partially negligent. Based on the clear language of the contract, the contractor brought a third-party claim against the subcontractor for indemnity. The court held that the indemnity provision was void as against public policy as announced in Rhode Island General Law § 6-34-1.[15] But rather than invalidate the entire indemnity provision, the court modified the indemnity provision and enforced only the portion in compliance with Rhode Island General Law § 6-34-1, specifically, that portion requiring the subcontractor to indemnify the general contractor to the extent of the subcontractor's negligence.[16]

3. INDEMNITY AGREEMENTS AS INSURED CONTRACTS

Rhode Island law is inconclusive as to whether an agreement to indemnify is an "insured contract" within the meaning of a general liability insurance policy. In the only case to touch upon the issue, the federal court for the District of Rhode Island recognized that other jurisdictions have allowed coverage for contractually assumed liability, but ultimately determined that an employment contract would not amount to such a contract.[17]

---

11. *Cosentino*, 485 A.2d at 107.
12. *Id.*
13. Gormly v. I. Lazar & Sons, Inc., 926 F.2d 47, 50 (1st Cir. 1991).
14. Cosimini v. Atkinson-Kiewit Joint Venture, 877 F. Supp. 68 (D.R.I. 1995).
15. *Id.* at 71.
16. *Id.* ("In the event that the contract calls for a subcontractor to indemnify the general contractor for its own negligence and for that of the general contractor, the former obligation is enforceable, while the latter obligation is unenforceable. First Circuit law permits a court to modify an illegal contract and enforce the revised version, even selectively enforcing some components of a seemingly indivisible clause.").
17. Foxon Packaging Corp. v. Aetna Casualty & Surety Co., 905 F. Supp. 1139, 1145 (D.R.I. 1995) (further holding that insurance cannot be afforded for intentional discrimination).

4. OPERATION OF AN AGREEMENT TO INDEMNIFY REFERRING TO OR REQUIRING INSURANCE

Rhode Island courts have not explicitly addressed the operation of Rhode Island General Law § 6-34-1, where an indemnity obligation is joined with an insurance-procurement requirement.[18] It appears, however, that if an agreement to procure insurance is linked to an otherwise void indemnity agreement, Rhode Island General Law § 6-34-1 does not nullify the insurance procurement clause.[19] As stated above, the court may limit the scope of the indemnity obligation and thereby narrow the scope of the insurance coverage.[20]

In *Cosimini*, the court also analyzed whether the insurance procurement obligation should be limited to the scope of indemnity. The insurance procurement clause indicated that "insurance shall cover performance of the above indemnity obligation[.]"[21] The court reasoned that "[t]he scope of the insurance that [the subcontractor] was obligated to procure is determined by the scope of the indemnity obligation, as it is legally required to be performed."[22] Because the court narrowed the subcontractor's performance obligation under the indemnity clause, the insurance clause, by its own language, was equally limited.[23]

A more recent case, *A.F. Lusi Construction, Inc. v. Peerless Insurance Co.*,[24] implies that insurance procurement clauses containing an agreement to indemnify a contractor for its own negligence will not be struck down by operation of Rhode Island General Law § 6-34-1.[25] Although the court in *Peerless* did not ultimately decide whether § 6-34-1 invalidates insurance procurement agreements, it cited to other jurisdictions with similar statutory provisions that have upheld agreements by a subcontractor to purchase insurance for a general contractor, even though the insurance would have the practical effect of indemnifying the general contractor against the claims for damages resulting from the general contractor's own negligence.[26]

18. A.F. Lusi Constr., Inc. v. Peerless Ins. Co., 847 A.2d 254, 265–66 (R.I. 2004).
19. *Cosimini*, 877 F. Supp. at 72.
20. *Id.*
21. *Id.* at 71.
22. *Id.* at 72–73.
23. *Id.*
24. *A.F. Lusi Constr., Inc.*, 847 A.2d at 265–66.
25. *Id.*
26. *Id.*

South Carolina

Brannon Arnold
Weinberg, Wheeler, Hudgins, Gunn & Dial

1. GENERAL RULES OF CONTRACTUAL INDEMNITY

South Carolina law allows a party to contractually relieve itself from liability for ordinary negligence, except where such an agreement is against public policy.[1] As a result, a contract that includes a provision "in which a first party is liable to a second party for a loss or damage the second party might incur to a third party" is enforceable.[2]

A contract of indemnity is construed "in accordance with the rules for the construction of contracts generally,"[3] and the courts focus primarily on the intent of the parties,[4] which is determined from the language used in the contract.[5] "If that language is clear and unambiguous, it must be given its plain and usual meaning."[6] If coverage for a loss appears to be reasonably within the contemplation of the parties, the court will interpret the contract of indemnity to cover such losses.[7]

As it is unusual, however, for an indemnitor to indemnify an indemnitee for losses resulting from the indemnitee's own negligence, a contract containing an indemnity provision that purports to relieve an indemnitee from the consequences of its own negligence will be strictly construed.[8] A contract of indemnity will not be construed to indemnify the indemnitee against losses resulting from its own negligent acts unless such intention is expressed in clear and unequivocal terms.[9]

Whether an agreement to indemnify for "any and all claims" reaches the sole negligence of the indemnitee is uncertain.[10] Indeed, the South Carolina Court of Appeals has noted that there are no less than three different interpretations of this phrase.[11]

In *Federal Pacific Electric v. Carolina Production Enterprises*, the Court of Appeals noted that the "Supreme Court has yet to choose which of the views it favors on the question of what constitutes a sufficient expression of the intent of the parties concerning the indemnification of the indemnitee for its own negligence."[12] In finding that the indemnity clause at

1. Laurens Emergency Med. Specialist v. M.S. Bailey & Sons Bankers, 584 S.E.2d 375, 377 (S.C. 2003).
2. *Id.* (citing Campbell v. Beacon Mfg. Co., Inc., 438 S.E.2d 271, 272 (S.C. Ct. App. 1993)).
3. *Campbell*, 438 S.E.2d at 272.
4. *Id.*
5. *Id.*
6. *Id.*
7. *Id.*
8. Fed. Pac. Elec. v. Carolina Prod. Enters., 378 S.E.2d 56, 57 (S.C. Ct. App. 1989).
9. *Id.* at 57 (citing Murray v. The Texas Co., 174 S.E. 231, 232 (S.C. 1934) ("[A] provision [in] a contract relieving one of the parties thereto from liability for . . . its own negligence should be clear and explicit.")). The Supreme Court of South Carolina has refused to extend this general rule to bar an indemnitee's claim for Comprehensive Environmental Response Compensation and Liability Act (CERCLA) cleanup costs since the determination of CERCLA liability is not fault-based, and therefore application of the rule would not serve the rule's purpose of deterring future negligent conduct. *See* Ashley II of Charleston, LLC v. PCS Nitrogen, Inc., 763 S.E.2d 19 (S.C. 2014).
10. *Fed. Pac. Elec.*, 378 S.E.2d at 57.
11. Some courts hold that "the 'clear and unequivocal terms' requirement is satisfied only by a specific reference in the indemnity clause to the indemnitee's negligence." *Id.* Other courts take the view that "words of general import are sufficient to satisfy the 'clear and unequivocal terms' requirement and that a specific reference to the indemnitee's negligence is therefore not necessary." *Id.* Still other courts "look at the entire contract and any other factors manifesting the intention of the parties to determine whether they 'clearly and unequivocally' expressed the intent to indemnify the indemnitee for its own negligence." *Id.* at 58.
12. *Id.*

issue in *Federal Pacific* did not satisfy the "clear and unequivocal" standard, the court held that "the use of the general terms 'indemnify . . . against any damage suffered or liability incurred . . . or any loss or damage of any kind in connection with the Leased Premises during the term of [the] lease' does not disclose an intention to indemnify for consequences arising from [the indemnitee's] own negligence."[13] In reaching its conclusion, the court in *Federal Pacific* relied upon an earlier decision, which held:

> While it is true that the language used in the [indemnity] provision . . . is broad and comprehensive, it is . . . provocative of some doubt. The [oil company] itself wrote the provision into the contract for its own benefit. It could have plainly stated, if such was the understanding of the parties, that the [distributor] agreed to relieve it in the matter from all liability for its own negligence. As it did not do so, we resolve all doubt . . . in favor of the [distributor], and hold that it was not the intent of the parties to give to the contract as written the effect claimed by the [oil] company.[14]

At the very least then, this holding was a rejection of the notion that words generally describing indemnity for the indemnitee's own negligence is sufficient.

2. EXCEPTIONS TO GENERAL RULES OF CONTRACTUAL INDEMNITY

Contracts "that are in violation of law or opposed to sound public policy" are void in South Carolina, and the courts will not enforce them.[15] On the other hand, South Carolina courts are cautioned not to void contracts on "doubtful grounds of public policy."[16] Rather, it is better for the legislature to first determine what types of contracts should be void as against public policy.[17]

"Public policy" in South Carolina is derived from the state's "established law . . . as found in its Constitution, statutes, and judicial decisions."[18] A statute provides that hold harmless clauses in construction contracts, where a party is indemnified for his or her sole negligence, are void as against public policy.[19] South Carolina Code Annotated § 32-2-10 provides in pertinent part, that "a promise or agreement in connection with the design, planning, construction, alteration, repair or maintenance of a building, structure, highway, road, appurtenance or appliance . . . purporting to indemnify the promisee . . . against liability for damages . . . resulting from the sole negligence of the promisee . . . is against public policy and unenforceable."[20] But this statutory limitation does not affect broader coverage that might be actually provided by an insurance policy that does not preclude coverage for sole negligence.[21]

---

13. *Id.* at 58–59.

14. *Id.* at 58 (quoting Murray v. The Texas Co., 174 S.E. 231, 232 (S.C. 1934)).

15. Batchelor v. American Health Ins. Co., 107 S.E.2d 36, 38–39 (S.C. 1959) (citing Weeks v. New York Life Ins. Co., 122 S.E. 586 (S.C. 1924)).

16. *Id.* at 39 (citing Crosswell v. Connecticut Indem. Ass'n, 28 S.E. 200, 205 (S.C. 1897)).

17. *Id.*

18. *Id.* at 38.

19. *See generally* S.C. CODE ANN. § 32-2-10.

20. *Id.*

21. *See id.* ("The provisions of this section shall not affect any insurance contract . . . ."); Standard Pac. of the Carolinas, LLC v. Amerisure Ins. Co., 2011 WL 31289 (D.S.C. 2011) (stating that the anti-indemnity statute "does not apply to insurance contracts"), *overruled on other grounds*, 500 Fed. App'x 237, 239 n.2 (4th Cir. 2012); Philip L. Bruner, Patrick J. O'Connor, Jr., *Anti-Indemnity Statutes—Statutes Prohibiting Indemnity Against Loss Due to the Indemnitee's Sole Negligence*, BOCL § 10:90 (July 2014) ("The majority of 'sole negligence' prohibitions by their terms do not affect the validity of an insurance product. Thus, if an indemnitor procured an insurance policy that provided protection for the indemnitee's sole negligence, then the indemnitee should be protected, notwithstanding the statutory bars.").

Another South Carolina statute prohibits a tenant from limiting the liability of a landlord or indemnifying the landlord for liability in a rental agreement.[22] Under South Carolina Code Annotated § 27-40-330(a)(3), "[a] rental agreement may not provide . . . that the tenant agrees to the exculpation or limitation of any liability of the landlord arising under law or to indemnify the landlord for that liability or the costs connected therewith."[23]

3. INDEMNITY AGREEMENTS AS INSURED CONTRACTS

The South Carolina courts have not specifically addressed whether and when an indemnity agreement is an "insured contract" within the meaning of a liability insurance policy. In *BP Oil Co. v. Federated Mutual Ins. Co.*, Federated Mutual Insurance Company (Federated) had a duty to defend one of BP Oil Company's (BP) distributors, Wilkerson Fuel Company, Inc. (Wilkerson), in any suit alleging damages covered by the policy.[24] BP's complaint against Wilkerson alleged that Wilkerson was liable to BP based upon indemnity provisions contained in two written agreements BP and Wilkerson had entered into for Wilkerson to distribute BP petroleum products in South Carolina.[25] Federated *admitted* that the two written agreements were "insured contracts" within the meaning of its policy.[26] Because the Federated policy covered "insured contracts," the court held that Federated had a duty to defend Wilkerson.[27]

4. OPERATION OF AN AGREEMENT TO INDEMNIFY REFERRING TO OR REQUIRING INSURANCE

There do not appear to be any decisions specifically addressing the effect of an indemnification agreement requiring the purchase of insurance or requiring the indemnitee to be named as an additional insured under the indemnitor's liability policy.

However, where parties mutually agree to shift the risk of loss or damage to an insurance company as opposed to each other, South Carolina recognizes that such an agreement does not violate public policy and is enforceable.[28] In addition, waiver of subrogation clauses are consistently upheld because "they apply only to property losses, they waive subrogation only to the extent covered by first party insurance, and they merely give effect to the parties' agreement to allocate risk."[29]

In *Summit Contractors v. General Heating & Air Conditioning, Inc.*, a subcontractor and general contractor entered into an agreement with a waiver of subrogation provision.[30] While working at the construction site, the subcontractor's employee caused a fire by negligent soldering, which caused extensive property damage.[31] The insurer paid the contractor $935,000 under its property loss policy.[32] The insurer then pursued subrogation rights against the subcontractor for the fire damage to the construction site.[33] The subcontractor, in turn, asserted as a defense the waiver of subrogation clause found in its contract with the contractor.[34]

---

22. S.C. Code Ann. § 27-40-330(a)(3).
23. *Id.*
24. BP Oil Co. v. Federated Mut. Ins. Co., 496 S.E.2d 35 (S.C. Ct. App. 1998).
25. *Id.* at 40–41.
26. *Id.*
27. *Id.*
28. Summit Contractors Inc. v. Gen. Heating & Air Conditioning, Inc., 595 S.E.2d 472 (S.C. 2004).
29. *Id.* at 476.
30. *Id.* at 474.
31. *Id.* at 473.
32. *Id.* at 473–74.
33. *Id.* at 473.
34. *Id.*

The court upheld the subcontractor's argument and enforced the waiver of subrogation clause.[35] In reaching its decision, the court noted that the contract provisions provided that "even though Subcontractor must fully indemnify Contractor for damage to the *property of others*, Contractor waives subrogation for damage *to the construction site to the extent covered by property insurance*."[36] As a result, the court found "no conflict within the waiver of subrogation clause."[37]

35. *Id.* at 476.
36. *Id.* (emphasis added).
37. *Id.*

South Dakota

Matthew Lawlyes
Wilson Law Group

1. GENERAL RULES OF CONTRACTUAL INDEMNITY

Contracts of indemnity are permitted in South Dakota but are subject to "close scrutiny" as to whether the intent to indemnify is present within the contract.[1] If the parties' intent as to the scope of indemnification is not expressed, South Dakota applies statutory rules of interpretation for contracts of indemnity.[2] Recovery is only permissible upon the indemnified party becoming liable[3] and, unless otherwise expressed, the indemnitor may be bound to defend the person indemnified.[4] Indemnification for an indemnitee's *sole* negligence is disallowed.[5]

Generally, "to relieve a party of the consequences of its own negligence, the language of an indemnity or hold harmless agreement must be clear and unequivocal."[6] "Any doubts are to be resolved in favor of the indemnitor."[7] The key to interpreting an indemnity agreement is the intention of the parties.[8] Courts applying South Dakota law have found the "intent to indemnify against a party's negligence, even though the term 'negligence' is not actually used, where such intent is clearly expressed."[9] In the construction context, "[c]ontracts of indemnity are strictly construed in favor of a subcontractor as against the contractor and unless the language employed clearly and definitely shows an intention to indemnify courts do not read into a written contract indemnity provisions not expressly set forth therein."[10]

As an example of South Dakota's analysis of controversial provisions, the court in *Chicago & N. W. Transp. Co. v. V & R Sawmill, Inc.*,[11] considered two separate indemnity clauses before declaring both invalid. The case involved both a lease and a licensing agreement between a railroad (lessor/licensor) and an adjacent sawmill (lessee/licensee). A train injured the sawmill's employee, and the railroad settled the case with the employee. Prior to settlement, the railroad never contacted the sawmill or tendered the defense, but then filed suit against the sawmill to recover the amount paid the employee plus fees and costs pursuant to the alleged indemnification agreements.[12] The United States District Court for the District of South Dakota considered whether the railroad was entitled to indemnity from the sawmill pursuant to the indemnity provisions of the lease and/or licensing agreement.[13] The court held the lease agreement lacked a clear manifestation of intent to

1. *See generally* Schull Constr. Co. v. Koenig, 121 N.W.2d 559 (S.D. 1963).
2. S.D. Codified Laws § 56-3-7.
3. S.D. Codified Laws § 56-3-8.
4. S.D. Codified Laws § 56-3-11.
5. S.D. Codified Laws § 56-3-18.
6. Chi. & N. W. Transp. Co. v. V & R Sawmill, Inc., 501 F. Supp. 278, 281 (D. S.D. 1980); Schull Constr. Co. v. Koenig, 121 N.W.2d 559, 562 (S.D. 1963).
7. Becker v. Black & Veatch Consulting Eng'rs, 509 F.2d 42, 46 (8th Cir. 1974).
8. U.S. v. Seckinger, 397 U.S. 203 (1970); *Becker*, 509 F.2d at 46.
9. *Chi. & N.W. Transp. Co.*, 501 F. Supp. at 281 (holding language of contract not clear enough to warrant indemnity against another party's negligence) (citing *Becker*, 509 F.2d 42).
10. *Schull Constr. Co.*, 121 N.W.2d at 562.
11. *Chi. & N.W. Transp. Co.*, 501 F. Supp. 278.
12. *Id.* at 279–80.
13. *Id.* at 281–83.

indemnify for the railroad's own negligence but found otherwise in regards to the pertinent license provision.[14]

These conflicting findings were based on the specific language of each provision. The lease language was quite general, providing that "Lessee also agrees to indemnify and hold harmless the Lessor against loss, damage or injury to the person or property of the Lessee, or any other person, while on or about the leased premises."[15] Conversely, the license was more specific:

> Licensee agrees to assume and pay for all loss or damage to property whatsoever, and injury to or death of any person, . . . however arising from or in connection with the existence, construction, maintenance, repair, renewal, reconstruction, operation, use or removal of said facility . . . and the Licensee forever indemnifies the Railway Company against . . . any and all claims, demands, law suits or liability for any such loss . . . *even though the operation of the Railway Company's railroad may have caused or contributed thereto.*[16]

Despite the clear manifestation of an intent to indemnify for the railroad's sole negligence, the court held the provision void under South Dakota law because it required indemnification in a situation where the railroad was *solely* negligent.[17] The court reasoned that it had to first determine whether an indemnity claim could even be made.[18] "To sustain an indemnity claim against the indemnitor, the indemnitee must prove legal liability to the injured party unless the defense has been tendered and refused by the indemnitor."[19]

Since there was no tender, the railroad had to prove its liability to the injured party.[20] The requisite proof of liability was established through evidence that the train did not sound a warning device prior to approaching the intersection, in violation of South Dakota Codified Laws § 49-25-2. Although the court relied on South Dakota Codified Laws § 56-3-18[21] to invalidate the indemnity, its opinion seemingly acknowledged an alternative basis for voiding the clause due to South Dakota Codified Laws § 53-9-3, which, as a matter of public policy, prohibits persons from contracting to exempt anyone from responsibility for violation of a law whether willful or negligent.[22]

2. EXCEPTIONS TO GENERAL RULES OF CONTRACTUAL INDEMNITY

The South Dakota legislature has declared several types of contractual provisions void, including:

1. **Indemnification agreements for a promisee's *sole negligence***
"A covenant, promise, agreement or understanding in, or in connection with or collateral to, a contract or agreement relative to the construction, alteration, repair or maintenance of a building, structure, appurtenance and appliance, including moving, demolition and excavating connected therewith, purporting to indemnify the promisee against liability for damages arising out of bodily injury to persons or damage to

14. *Id.* at 282.
15. *Id.* at 279.
16. *Id.* at 279–80 (emphasis added).
17. *Id.* at 283–84 (based on the evidence at trial, the only way the railroad could have been liable to the injured employee was if the train failed to sound its bell or whistles).
18. *Id.* at 282.
19. *Id.* (citing S.D. Codified Laws § 56-3-13 and Missouri Pac. R.R. Co. v. Arkansas Oak Flooring Co., 434 F.2d 575, 580 (8th Cir. 1970)).
20. *Id.*
21. S.D. Codified Laws § 56-3-18 provides that agreements to indemnify others for their sole negligence in the construction context are void as against public policy.
22. *Chi. & N.W. Transp. Co.*, 501 F. Supp. at 283.

property caused by or resulting from the *sole negligence* of the promisee, his agents or employees, or indemnitee, is against the policy of the law and is void and unenforceable."[23]

2. **Contract provisions contrary to law**
"A contract provision contrary to an express provision of law or to the policy of express law, though not expressly prohibited or otherwise contrary to good morals, is unlawful."[24]
3. **Contracts against public policy**
"All contracts which have for their object, directly or indirectly, to exempt anyone from responsibility for his own fraud or willful injury to the person or property of another or from violation of law whether willful or negligent, are against the policy of the law."[25]
4. **Contracts to exempt a common carrier for willful or wanton misconduct or fraud**
"A common carrier cannot be exonerated from liability for willful or wanton misconduct, fraud, or willful wrong of himself or his servant by any agreement made in anticipation thereof."[26]

3. INDEMNITY AGREEMENTS AS INSURED CONTRACTS

The South Dakota courts have not addressed whether and under what circumstances an agreement to indemnify is an "insured contract" within the meaning of the exception to the form exclusion for contractually assumed liability.

4. OPERATION OF AN AGREEMENT TO INDEMNIFY REFERRING TO OR REQUIRING INSURANCE

South Dakota has not had occasion to address the impact of insurance requirements on the application of enforceability of related indemnity provisions.

23. S.D. Codified Laws § 56-3-18 (emphasis added).
24. S.D. Codified Laws §§ 53-9-1, 56-3-2.
25. S.D. Codified Laws § 53-9-3.
26. S.D. Codified Laws § 49-2-9.

Tennessee

Matt Woolf and Ryan Freeman
Baker, Donelson, Bearman, Caldwell & Berkowitz, P.C.

1. GENERAL RULES OF CONTRACTUAL INDEMNITY

Tennessee courts will enforce contractual indemnity agreements.[1] The Tennessee Supreme Court, in *Planters Gin Co. v. Federal Compress & Warehouse Co., Inc.*, specifically noted that "the allocation of risk agreed to by parties with equivalent bargaining powers in a commercial setting serves a particularly valid purpose where, as here, the contract delineates the parties' duty to obtain and bear the cost of insurance . . . . Thus, even broad transfers of liability, where unambiguous, should be honored."[2]

However, courts strictly construe contracts that provide indemnification against one's own negligence.[3] In this context, the intention of the parties must be expressed in clear and unequivocal terms.[4] For example, where an agreement only provided that "[l]iability for injury, disability and death of workmen and other persons caused by the operation, handling or transportation of the equipment during the Rental Period shall be assumed by the [lessee-indemnitee],"[5] the agreement was held not to reach the indemnitor's own negligence.[6] "'Mere general, broad, and all inclusive language in the indemnifying agreement has been said not to be sufficient to impose liability for the indemnitee's own negligence.'"[7]

One indemnity agreement can address separate indemnity obligations. For example, the first paragraph of the following agreement did not reach anything but the indemnitor's negligence, but the second paragraph, relating to claims by the indemnitor's employer, covered even the indemnitee's negligence:

> INDEMNITY: Contractor shall indemnify and save Purchaser harmless from and against all losses or damages, and all claims, demands, suits, actions, payments and judgments, including attorney's fees, arising from personal injuries (including death), losses or damages to property, or otherwise, brought or recovered against Purchaser by reason of any act or omission of Contractor (or any of his sub-contractors) in the execution or guarding of the work, or by reason of any liens, claims, demands and debts for all labor performed and for all equipment and materials furnished under this Contract.
>
> Contractor shall be responsible for the conduct and safety of his employees and his sub-contractors and the employees thereof in the performance of the work hereunder and while on the premises of the Purchaser, and the Contractor agrees that he will hold the Purchaser and his officers and employees harmless and indemnify them from and against any and all claims of any of such employees for personal

1. Pitt v. Tyree Org. Ltd., 90 S.W.3d 244, 252 (Tenn. Ct. App. 2002); Greene v. Greene, No. E2005-01394-COA-R3-CV, 2006 Tenn. App. LEXIS 158, at *7 (Tenn. Ct. App. Mar. 7, 2006) (quoting Honeycutt v. Honeycutt, 152 S.W.2d 556, 561 (Tenn. Ct. App. 2003)).
2. Planters Gin Co. v. Federal Compress & Warehouse Co., Inc., 78 S.W.3d 885, 892–93 (Tenn. 2002).
3. Power Equip. Co. v. J. A. Jones Constr. Co., No. 844, 1989 Tenn. App. LEXIS 108, at *4 (Tenn. Ct. App. Feb. 10, 1989).
4. *Id.* at *4–5.
5. *Id.* at *3–4.
6. *Id.* at *5–6.
7. *Id.* at *5 (quoting Wajtasiak v. Morgan Cty., 633 S.W.2d 488, 490 (Tenn. Ct. App. 1982)); *see also* Crum v. Colman-Cocker Textile Mach. Co., 467 F. Supp. 6, 7 (E.D. Tenn. 1978).

> injuries suffered by any of such employees in the performance of such work or while on the premises of the Purchaser.[8]

Tennessee also recognizes the purportedly "universal rule that there can be no recovery where there was concurrent negligence of both indemnitor and indemnitee unless the indemnity contract provides for indemnification in such case by 'clear and unequivocal terms.'"[9] Thus, a clause that "[t]he contractor shall continuously maintain adequate protection of all his work from damage and shall protect the owner's property from injury arising in connection with this contract" did not reach the concurrent negligence of the indemnitor and indemnitee.[10]

An employer can be held liable pursuant to a contract for indemnity, despite the "exclusive remedy" provision of the Tennessee Workers' Compensation Act, Tennessee Code Annotated § 50-6-108.[11]

2. EXCEPTION TO GENERAL RULES OF CONTRACTUAL INDEMNITY

Tennessee has adopted several exceptions to the general rule permitting agreements to indemnify for one's own negligence.

By statute, indemnity agreements relative to construction contracts, wherein a party is indemnified for his or her sole negligence, are deemed void as against public policy:[12]

> A covenant promise, agreement or understanding in or in connection with or collateral to a contract or agreement relative to the construction, alteration, repair or maintenance of a building, structure, appurtenance and appliance, including moving, demolition and excavating connected therewith, purporting to indemnify or hold harmless the promisee against liability for damages arising out of bodily injury to persons or damage to property caused by or resulting from the sole negligence of the promisee, the promisee's agents or employees, or indemnitee, is against public policy and is void and unenforceable.[13]

This statute is broadly construed. "Looking at the natural and ordinary meaning of this statute, we interpret it to include any agreement relative to the construction of a building. Thus, a contract to provide certain services relative to a building under construction under a separate contract would be included under T.C.A. § 62-6-123 and any provision purporting to indemnify or hold harmless the promisee against liability arising out of bodily injury to persons or damage to property caused by or resulting from the sole negligence of the promisee is against public policy and is void and unenforceable."[14]

In addition, residential rental agreements in certain counties may not limit the liability of the landlord or indemnify the landlord for liability.[15] Under Tennessee Code Annotated § 66-28-203(a)(2), "[n]o rental agreement may provide that the tenant . . . (2) Agrees to the exculpation or limitation of any liability of the landlord to the tenant arising under law or to

---

8. Kellogg Co. v. Sanitors, Inc., 496 S.W.2d 472, 473 (Tenn. 1973).

9. Kroger Co. v. Giem, 387 S.W.2d 620, 626 (Tenn. 1964); Farmers Mut. of Tenn. v. Athens Ins. Agency, 145 S.W.3d 566, 569 (Tenn. Ct. App. 2004).

10. *Kroger Co.*, 387 S.W.2d at 622.

11. Easter v. Exxon Co., 699 S.W.2d 168, 170 (Tenn. Ct. App. 1985); *but see* Summers v. Command Systems, Inc., No. 02A01-9104-CV-0054, 1991 Tenn. App. LEXIS 803, at *4 (Tenn. Ct. App. Oct. 10, 1991) (holding that, where no such agreement exists, Tennessee Code Annotated § 50-6-108 will bar noncontractual indemnity).

12. *Planters Gin*, 78 S.W.3d at 893; *see also* Elliott Crane Serv., Inc. v. H. G. Hill Stores, Inc., 840 S.W.2d 376 (Tenn. Ct. App. 1992); Trinity Indus. v. McKinnon Bridge Co., 77 S.W.3d 159, 174 (Tenn. Ct. App. 2001); Tenn. Code Ann. § 62-6-123.

13. Tenn. Code Ann. § 62-6-123.

14. Carroum v. Dover Elevator Co., 806 S.W.2d 777, 780 (Tenn. Ct. App. 1990).

15. *Planters Gin*, 78 S.W.3d at 893; Tenn. Code Ann. § 66-28-203(a)(2).

indemnify the landlord for that liability or the costs connected with such liability." This statute applies to "counties having a population of more than seventy-five thousand (75,000) according to the 2010 federal census or any subsequent federal census," but does not apply to "any occupancy in a public housing unit or other housing unit that is subject to regulation by the department of housing and urban development and owned by a governmental entity or non-profit corporation to the extent such regulation conflicts with state law, but shall apply to the extent that any such regulations defer to the application of state law."[16]

In *Crawford v. Buckner*, the court held that an exculpatory clause in a residential lease releasing a landlord from liability for future acts of negligence, even when executed in a county not covered by Tennessee Code Annotated § 66-28-203, was void as contrary to public policy.[17] Likewise, in *Olsen v. Molzen*, the court found that an exculpatory contract signed by a patient as a condition of receiving medical treatment was contrary to public policy and void.[18] And in *Adams v. Roark*, the court held that indemnity clauses as to damages caused by gross negligence or willful conduct on the part of the indemnified party were invalid.[19]

3. INDEMNITY AGREEMENTS AS INSURED CONTRACTS

Tennessee recognizes an agreement to indemnify a third party for the third party's tort liability by an insured as an "insured contract" within the meaning of a liability insurance policy excepting such assumption of liability from an exclusion for contractually assumed liability.[20]

4. OPERATION OF AN AGREEMENT TO INDEMNIFY REFERRING TO OR REQUIRING INSURANCE

A facially unambiguous agreement in a lease, whereby the lessee agrees to hold the lessor harmless, ascribes a meaning that is "inescapable" when joined with an agreement on the part of the lessee to insure the contents of items stored on the leased property, and when joined with a waiver of subrogation provision.[21] Consequently, where the lessee received payment for its loss from its property insurance carrier, and the carrier then pursued a subrogation action in the name of the lessee against the lessor, the hold harmless and waiver of subrogation provisions precluded the subrogation action.[22] The broad hold harmless provision was held to apply notwithstanding that the alleged negligence of the lessor causing the damage arose out of the lessor's maintenance of premises other than that leased by the lessor.[23]

An insurance carrier owes direct duties of defense and indemnity to a party who is the beneficiary of a policy that assumes the liability of an "insured contract," which may cover any contract or agreement under which the policyholder has assumed "the tort liability of another party to pay for 'bodily injury' or 'property damage' to a third person or organization."[24] For example, when a subcontractor enters into a subcontract agreement requiring it to indemnify a contractor and purchase insurance coverage to accomplish such indemnification, the insurance carrier who provides the policy obtained by the subcontractor owes a direct duty to defend and indemnify the contractor unless "it is plain from the face of the complaint that the allegations failed to state facts that bring the case within or potentially within the policy's coverage."[25]

16. Tenn. Code Ann. § 66-28-102.
17. Crawford v. Buckner, 839 S.W.2d 754, 760 (Tenn. 1992); *see also Planters Gin*, 78 S.W.3d at 893.
18. Olsen v. Molzen, 558 S.W.2d 429, 431 (Tenn. 1977); *see also Planters Gin*, 78 S.W.3d at 893.
19. Adams v. Roark, 686 S.W.2d 73, 75–76 (Tenn. 1985); *see also Planters Gin*, 78 S.W.3d at 893.
20. York v. Vulcan Materials Co., 63 S.W.3d 384, 387 (Tenn. Ct. App. 2001).
21. *Id.* at 390; *Planters Gin*, 78 S.W.3d at 893.
22. *Id.*
23. *Id.*
24. *York*, 63 S.W.3d 384.
25. *Id.*

Texas

Gregory E. Van Houten
Haynes and Boone, LLP

1. GENERAL RULES OF CONTRACTUAL INDEMNITY

Ordinarily, the Texas courts "construe indemnity agreements under the normal rules of contract construction" in their attempt to determine the parties' intent.[1] Determining that intent requires the courts to examine and consider the entire writing in an effort to "harmonize and to give effect to all the provisions of the contract so that none will be rendered meaningless."[2] Thus, no provision taken alone will be given controlling effect. Rather, all the provisions will be construed with reference to the whole instrument.[3]

Various courts of appeals have held that indemnity obligations are not lightly inferred.[4] "[A]s a general rule," indemnity contracts will be strictly construed in favor of the indemnitor.[5]

In contrast to other indemnity agreements, Texas law views contracts that "exculpate a party from the consequences of its own negligence" to constitute an "extraordinary shifting of risk."[6] Thus, Texas has developed two types of fair notice requirements for such agreements: the express negligence doctrine and the conspicuousness requirement.[7] Whether an indemnity agreement meets the express negligence test and is sufficiently conspicuous is a question of law for the court.[8] If the indemnitor has actual notice or knowledge of the indemnity agreement, then the "fair notice requirements are not applicable."[9] Furthermore, in 2005, the Texas Court of Appeals emphasized that, "[t]he application of the fair notice requirements has been 'explicitly limited to releases and indemnity clauses in which one party exculpates itself from its own future negligence.'"[10]

In 1987, Texas abandoned the "clear and unequivocal" rule and adopted the "express negligence" rule in *Ethyl Corp. v. Daniel Construction Co.*[11] The express negligence test requires "that parties seeking to indemnify the indemnitee from the consequences of its own negligence must express that intent in specific terms. Under the doctrine of express negligence, the intent of the parties must be specifically stated within the four corners of the contract."[12]

The express negligence rule applies to any agreement that relieves a party in advance of responsibility for its own negligence, whether that agreement is labeled an indemnity or a release.[13] The doctrine will also be applied to indemnity agreements that cover strict

1. Associated Indem. Corp. v. CAT Contracting, Inc., 964 S.W.2d 276, 284 (Tex. 1998).
2. Universal C.I.T. Credit Corp. v. Daniel, 243 S.W.2d 154, 158 (Tex. 1951).
3. *See* Myers v. Gulf Coast Minerals Mgmt. Corp., 361 S.W.2d 193, 196 (Tex. 1962).
4. Turboff v. Gertner, Aron & Ledet Invs., 840 S.W.2d 603, 612 (Tex. App. 1992, *writ dism'd*).
5. *See, e.g.*, Webb v. Lawson-Avila Constr., Inc., 911 S.W.2d 457, 461 (Tex. App. 1995, *writ dism'd*); Safeco Ins. Co. of America v. Gaubert, 829 S.W.2d 274, 281 (Tex. App. 1992, *writ denied*); Atchison, Topeka & Santa Fe Ry. Co. v. Denton, 475 S.W.2d 821, 832 (Tex. Civ. App. 1971, *writ ref'd n.r.e.*).
6. Dresser Indus., Inc. v. Page Petroleum, Inc., 853 S.W.2d 505, 508 (Tex. 1993).
7. *Id.*; *see also* Green Int'l, Inc. v. Solis, 951 S.W.2d 384, 386 (Tex. 1997).
8. *Dresser Indus.*, 853 S.W.2d at 509.
9. *Id.* at 508 n.2.
10. OXY USA, Inc. v. Sw. Energy Prod. Co., 161 S.W.3d 277, 283 (Tex. App. 2005, *pet. denied*).
11. Ethyl Corp. v. Daniel Construction Co., 725 S.W.2d 705, 706 (Tex. 1987).
12. *Id.* at 708.
13. *See Dresser Indus.*, 853 S.W.2d at 509.

liability claims and agreements for comparative indemnity.[14] The express negligence test *does not* apply to additional insured provisions in insurance policies.[15]

The conspicuousness requirement mandates "that something must appear on the face of the [contract] to attract the attention of a reasonable person when he looks at it."[16] In 1993, the Texas Supreme Court adopted the requirements of the Uniform Commercial Code for indemnities that relieve a party in advance from the consequences of its own negligence:

> A term or clause is conspicuous when it is so written that a reasonable person against whom it is to operate ought to have noticed it. A printed heading in capitals (as: NON-NEGOTIABLE BILL OF LADING) is conspicuous. Language in the body of a form is "conspicuous" if it is in larger or other contrasting type or color. But in a telegram any stated term is "conspicuous."[17]

Thus, language in capitalized headings and language in contrasting type is conspicuous.[18]

One Texas court has held that the conspicuousness of an indemnity agreement is shown by objective factors on the face of the contract and does not vary according to "the subjective sophistication and experience of each party against whom the agreement may be asserted."[19]

Ultimately, "[i]n the absence of an extraordinary shifting of risk, the Supreme Court has 'resisted expanding the fair notice requirements.'"[20]

2. EXCEPTIONS TO GENERAL RULES OF CONTRACTUAL INDEMNITY

While Texas has several statutes that limit the enforceability of indemnity contracts,[21] there are two statutory exceptions that have the most potential significance to insurance agreements: the Oilfield Anti-Indemnity Act[22] and the architects and engineers' anti-indemnity statute.[23]

The Oilfield Anti-Indemnity Act "provides that an agreement pertaining to an oil or gas well is void if it purports to indemnify a party from loss or liability for damage arising out of its own negligence."[24] The prohibition applies to contracts involved in drilling or servicing of oil, gas, or water wells and mineral mines.[25]

The Act makes unenforceable any indemnity that protects a party from damages resulting from the "sole or concurrent negligence of the indemnitee, his agent or employee, or an individual contractor directly responsible to the indemnitee."[26] If there is insurance supporting the indemnification agreement, the agreement will be enforceable: (1) to the full extent of the indemnity if the agreement is "mutual," or (2) to $500,000 if the indemnity is "unilateral."[27] A "mutual" indemnity is an agreement in which the parties agree to indemnify

---

14. Hous. Lighting & Power Co. v. Atchison, Topeka & Santa Fe Ry. Co., 890 S.W.2d 455, 459 (Tex. 1994).
15. Getty Oil Co. v. Ins. Co. of N. Am., 845 S.W.2d 794, 806 (Tex. 1992).
16. *Dresser Indus.*, 853 S.W.2d at 508 (quoting Ling & Co. v. Trinity Sav. & Loan Ass'n, 482 S.W.2d 841, 843 (Tex. 1972)).
17. *Id.* at 511 (quoting Tex. Bus. & Com. Code Ann. § 1.201(10)).
18. *Id.*
19. U.S. Rentals, Inc. v. Mundy Serv. Corp., 901 S.W.2d 789, 792 (Tex. App. 1995, *writ denied*).
20. *OXY USA*, 161 S.W.3d at 283 (quoting Storage & Processors, Inc. v. Reyes, 134 S.W.3d 190, 193 (Tex. 2004)).
21. Tex. Labor Code Ann. § 417.004 (West 2015) (worker's compensation); Tex. Transp. Code Ann. § 623.0155 (West 2015) (common carrier as condition of hire).
22. Tex. Civ. Prac. & Rem. Code Ann. § 127.003 (West 2015).
23. *Id.* § 130.002.
24. *Getty Oil Co.*, 845 S.W.2d at 802–03.
25. Tex. Civ. Prac. & Rem. Code Ann. § 127.001(3).
26. *Id.* § 127.003.
27. *Id.* § 127.005.

each other and each other's contractors completely.[28] A "unilateral" indemnity, as the name implies, operates to the favor of only the indemnitee; it is not reciprocal to the indemnitor.[29]

The Act only regulates agreements for the purchase of insurance if they are in support of indemnity agreements. It does not "prohibit 'insurance shifting' schemes that do not fall within its parameters; rather it *permits* certain indemnity agreements if they are supported by liability insurance and meet the section's other requirements."[30] Thus, the Act will not prohibit an independent contractual obligation to provide a party with additional insured status.[31] Additional insured status will not be prohibited by the Act even if the effect of such an endorsement is to relieve a party for responsibility for its sole negligence.[32]

The architects and engineers' anti-indemnity statute makes unenforceable some indemnity agreements running from a contractor, some landowners, or building suppliers in favor of a registered architect or engineer.[33] The statute applies to indemnification for damage resulting from defects in plans "prepared, approved, or used" by the architect or engineer or from the negligence of the architect or engineer.[34] Indemnification of an architect or engineer for liability resulting from the negligent acts of another, including a contractor, is specifically permitted under the statute[35] and, as would be expected, the courts have enforced such indemnity agreements.[36]

The Texas Anti-Indemnity Act further limits the enforceability of indemnity agreements in the construction context.[37] Section 151.102 provides:

> [A] provision in a construction contract, or in an agreement collateral to or affecting a construction contract, is void and unenforceable as against public policy to the extent that it requires an indemnitor to indemnify, hold harmless, or defend a party, including a third party, against a claim caused by the negligence or fault, the breach or violation of a statute, ordinance, governmental regulation, standard, or rule, or the breach of contract of the indemnitee, its agent or employee, or any third party under the control or supervision of the indemnitee, other than the indemnitor or its agent, employee, or subcontractor of any tier.[38]

There are several exceptions to the Texas Anti-Indemnity Act. Most notably, the Act does not apply "to a provision in a construction contract that requires a person to indemnify, hold harmless, or defend another party to the construction contract or a third party against a claim for the bodily injury or death of an employee of the indemnitor, its agent, or its subcontractor of any tier."[39] Section 151.105 sets out the other statutory exceptions.[40]

---

28. *Id.* § 127.001(3).
29. *Id.* § 127.001(6).
30. *Getty Oil Co.*, 845 S.W.2d at 804 (citing Tex. Civ. Prac. & Rem. Code Ann. § 127.005).
31. *Id.* at 806.
32. *Id.*
33. Tex. Civ. Prac. & Rem. Code Ann. §§ 130.001, 130.002.
34. *Id.* § 130.002(a)(1).
35. *Id.* § 130.005.
36. Foster, Henry, Henry & Thorpe, Inc. v. J.T. Constr. Co., 808 S.W.2d 139, 141 (Tex. App. 1991, *writ denied*).
37. Tex. Ins. Code Ann. §§ 151.001 *et seq.* (West 2015).
38. *Id.* § 151.102.
39. *Id.* § 151.103.
40. Section 151.105 provides that "[t]his subchapter does not affect:

(1) an insurance policy, including a policy issued under an owner-controlled or owner-sponsored consolidated insurance program or a contractor-controlled or contractor-sponsored consolidated insurance program, except as provided by Section 151.104;

(2) a cause of action for breach of contract or warranty that exists independently of an indemnity obligation, including an indemnity obligation in a construction contract under a construction project for which insurance is provided under a consolidated insurance program;

(3) indemnity provisions contained in loan and financing documents, other than construction contracts to which the contractor and owner's lender are parties as provided under Section 151.001(5);

3. INDEMNITY AGREEMENTS AS INSURED CONTRACTS

Texas will find that an indemnity agreement is covered in a general liability policy that provides insured contract coverage.[41]

4. OPERATION OF AN AGREEMENT TO INDEMNIFY REFERRING TO OR REQUIRING INSURANCE

A risk-shifting agreement that contains both an indemnity and an agreement to procure insurance will ordinarily be enforced as two separate and independent obligations.[42] In 1992, the Texas Supreme Court decided *Getty Oil Co. v. Insurance Co. of North America*, which concerned an indemnity agreement containing an agreement to add the indemnitee as additional insured. While the indemnitee was denied indemnification on the basis of res judicata, it was permitted to pursue additional insured status. The court noted: "[i]t was determined [in a prior suit] that Getty had no right of indemnity from NL, *but Getty is not attempting to relitigate that issue here. Rather, it is seeking damages for NL's failure to extend insurance coverage to Getty.*"[43]

As should be evident from the last two sections, Texas will not allow an indemnity agreement to limit additional insured coverage. Under Texas law, limitations that might be found in an indemnity agreement will not be imported into a policy of insurance that adds an indemnitee as an additional insured.[44]

---

(4) general agreements of indemnity required by sureties as a condition of execution of bonds for construction contracts;
(5) the benefits and protections under the workers' compensation laws of [Texas];
(6) the benefits or protections under the governmental immunity laws of [Texas];
(7) agreements subject to Chapter 127, Civil Practice and Remedies Code;
(8) a license agreement between a railroad company and a person that permits the person to enter the railroad company's property as an accommodation to the person for work under a construction contract that does not primarily benefit the railroad company;
(9) an indemnity provision pertaining to a claim based upon copyright infringement;
(10) an indemnity provision in a construction contract, or in an agreement collateral to or affecting a construction contract; pertaining to:
 (A) a single family house, townhouse, duplex, or land development directly related thereto; or
 (B) a public works project of a municipality; or
(11) a joint defense agreement entered into after a claim is made."

41. Travelers Ins. Co. v. Chi. Bridge & Iron Co., 442 S.W.2d 888, 898 (Tex. Civ. App. 1969, *writ ref'd n.r.e.*); Mid-Continent Cas. Co. v. Swift Energy Co., 206 F.3d 487, 492–96 (5th Cir. 2000); Gibson & Assocs., Inc. v. Home Ins. Co., 966 F. Supp. 468, 476–77 (N.D. Tex. 1997).

42. *See Getty Oil Co.*, 845 S.W.2d at 798–802; Coastal Transp. Co. v. Crown Cen. Petroleum Corp., 20 S.W.3d 119, 125–29 (Tex. App. 2000, *pet. denied*); Certain Underwriters at Lloyds v. Oryx Energy Co., 142 F.3d 255, 259–60 (5th Cir. 1998); *see also* Helmerich & Payne Int'l Drilling Co. v. Swift Energy Co., 180 S.W.3d 635, 644 (Tex. App. 2005) (citing Getty Oil Co. v. Ins. Co. of N. Am., 845 S.W.2d 794, 806 (Tex. 1992)).

43. *Getty Oil Co.*, 845 S.W.2d at 802 (emphasis added).

44. *Mid-Continent Cas.*, 206 F.3d at 494 n.8 ("But it is the Policy's language, not the language in the MSA, which governs the scope of the Policy."); *see also Helmerich & Payne Int'l Drilling*, 180 S.W.3d at 645, (citing *Mid-Continent Cas. Co.*, 206 F.3d at 492–95, to buttress the position that "the language of additional-insured provisions in the contracts at issue were not tied to the validity of the indemnity provisions of the contract and therefore were not affected by the alleged invalidity of the indemnity provisions under applicable anti-indemnity statutes").

Utah

Nicholas Panayotopoulos
Weinberg, Wheeler, Hudgins, Gunn & Dial

1. GENERAL RULES OF CONTRACTUAL INDEMNITY

In Utah, the right to indemnification by an express agreement is enforceable if the contract language clearly and unequivocally expresses the parties' intent for one to indemnify the other.[1] The language of such provisions must clearly and unequivocally express the parties' intent to release, shift, or avoid potential liability for loss or injury resulting from particular transactions or occurrences.[2]

To constitute a clear and unequivocal expression of intent to indemnify for a party's own negligence, an indemnity agreement need not contain specific language, but must provide a sufficiently clear and unequivocal expression of the parties' intent.[3] For example, a provision that holds a party harmless for "any and all claims, damages, loss and expenses, to the fullest extent permitted by law" for "any death, accident, injury or other occurrence" from visits to a specific location, meets the test for enforceability.[4] When interpreting indemnity agreements, Utah courts look at the objectives of the parties and the surrounding facts and circumstances.[5]

Historically, such express indemnity agreements were strictly construed by the courts.[6] Utah courts have more recently relaxed the rule of strict construction and adopted the more lenient "clear and unequivocal" test for enforcing indemnity agreements.[7]

Express agreements by which one person obtains another person's agreement to indemnify him or her from the results for his or her own negligence are not favored under Utah law and are strictly construed against the indemnitee.[8] Since relieving one from his or her own negligence is sometimes declared invalid as being against public policy, such intention is not achieved by inference or implication from general language.[9] But where the intention to indemnify a person from losses attributable to his or her own negligence is "clearly and unequivocally expressed" in the contract language, such an indemnity agreement will be upheld.[10]

---

1. Ervin v. Lowe's Cos., 128 P.3d 11, 15 (Utah Ct. App. 2005); Russ v. Woodside Homes, Inc., 905 P.2d 901, 904–05 (Utah Ct. App. 1995); Shell Oil Co. v. Brinkerhoff-Signal Drilling Co., 658 P.2d 1187, 1190–91 (Utah 1983).

2. *Russ*, 905 P.2d at 906.

3. Healey v. J.B. Sheet Metal, Inc., 892 P.2d 1047, 1049 (Utah Ct. App. 1995).

4. *Russ*, 905 P.2d at 906.

5. *Ervin*, 128 P.3d at 15.

6. *Russ*, 905 P.2d at 905.

7. *Id.*; *see also Ervin*, 128 P.3d at 15; Pichover v. Smith's Mgmt. Corp., 771 P.2d 664, 667–68 (Utah Ct. App. 1989) (discussing trend to limit rule of strict construction for indemnity agreement).

8. Utah Transit Auth. v. Greyhound Lines, Inc., 355 P.3d 947, 953 (Utah 2015); *Shell Oil*, 658 P.2d at 1189; Jankele v. Tex. Co., 54 P.2d 425 (Utah 1936) (stating that it has been declared to be good doctrine that no person may contract against his or her own negligence).

9. Union Pac. R.R. Co. v. El Paso Natural Gas Co., 408 P.2d 910 (Utah 1965).

10. *Shell Oil*, 658 P.2d at 1189.

2. EXCEPTIONS TO GENERAL RULES OF CONTRACTUAL INDEMNITY

Gross or wanton negligence or intentional misconduct will nullify an indemnity agreement.[11] An indemnity agreement may also be invalidated on public policy grounds where it is shown to have resulted from duress, deception, a disparity of bargaining power, or negotiations conducted at less than arm's length.[12] When determining whether an indemnity provision offends public policy, Utah courts look to the provision's context, subject, and overall purpose.[13] For example, while releases of liability for prospective negligence are generally enforceable, the Utah Supreme Court recently held that, as a matter of public policy, a parent may not release a minor's prospective claim to recover damages for negligence caused by another.[14]

An indemnity agreement that contravenes a statute or rule may also violate public policy.[15] Such a limitation is exemplified by Utah Code Annotated § 13-8-1, which provides that an agreement for the construction, repair, or maintenance of a building that purports to indemnify the promisee for liability resulting from the promisee's "sole negligence" is void and unenforceable as against public policy.[16] However, since building code violations, negligent construction, or other liabilities can arise from their finished product, builders and buyers may contract to place potential liability for inherent risks of construction sites and similar risks on one of the parties.[17]

Generally, public servants may not contract to escape potential liabilities for their ordinary negligence,[18] including state agencies, utilities, innkeepers, common carriers, and public warehousers.[19] Public servants are persons and entities that provide essential and indispensable services such as hospital care and police protection,[20] and include those who are duty bound to contract with all comers.[21]

3. INDEMNITY AGREEMENTS AS INSURED CONTRACTS

No Utah court has discussed whether an indemnity agreement is an "insured contract" under a liability insurance policy. Such an argument was advanced in *Smith v. United States Fidelity & Guarantee Co.*, but the court did not reach the issue.[22] Nevertheless, the case indicates that Utah courts might be receptive to such an argument in the proper factual situation.

4. OPERATION OF AN AGREEMENT TO INDEMNIFY REFERRING TO OR REQUIRING INSURANCE

Utah courts have held that where the parties have chosen by clear and equivocal language to require one party to indemnify the other from liability arising from any cause, including the indemnitee's own negligence, a further provision funding that indemnification by the purchase of liability insurance should be construed as any other contractual language,

11. Hawkins v. Peart, 37 P.3d 1062, 1065 (Utah 2001), *superseded on other grounds by*, Utah Code Ann. § 78B-4-203.
12. *Shell Oil*, 658 P.2d at 1189.
13. *Russ*, 905 P.2d at 907.
14. *Hawkins*, 37 P.3d at 1066.
15. *See id.* at 1066–67.
16. Utah Code Ann. § 13-8-1.
17. *Russ*, 905 P.2d at 907.
18. *Id.*
19. *Id.*
20. *Id.*
21. *Id.*
22. Gibbs M. Smith, Inc. v. U.S. Fidelity & Guar. Co., 949 P.2d 337, 342 (Utah 1997).

and is not subject to the strict construction rule.[23] Contracts to obtain insurance coverage to cover liability arising from an additional insured's own negligence will be upheld.[24]

Utah permits agreements to procure insurance on behalf of another, and such agreements do not violate Utah Code Annotated § 13-8-1, which prohibits indemnity for a contractor's sole negligence.[25] An agreement to obtain insurance is not an agreement of insurance; a person promising to obtain insurance does not by that promise become an insurer and is not responsible for personally insuring or indemnifying another for its own negligence.[26] An agreement to purchase insurance does not make the party agreeing to provide the insurance an indemnitor.[27]

The Utah Supreme Court distinguished the expansive duty of indemnity with no limits or bounds from an insurance procurement provision, which is "normally limited in substantive ways."[28] Thus, a mere agreement to purchase insurance does not constitute indemnity.

---

23. Utah Transit Auth. v. Greyhound Lines, Inc., 355 P.3d 947, 953 (Utah 2015).
24. *Id.* at 958; Freund v. Utah Power & Light Co., 793 P.2d 362, 373 (Utah 1990).
25. *Utah Transit Auth.*, 355 P.3d at 957.
26. *Id.*
27. *Id.*
28. *Id.*

Vermont

Julianna Malogolowkin
Hinckley, Allen, & Snyder LLP
Kurt Mullen and Sydney Pritchett
Nixon Peabody, LLP

1. GENERAL RULES OF CONTRACTUAL INDEMNITY

Vermont courts generally recognize the enforceability of express indemnification agreements contained within commercial contracts. Where the language of an indemnity agreement is clear, the intention and understanding of the parties must be taken to be that which their agreement declares.[1] "We interpret the indemnification provisions of a document as we do all other contract provisions—to give effect to the intent of the parties as their intent is expressed in their writing."[2] Thus, indemnification clauses expressly covering liability for an indemnitee's own negligence are enforceable.[3]

Where the language of an indemnity agreement "'clearly and unequivocally indicates that one party is to be indemnified, regardless of whether or not that injury was caused in part by that party, indemnification is required notwithstanding the indemnitee's active negligence.'"[4] Courts have not required specific or express language referring to the indemnitee's negligence in order to uphold an absolute indemnification clause.[5] Rather, broad, absolute indemnity language will be enforced if the intent of the parties is clear. Thus, the following clause in a lease agreement was enforced despite the landlord's own negligence: "Tenant agrees to indemnify, hold harmless, and defend Landlord from and against any and all losses, claims, liabilities, and expenses, including reasonable attorney's fees, if any, which Landlord may suffer or incur in connection with Tenant's use or misuse of premises."[6]

Even where the language of an indemnity agreement is clear and unambiguous, courts will only enforce such language in arm's-length business deals between commercial parties dividing risks and responsibilities.[7] Where there are issues of unequal bargaining power, fairness, and risk spreading, the courts may not enforce an absolute indemnity provision on public policy grounds.[8]

Also, since the courts are more likely to enforce contracts of indemnity where the parties are sophisticated entities with equal bargaining power, a federal district court has held that a third party may sustain an action for contractual indemnification against the employer of an injured party. The worker's compensation bar of Vermont Statutes Annotated, tit. 21, § 622 is not a bar to a claim for contractual indemnity from the employer.[9]

1. Folino v. Hampden Color & Chem. Co., 832 F. Supp. 757, 760–61 (D. Vt. 1993); Lamoille Grain Co. v. St. Johnsbury & Lamoille Cty. R.R., 369 A.2d 1389, 1390 (Vt. 1976).
2. Hamelin v. Simpson Paper (Vt.) Co., 702 A.2d 86, 88 (Vt. 1997).
3. Furlon v. Haystack Mountain Ski Area, 388 A.2d 403, 405 (Vt. 1978).
4. Hart v. Amour, 776 A.2d 420, 424 (Vt. 2001) (quoting and agreeing with Arizona Supreme Court in Cunningham v. Goettl Air Conditioning, Inc., 980 P.2d 489, 493 (Ariz. 1999)).
5. *Id.* at 422; *Hamelin*, 702 A.2d at 89; Loli of Vt., Inc. v. Stefandl, No. 2:94-CV-5, 1995 U.S. Dist. LEXIS 20235, at *6 (D. Vt. 1995) ("[A]lthough a specific reference to negligence liability is not essential to effectively immunize a party from such liability, in order for the agreement to have such an effect, "words conveying a similar import must appear." (quoting Colgan v. Agway, Inc., 553 A.2d 143, 146 (Vt. 1988)); *Lamoille*, 369 A.2d at 1390 ("We do not find that the failure of the contract to literally and specifically excuse the railroad for its own negligence precludes other verbiage from having that same effect.").
6. *Hart*, 776 A.2d at 422.
7. *Hamelin*, 702 A.2d at 89.
8. *Id.*
9. New England Tel. & Tel. Co. v. Central Vt. Pub. Serv. Corp., 391 F. Supp. 420, 428 (D. Vt. 1975).

2. EXCEPTIONS TO GENERAL RULES OF CONTRACTUAL INDEMNITY

Vermont is in the minority of states that have not passed legislation limiting the enforceability of contractual indemnity provisions in certain contexts.

3. INDEMNITY AGREEMENTS AS INSURED CONTRACTS

No Vermont court has specifically addressed the extent to which an insured is covered for its indemnification of another's tort liability where a policy specifically excludes contractually assumed liability, but excepts from this exclusion "insured" or "incidental" contracts. However, a clause in a liability insurance policy that excludes liability assumed by the insured by a contract does not exclude coverage of claims for which the law imposes primary liability on the insured where the insured agrees to protect another against secondary liability.[10]

4. OPERATION OF AN AGREEMENT TO INDEMNIFY REFERRING TO OR REQUIRING INSURANCE

Where parties agree that one of the parties will purchase insurance as part of an underlying agreement, "it is only natural that they assume that the insurance is for their mutual benefit and that the parties will look only to the insurance for loss coverage."[11] In the landlord-tenant context, the agreement of the parties that the landlord will procure insurance is interpreted to mean that the tenant is an additional insured on the insurance policy.[12] Thus, the tenant is protected against subrogation claims by the insurer.[13] The rationale for this rule is that "multiplicity of insurance policies and overlapping coverage in commercial settings is economically inefficient and results in higher overall costs."[14]

Vermont courts have not specifically addressed whether the existence of an insurance policy naming the indemnitee as an "additional insured" and providing coverage in an amount greater than the amount required to be procured in the underlying indemnification agreement entitles the indemnitee to coverage beyond the scope of the original agreement.

Vermont courts have addressed a similar situation regarding the right of an insurer to make a subrogation claim for insurance coverage paid that exceeded the amount of the insurance coverage required under an underlying construction contract. In *Behr v. Hook*, the owner of a home under construction was required under the standard AIA contract to purchase and maintain property insurance "in the amount of the initial contract plus any later modifications thereto for the entire work."[15] The contract also included a waiver of subrogation provision that required the owner, general contractor, and subcontractors to waive all rights against each other for damages "to the extent that there is property insurance obtained pursuant to" the contract.[16]

After paying the owner for the owner's entire loss following a fire, the insurer brought suit against the subcontractors, arguing that $181,000 of the $1.4 million paid to the owner was in excess of the contract provision that required the owner to obtain property insurance.[17] This amount covered cabinets, plumbing, and landscaping, which were specifically

10. Abajian v. Aetna Cas. & Ins. Co., 232 F. Supp. 710, 712 (D. Vt. 1964).
11. Fairchild Square Co. v. Green Mountain Bagel Bakery, Inc., 658 A.2d 31, 37 (Vt. 1995).
12. Union Mut. Fire Ins. Co. v. Joerg, 824 A.2d 586, 590 (Vt. 2003).
13. *Id.*
14. *Fairchild*, 658 A.2d at 37; *Joerg*, 824 A.2d at 591.
15. Behr v. Hook, 787 A.2d 499, 501 (Vt. 2001).
16. *Id.* at 501, 506.
17. *Id.* at 506.

excluded from the contract.[18] The insurer thus argued that since the contract provision only required the owner to obtain insurance "in the amount of the initial contract plus any later modifications," the amount for which the owner was compensated for that specifically excluded items was recoverable from the subcontractors.[19] The court disagreed. While the owner was not required to obtain insurance that would compensate him for anything more than "the initial contract plus any later modifications," the owner had gone beyond the requirement and obtained additional insurance coverage.[20] Since the waiver of subrogation provision applied to the extent of "property insurance obtained pursuant to the contract," the subcontractors received the benefit of the additional coverage procured by the owner.[21] Thus, the insurer could not bring a subrogation action against the subcontractors for the difference between the insurance provided and the insurance required.[22]

---

18. *Id.*
19. *Id.* at 501.
20. *Behr*, 658 A.2d at 506.
21. *Id.*
22. *Id.*

Virginia

Kathryn Kasper
Hancock, Daniel & Johnson, P.C.

1. GENERAL RULES OF CONTRACTUAL INDEMNITY

"'Virginia courts adhere to the 'plain meaning' rule of interpreting contracts, whereby clear and explicit language in a contract is to be taken in its ordinary signification, and, if the meaning is plain when so read, the instrument must be given effect accordingly.' . . . And, of course, '[i]ndemnity agreements are subject to general rules of contract construction.'"[1] In assessing a contractual right of indemnification under Virginia law, the language of the contract must be viewed as a whole, and clear and unambiguous terms should be construed "according to their plain meaning."[2] Of greatest importance are the parties' intentions, and courts must not insert by construction a term not specifically expressed in the agreement.[3]

An "indemnity agreement is enforceable even if it protects a party from its own negligence, so long as the terms of the agreement are 'clear and explicit.'"[4] "It is apparently not against the public policy of Virginia for one to contract against his own negligence in some situations, . . . [but] neither is there a strong policy supporting such agreements to the extent that they should be read into a contract which shows no ambiguity on its face."[5] When an agreement indemnifies the indemnitee "from and against all liability for injury or death" and only excepts the indemnitee's sole negligence, the agreement will be construed to cover the concurrent negligence of the indemnitor and indemnitee.[6]

Moreover, the exclusive remedy provision of the Virginia Workers' Compensation Act "does not invalidate an express indemnification agreement between an employer and a third party" and an action will still lie against the employer for contractual indemnity based on injuries sustained by an employee.[7] Similarly, although a common carrier cannot contract to relieve itself of its own negligence when acting as a common carrier, it can contract to be indemnified for its own negligence when it is not acting as a common carrier or transporter.[8]

2. EXCEPTIONS TO GENERAL RULES OF CONTRACTUAL INDEMNITY

Various public policy considerations place limits on the boundaries of enforceable indemnification in Virginia.

As stated above, common carriers and public utilities may not contract against liability for their own negligence in performing duties in their public capacities, but may enter into an indemnification agreement against their own negligence if they are acting in a purely private capacity.[9] Even if contracting as a private party, however, a common carrier or

1. Kraft Foods N. Am. v. Banner Eng'g & Sales, 446 F. Supp. 2d 551, 577 (E.D. Va. 2006) (internal citations omitted).
2. Am. Spirit Ins. Co. v. Owens, 541 S.E.2d 553, 555 (Va. 2001).
3. *Id.*
4. *In re Complaint of Christiansen Marine, Inc.*, No. 2:95cv896, 1996 U.S. Dist. LEXIS 10920, at *28 (E.D. Va. Apr. 11, 1996) (internal citations omitted). *See also* Estes Express Lines, Inc. v. Chopper Express, Inc., 641 S.E.2d 476 (Va. 2007).
5. Nat'l Motels, Inc. v. Howard Johnson, Inc., 373 F.2d 375, 379 (4th Cir. 1967).
6. Richardson-Wayland Elec. Corp. v. Va. Elec. & Power Co., 247 S.E.2d 465, 466 (Va. 1978).
7. Garrison v. Mustang Mfg. Co., 28 Va. Cir. 109 (Va. Cir. Ct. 1992).
8. C. & O. Ry. Co. v. Tel. Co., 224 S.E.2d 317, 322 (Va. 1976).
9. *Richardson-Wayland*, 219 Va. at 201–03.

public utility may not be indemnified for its own negligence in performing a duty owed to the public.[10] The statute applicable to common carriers provides as follows:

> No contract, receipt, rule, or regulation shall exempt any transportation company from the liability of a common carrier which would exist had no contract been made or entered into and no such contract, receipt, rule, or regulation for exemption from liability for injury or loss occasioned by the neglect or misconduct of such transportation company as a common carrier shall be valid. The liability referred to in this section shall mean the liability imposed by law upon a common carrier for any loss, damage, or injury to freight or passengers in its custody and care as a common carrier.[11]

Similarly, any provision in a construction contract that provides for indemnification for injury or damage caused solely by the indemnitee's negligence is void as against public policy. The applicable code section provides:

> Any provision contained in any contract relating to the construction, alteration, repair or maintenance of a building, structure or appurtenance thereto, including moving, demolition and excavation connected therewith, or any provision contained in any contract relating to the construction of projects other than buildings by which the contractor performing such work purports to indemnify or hold harmless another party to the contract against liability for damage arising out of bodily injury to persons or damage to property suffered in the course of performance of the contract, caused by or resulting solely from the negligence of such other party or his agents or employees, is against public policy and is void and unenforceable. This section applies to such contracts between contractors and any public body, as defined in § 2.2-4301.
>
> This section shall not affect the validity of any insurance contract, workers' compensation, or any agreement issued by an admitted insurer.[12]

Finally, certain indemnification clauses in contracts involving design professionals are void as against public policy. More specifically:

> Any provision contained in any contract relating to the planning or design of a building, structure or appurtenance thereto, including moving, demolition or excavation connected therewith, or any provision contained in any contract relating to the planning or design of construction projects other than buildings by which the architect or professional engineer performing such work purports to indemnify or hold harmless another party to the contract against liability for damage arising out of bodily injury to persons or damage to property suffered in the course of the performance of the contract, caused by or resulting solely from the negligence of such other party, his agents or employees, is against public policy and is void and unenforceable.
>
> This section shall apply to such contracts between an architect or professional engineer and any public body as defined in § 2.2-4301. Every provision contained in a contract between an architect or professional engineer and a public body relating to the planning or design of a building, structure, or appurtenance thereto, including moving, demolition, or excavation connected therewith, or relating to the planning or design of construction projects other than buildings by which the

10. *Id.*

11. VA. CODE ANN. § 56-119 (2006).

12. VA. CODE ANN. § 11-4.1 (The provisions of this section do not apply to any provision of any contract entered into prior to July 1, 1973.).

architect or professional engineer performing such work purports to indemnify or hold harmless the public body against liability is against public policy and is void and unenforceable. This section shall not be construed to alter or affect any provision in such a contract that purports to indemnify or hold harmless the public body against liability for damage arising out of the negligent acts, errors or omissions, recklessness, or intentionally wrongful conduct of the architect or professional engineer in performance of the contract.

This section shall not affect the validity of any insurance contract, worker's compensation, or any agreement issued by an admitted insurer.[13]

3. INDEMNITY AGREEMENTS AS INSURED CONTRACTS

The Fourth Circuit, applying Virginia law, has held with little discussion that an indemnity agreement by which the insured assumes the tort liability of another is an "insured contract" for purposes of the exception in the form commercial general liability insurance policy to the exclusion for contractually assumed liability.[14]

4. OPERATION OF AN AGREEMENT TO INDEMNIFY REFERRING TO OR REQUIRING INSURANCE

Although not addressed by any Virginia court, the Fourth Circuit has predicted that Virginia courts would rely on valid, enforceable indemnification agreements to give context to and determine the allocation of liability in an insurance dispute.[15] Relying on an Eighth Circuit decision, the Fourth Circuit adopted the view that an indemnity agreement between the insureds or a contract with an indemnification clause may shift an entire loss to a particular insurer. In *St. Paul Fire & Marine Ins. Co. v. Am. Int'l Specialty Lines Ins. Co.*, the Fourth Circuit relied on an indemnity clause to place the risk of loss for all claims on the indemnitee's insurer, even though the indemnitors had procured their own policies for their liabilities. Holding that the scope of the underlying indemnity agreement should be decided simultaneously with the coverage issues, the Fourth Circuit predicted that a Virginia court would give priority to the underlying indemnity agreement to allocate responsibility among insurers where there was a concomitant agreement by the parties to purchase insurance to cover losses under the contract.[16]

---

13. VA. CODE ANN. § 11-4.4.

14. *See* KBS, Inc. v. Great Am. Ins. Co., No. 3:04cv730, 2006 U.S. Dist. LEXIS 88520 (E.D. Va. Nov. 7, 2006); St. Paul Fire & Marine Ins. Co. v. Am. Int'l Specialty Lines Ins. Co., 365 F.3d 263, 276 (4th Cir. 2004).

15. *Id.*

16. *Id.*

Washington

Bryana L. Blessinger
Bullivant Houser Bailey, P.C.

1. GENERAL RULES OF CONTRACTUAL INDEMNITY

In Washington, the general rule is that contracting parties may agree to indemnify as they choose according to Washington's general rules of contract construction.[1] The parties' intent controls the interpretation of the indemnification provision, and the intent typically must be gathered from the contract as a whole.[2] Indemnity clauses are "to be viewed realistically, recognizing the intent of the parties to allocate as between them the cost or expense of the risk of losses or damages arising out of performance of the contract."[3] If the contractual language is clear and unambiguous, ambiguity will not be read into the contract.[4] And if the indemnity provision is ambiguous, the ambiguity will be resolved against the drafter of the contract.[5]

Indemnification for an indemnitee's sole negligence is permissible so long as the arrangement is not prohibited by statute or public policy.[6] However, these clauses "are not favored and are to be clearly drawn and strictly construed, with any ambiguity resolved against the indemnitor.[7] "[T]he general rules that disfavor an agreement to indemnify an indemnitee against its own negligence do not render such a clause void or unenforceable as a matter of law. Instead, what these rules require is that . . . the agreement must be clearly spelled out."[8] These provisions are enforceable where the language of the agreement unquestionably demonstrates that the intent of the parties was to provide for indemnification of an indemnitee's sole negligence.[9] Such intention must be "expressed in clear and unequivocal terms."[10] Washington courts currently require "that more specific language be used to evidence a clear and unequivocal intention to indemnify the indemnitee's own negligence."[11] This requirement represents a departure from the more general rule of looking at "the entire[ty] of the contract" to determine the parties' intent.[12]

When contracting parties agree that indemnity will be provided "whether or not caused by [the indemnitee's] . . . negligence," such language is sufficient to meet the more specific requirement permitting indemnification for sole negligence.[13] Keeping in mind that the focus of the triggering of indemnification clauses is causation and not negligence,[14] liability rather than negligence may be the "triggering mechanism of an indemnity contract."[15]

---

1. Jones v. Strom Const. Co., Inc., 527 P.2d 1115, 1117–18 (Wash. 1974); *see also* Donner v. Blue, 347 P.3d 881, 885–86 (Wash. Ct. App. 2015); Nunez v. Am. Bldg. Maint. Co. W., 190 P.3d 56, 58 (Wash. Ct. App. 2008).
2. *Jones*, 527 P.2d at 1117.
3. *Id.* at 1118; *see also Donner*, 347 P.3d at 885 (quoting *Jones*).
4. *Jones*, 527 P.2d at 1118.
5. *Id.*
6. *See* Nw. Airlines v. Hughes Air Corp., 702 P.2d 1192, 1193 (Wash. 1985); *see also* Snohomish Cty. Pub. Transp. Benefit Area Corp. v. FirstGroup Am., Inc., 271 P.3d 850, 852–53 (Wash. 2012).
7. *Jones*, 527 P.2d at 1118; *see also Donner*, 347 P.3d at 885 (quoting *Jones*).
8. McDowell v. Austin Co., 710 P.2d 192, 196 (Wash. 1985) (internal citations and punctuation omitted).
9. Newport Yacht Basin Ass'n of Condo. Owners v. Supreme Nw., Inc., 285 P.3d 70, 79 (Wash. Ct. App. 2012).
10. *Nw. Airlines*, 702 P.2d at 1194 (citing 41 AM. JUR. 2d *Indemnity* § 15 (1968) and 42 C.J.S. *Indemnity* § 7 (1944)).
11. *See id.* (citing Dirk v. Amerco Mktg. Co., 565 P.2d 90 (Wash. 1977)).
12. *Id.*
13. *Id.*
14. *Nunez*, 190 P.3d at 59 (citing Cont'l. Cas. Co. v. Municipality of Metro. Seattle, 405 P.2d 581, 584 (Wash. 1965)).
15. *McDowell*, 710 P.2d at 194.

Thus, an agreement in which one agrees to "indemnify and save harmless . . . against *all liability* for personal injury, including death resulting therefrom, . . . *caused* or alleged to have been caused, directly or indirectly, by an act or omission, negligent or otherwise," is enforceable because it clearly spells out the contracting parties' allocation of responsibilities.[16]

In general, a third party can enforce a written indemnity agreement against an employer for losses the third party has paid to the employer's employee.[17] In the construction context, the Revised Code of Washington § 4.24.115 (2012) allows for the exclusive remedy provision in the worker's compensation laws to be circumvented in a written indemnity agreement by an express statement that the employer waives immunity under the Washington State Industrial Insurance Act, with additional requirements to be valid and effective.[18]

2. EXCEPTIONS TO GENERAL RULES OF CONTRACTUAL INDEMNITY

Revised Code of Washington § 4.24.115 limits parties' abilities to enter into indemnity agreements regarding construction contracts. Section 4.24.115(1)(a) specifically renders void and unenforceable as against public policy indemnity provisions that involve the sole negligence of the indemnitee in the contexts enumerated in § 4.24.115(1).[19] Subsection 1 of the statute provides as follows:

> (1) A covenant, promise, agreement, or understanding in, or in connection with or collateral to, a contract or agreement relative to the construction, alteration, repair, addition to, subtraction from, improvement to, or maintenance of, any building, highway, road, railroad, excavation, or other structure, project, development, or improvement attached to real estate, including moving and demolition in connection therewith, a contract or agreement for architectural, landscape architectural, engineering, or land surveying services, or a motor carrier transportation contract, purporting to indemnify, including the duty and cost to defend, against liability for damages arising out of such services or out of bodily injury to persons or damage to property:
> (a) Caused by or resulting from the sole negligence of the indemnitee, his or her agents or employees is against public policy and is void and unenforceable;
> (b) Caused by or resulting from the concurrent negligence of (i) the indemnitee or the indemnitee's agents or employees, and (ii) the indemnitor or the indemnitor's agents or employees, is valid and enforceable only to the extent of the indemnitor's negligence and only if the agreement specifically and expressly provides therefor, and may waive the indemnitor's immunity under industrial insurance, Title 51 RCW, only if the agreement specifically and expressly provides therefor and the waiver was mutually negotiated by the parties. This subsection applies to agreements entered into after June 11, 1986.[20]

Upon a finding that an indemnity provision purports to indemnify for a party's sole negligence in the construction context, coupled with a factual finding that the injury at issue was caused by the indemnitee's sole negligence, § 4.24.115(1)(a) renders the agreement ineffective.[21] The purpose of the rule is to "prevent injustice, and to insure that a contracting

16. *Id.* at 193–94.
17. Redford v. City of Seattle, 615 P.2d 1285, 1287 (Wash. 1980); Truck Ins. Exch. v. BRE Props., Inc., 81 P.3d 929, 931 (Wash. Ct. App. 2003).
18. *See* WASH. REV. CODE § 4.24.115(1)(b) (2012) and discussion, *infra*.
19. WASH. REV. CODE § 4.24.115(1)(a).
20. WASH. REV. CODE § 4.24.115.
21. *See McDowell*, 710 P.2d at 194.

party has fair notice that a large and ruinous award can be assessed against it solely by reason of negligence attributable to the other contracting party."[22]

Section 4.24.115(1)(b) declares certain indemnification agreements regarding liability caused by or resulting from concurrent negligence of the indemnitee and indemnitor to be valid and enforceable, which would include an agreement by a subcontractor to indemnify a general contractor against liability for damages caused by the concurrent negligence of the subcontractor or its agents or employees.[23] However, § 4.24.115(1)(b) sets significant limits on this category of indemnification agreements, including the restriction that the subcontractor is permitted to indemnify the general contractor only to the extent of the subcontractor's negligence.[24] To satisfy the statute, contractual language must specifically state that the agreement provides indemnity for concurrent negligence to the extent of the indemnitor's negligence.[25] Furthermore, while § 4.24.115(1)(b) anticipates claims against a general contractor for workplace injury to a subcontractor's employee by allowing a waiver of the indemnitor's immunity under industrial insurance statutes, it requires that the indemnity agreement must "specifically and expressly provide" the specific waiver and the waiver must have been "mutually negotiated" by the parties.[26]

3. INDEMNITY AGREEMENTS AS INSURED CONTRACTS

General liability policies typically contain a specific exclusion for liabilities that a policyholder assumes through a contract with a third party. Many general liability policies also contain an exception to this exclusion, providing coverage for an "insured contract," a phrase that the insurance policy may or may not expressly define. Washington courts will construe the policy's "insured contract" exception to the exclusion to determine the scope of coverage provided by that exception.[27] The concept of an "insured contract" generally contemplates a contract in which the insured assumes tort liability it would not have had absent the subject contract.[28] An agreement to indemnify another for the other's tort liability is typically considered an "insured contract" within the exception to the exclusion. Washington courts will give effect to an "insured contract" provision to provide coverage for an indemnity agreement depending upon the scope of the "insured contract" provision.[29]

Even though an indemnity agreement may qualify as an "insured contract" pursuant to the provisions of an insurance policy, coverage is not automatic for tort liability assumed under the indemnity agreement. Washington courts will analyze whether other policy exclusions clearly exclude coverage for the particular liability at issue. For example, with respect to an insurance policy containing an "insured contract" exception to the contractual liability exclusion and defining "insured contract" as "a contract for a lease of premises," the Washington Court of Appeals has held the general exclusion for damage to property

---

22. *Id.* at 195 (citing Joe Adams & Son v. McCann Constr. Co., 475 S.W.2d 721, 722 (Tex. 1971)).

23. *Cf.* Millican v. N.A. Degerstrom, Inc., 313 P.3d 1215, 1221 (Wash. Ct. App. 2013) (citing Gilbert H. Moen Co. v. Island Steel Erectors, Inc., 912 P.2d 472, 480 (Wash. 1996)), *rev. denied*, 320 P.3d 718 (Wash. 2014).

24. Wash. Rev. Code § 4.24.115(1)(b).

25. *See Moen*, 912 P.2d at 474. The agreement at issue in *Moen* provided that "[Island's] duty to indemnify [Moen] for liability for damages arising out of bodily injury to persons or damage to property caused by or resulting from the concurrent negligence of (a) [Moen or its] agents or employees, and (b) [Island or its] agents or employees, shall apply only to the extent of negligence of [Island or its] agents or employees." *Id.*

26. Wash. Rev. Code § 4.24.115(1)(b).

27. *Cf.* Int'l Marine Underwriters v. ABCD Marine, LLC, 313 P.3d 395, 399–405 (Wash. 2013) (although the insurer conceded that the indemnity agreement at issue was an "insured contract," the Supreme Court analyzed policy language, extrinsic evidence, and relevant business entity statutes to determine whether a specific individual was covered under the "insured contract" definition).

28. *Truck Ins. Exch.*, 81 P.3d at 934–35.

29. *See, e.g.*, *id.* at 935.

rented by the insured is sufficient to overcome the extension of coverage for the insured contract.[30]

4. OPERATION OF AN AGREEMENT TO INDEMNIFY REFERRING TO OR REQUIRING INSURANCE

Several Washington cases analyzing indemnity agreements involve contracts that contain provisions regarding insurance policy procurement. However, Washington courts have not yet extensively discussed the effect a contractual provision requiring the procurement of insurance has on either the indemnity obligation itself or the scope of coverage provided by the procured insurance. Washington courts have noted that enforcing third-party indemnification agreements in certain situations, such as where liability may otherwise be barred due to worker's compensation immunity, "allows contractors to allocate 'responsibility to purchase insurance' according to their negotiated allocation of risk and potential liabilities."[31] Whether the indemnity contract is unenforceable due to a violation of Revised Code of Washington § 4.24.115 or some other limitation on indemnity agreements may not be relevant to the scope of the insurance policy's coverage.[32]

In *Truck Insurance Exchange v. BRE Properties, Inc.*, a contractor and subcontractor entered into an indemnification agreement whereby the subcontractor was contractually required to indemnify the contractor against claims caused by its acts, omissions, or negligence.[33] The subcontractor was further contractually required to procure an insurance policy naming the contractor as an additional insured.[34] Despite policy exclusions for injury to an employee of "the insured," the court held that the insurance policy extended coverage to both the contractor and the subcontractor where one of the subcontractor's employees was injured. The procured insurance policy covered the subcontractor's indemnity obligation because the indemnity agreement was an "insured contract" under the policy.[35]

A valid "waiver of subrogation" provision in an indemnification agreement insulates only the promisor from liability to the extent of the promisee's insurance coverage.[36] For example, an indemnification provision that requires that the owner and general contractor obtain insurance to cover all claims arising under the contract between the owner and general contractor, and expressly waives subrogation rights to the extent of insurance coverage, affords no relief to a subcontractor that is not a party to the contract itself.[37] Even when the parties arguably intend a "standard" waiver that would have included subcontractors and provided that the waiver applied to *all* claims, a subcontractor cannot take advantage of the waiver if the waiver as drafted does not actually include subcontractors.[38]

Washington courts reject the rule that "co-insured status for any loss under a builder's risk policy automatically insulates the co-insured from subrogation by the insurer for damage to all property covered therein."[39] Rather, the scope of protection rests soundly within the parameters of the indemnification agreement itself.[40]

30. Cle Elum Bowl, Inc. v. N. Pac. Ins. Co. Inc., 981 P.2d 872, 874, 876 (Wash. Ct. App. 1999); *cf.* Mut. of Enumclaw Ins. Co. v. Patrick Archer Constr., Inc., 97 P.3d 751, 757–59 (Wash. Ct. App. 2004) (finding that a specific exclusion overrides a general grant of coverage by endorsement, and no ambiguity results when the two provisions arguably cover the same subject matter).

31. *Truck Ins. Exch.* 81 P.3d at 934 (quoting *McDowell,* 710 P.2d at 196); *see also Moen*, 912 P.2d at 476 (quoting *McDowell*, 710 P.2d at 196).

32. *Int'l Marine,* 313 P.3d at 405 (discussing that a violation of Wash. Rev. Code § 4.24.115 or the principles of *McDowell* would be relevant to the underlying action between the parties to the indemnity agreement but not the declaratory judgment action regarding the scope of coverage).

33. 81 P.3d 929, 930–31 (Wash. Ct. App. 2003).

34. *Id.* at 930.

35. *Id.* at 931, 934–35 (insured contract was exception to the exclusion for injury to an employee of the insured).

36. *See* Touchet Valley Grain Growers, Inc. v. Opp & Seibold Gen. Constr., Inc., 831 P.2d 724, 725 (Wash. 1992).

37. *Id.* at 728–29.

38. *Id.*

39. W. Wash. Corp. of Seventh-Day Adventists v. Ferrellgas, Inc., 7 P.3d 861, 870 (Wash. Ct. App. 2000).

40. *Id.*

West Virginia

Grace E. Hurney and Al Emch
Jackson Kelly, PLLC

1. GENERAL RULES OF CONTRACTUAL INDEMNITY

Contractual agreements to indemnify are enforceable.[1] "Ordinary rules of contract construction apply" when interpreting the language of an indemnity contract.[2] This includes the rules governing the requisites and validity of contracts.[3] "[A] valid written agreement using plain and unambiguous language is to be enforced according to its plain intent and should not be construed."[4]

Except as discussed below, indemnity agreements are encouraged in West Virginia. "[P]ublic policy demands that indemnity agreements be permitted unless they go beyond a mere allocation of potential joint and several liability and indemnify against the sole negligence of the indemnitee without an appropriate insurance fund[.]"[5]

2. EXCEPTIONS TO GENERAL RULES OF CONTRACTUAL INDEMNITY

Agreements to indemnify a party against its sole negligence in connection with construction activities are void and unenforceable.[6] West Virginia Code § 55-8-14 states:

> A covenant, promise, agreement or understanding in or in connection with or collateral to a contract or agreement entered into on or after the effective date of this section [June 6, 1975], relative to the construction, alteration, repair, addition to, subtraction from, improvement to or maintenance of any building, highway, road, railroad, water, sewer, electrical or gas distribution system, excavation or other structure, project, development or improvement attached to real estate, including moving and demolition in connection therewith, purporting to indemnify against liability for damages arising out of bodily injury to persons or damage to property caused by or resulting from the sole negligence of the indemnitee, his agents or employees is against public policy and is void and unenforceable and no action shall be maintained thereon.

The code section does not affect indemnification agreements that exclude indemnification for an indemnitee's sole negligence.[7]

However, courts will not automatically void an agreement to indemnify, even for a party's sole negligence. Rather, the courts will "void a broad indemnity agreement *only*: (1) if the indemnitee is found by the trier-of-fact to be solely (100 percent) [at fault]; and (2) it cannot be inferred from the contract that there was a proper agreement to purchase insurance for the benefit of all concerned."[8] "A contract that provides in substance that A

1. *See* Dalton v. Childress Serv. Corp., 432 S.E.2d 98, 101 (W. Va. 1993).
2. *See* Vankirk v. Green Constr. Co., 466 S.E.2d 782, 788 (W. Va. 1995).
3. Dawson v. Norfolk & W. Ry. Co., 475 S.E.2d 10, 17 (W. Va. 1996).
4. *Id.*
5. *Dalton*, 432 S.E.2d at 101.
6. W. Va. Code § 55-8-14 (2017).
7. *Id.*; *Dalton*, 432 S.E.2d at 102.
8. *Dalton*, 432 S.E.2d at 101.

shall purchase insurance to protect B against actions arising from B's sole negligence *does not* violate the statute as public policy encourages both the allocation of risks and the purchase of insurance."[9] Consequently, a facially void indemnity agreement will be saved by an agreement to purchase insurance covering the indemnity obligation.

Employers who participate in the worker's compensation scheme are protected from common law liability for the negligent injury or death of an employee.[10] This protection extends to suits filed by third parties against the employer.[11] Liability against an employer is exclusive under the statute unless the employer waives the immunity by entering into a contractual agreement to indemnify.[12]

3. INDEMNITY AGREEMENTS AS INSURED CONTRACTS

Courts recognize that an insured's agreement to indemnify another constitutes an "insured contract" within the meaning of a general liability policy.[13] In a general commercial liability policy, a party with an "insured contract" stands in the shoes of the insured for coverage purposes.[14]

4. OPERATION OF AN AGREEMENT TO INDEMNIFY REFERRING TO OR REQUIRING INSURANCE

As noted above, a third party stands in the shoes of the insured pursuant to an "insured contract."[15] As also noted, the purchase of insurance will remedy an allegedly void indemnity agreement based upon the agreement to indemnify for another's sole negligence. In *Dalton v. Childress Service Corp.*, a party agreed to indemnify another against all liabilities attributed to the indemnitor, (arguably) including liability for the indemnitee's sole negligence.[16] The agreement further required the indemnitor to obtain insurance that covered all of the indemnitor's potential liability under the indemnity clause.[17] The ultimate issue was whether the indemnitee could enforce the indemnity agreement.[18] In finding the indemnity clause enforceable, the court characterized the clause as "really only an agreement to purchase insurance."[19]

---

9. *Id.*

10. W. Va. Code § 23-2-6 (2017).

11. Belcher v. J. H. Fletcher & Co., 498 F. Supp. 629, 631 (S.D. W. Va. 1980); Pasquale v. Ohio Power Co., 418 S.E.2d 738, 748 (W. Va. 1992) (citing Syl. Pt. 6, Sydenstricker v. Unipunch Prods., Inc., 288 S.E.2d 511 (W. Va. 1982)).

12. *Belcher*, 498 F. Supp. at 631; Valloric v. Dravo Corp., 357 S.E.2d 207, 210 n.3 (W. Va. 1987).

13. Marlin v. Wetzel Cty. Bd. of Educ., 569 S.E.2d 462, 468–69 (W. Va. 2002).

14. *Id.* at Syl. Pt. 4 (citing Syl. Pt. 7, Consolidation Coal Co. v. Boston Old Colony Ins. Co., 508 S.E.2d 102 (W. Va. 1998)).

15. *Id.*

16. *Dalton*, 432 S.E.2d at 99.

17. *Id.* at 100.

18. *See id.* at 99.

19. *Id.* at 102.

Wisconsin

Laura Hanson
Meagher & Geer, PLLP

1. GENERAL RULES OF CONTRACTUAL INDEMNITY

Wisconsin courts have consistently upheld the validity of indemnity contracts.[1]

> It is a settled rule in this state that indemnity agreements are to be broadly construed where they deal with the negligence of the indemnitor, but strictly construed where the indemnitee seeks to be indemnified for his own negligence . . . . The obligation to indemnify an indemnitee for its own negligence must be clearly and unequivocally expressed in the agreement. General language will not suffice.[2]

A contract of indemnity will not be construed so as to indemnify one against loss or damage resulting from one's own negligent acts unless such intention is expressed in clear and unequivocal terms.[3] If the parties agree to indemnify the indemnitee for its own negligence, such indemnity agreements are strictly construed and must satisfy the conspicuousness standards in Wisconsin Statutes § 401.201(f) (2014).[4] "'Conspicuous' with reference to a term, means so written, displayed, or presented that a reasonable person against which it is to operate ought to have noticed it."[5]

The rule of strict construction for contracts to indemnify an indemnitee for its own negligence cannot be used to defeat the clear intent of the parties:

> If the agreement clearly states that the indemnitee is to be covered for losses occasioned by his own negligent acts, the indemnitee may recover under the contract. Additionally, if it is clear that the purpose and unmistakable intent of the parties in entering into the contract was for no other reason than to cover losses occasioned by the indemnitee's own negligence, indemnification may be afforded.[6]

2. EXCEPTIONS TO GENERAL RULES OF CONTRACTUAL INDEMNITY

The Wisconsin Court of Appeals, in *Fabco Equipment, Inc. v. Kreilkamp Trucking, Inc.*, considered a contract of indemnity in the context of a multi-count lawsuit where some claims fell within the indemnity agreement while other claims did not.[7] The court held that the

1. Herchelroth v. Mahar, 153 N.W.2d 6 (Wis. 1967); Mustas v. Inland Constr., Inc., 120 N.W.2d 95 (Wis. 1963); Mikula v. Miller Brewing Co., 701 N.W.2d 613 (Wis. Ct. App. 2005).

2. Roto Zip Tool Corp. v. Design Concepts, 713 N.W.2d 191 (Wis. Ct. App. 2006) (quoting Deminsky v. Arlington Plastics Mach., 638 N.W.2d 331, 340 (Wis. Ct. App. 2001), *aff'd as modified and remanded*, 657 N.W.2d 411 (Wis. 2003), and Spivey v. Great Atl. & Pac. Tea Co., 255 N.W.2d 469, 472 (Wis. 1977)).

3. *Spivey*, 255 N.W.2d at 472; *but see Herchelroth*, 153 N.W.2d at 9 (construing an indemnification agreement drawn in general language as intending to protect the indemnitee for its own negligent acts; however, it was clear from the record that no other purpose could be served by the agreement other than to protect the indemnitee's responsibility for his negligent acts).

4. Deminsky v. Arlington Plastics Mach., 657 N.W.2d 411, 422–23 (Wis. 2003).

5. Wis. Stat. § 401.201(f) (2014) (formerly Wis. Stat. § 401.201(10)).

6. *Spivey*, 225 N.W.2d at 472; *see also* Hastreiter v. Karau Bldgs, Inc., 205 N.W.2d 162 (Wis. 1973) (reasoning it was the intent of the parties to hold the indemnitee harmless even though he was negligent, because there was an explicit provision requiring a public liability insurance that was intended to protect the indemnitee from the effects of his own negligence).

7. Fabco Equip., Inc. v. Kreilkamp Trucking, Inc., 841 N.W.2d 542 (Wis. Ct. App. 2013).

plain language of the indemnity contract required division of the indemnity obligation on a proportional basis between indemnified and non-indemnified claims. The specifics of *Fabco* begin with the relationship between the indemnitee and indemnitor: FABCO—the indemnitee—was a construction equipment leasing company and Kreilkamp—the indemnitor—was a transportation company hired to transport equipment for FABCO.[8] The dispute between the two companies arose after a Krielkamp employee was killed when a piece of FABCO rental equipment fell on him in the process of unloading the equipment with a forklift.[9] Following the death, the employee's estate and widow brought claims against FABCO and Terex, the manufacturer of the equipment, alleging that negligence by each caused the death.[10] FABCO sought defense and indemnity, which Kreilkamp denied.[11]

The indemnity agreement read:

> *Indemnity.* [Kreilkamp] agrees that it will defend, indemnify, and hold harmless [FABCO] from and against all claims, lawsuits, demands, liability, costs and expenses, including reasonable attorney's fees and other costs of defense, caused by, arising out of, or connected with the performance of [Kreilkamp] hereunder and which result in any injury to, or the death of any persons, damage to or loss of property, including cargo, and any disputes involving the performance of services hereunder by third parties; provided, however, that [Kreilkamp] shall not be required to defend, indemnify or hold harmless [FABCO] to the extent any claims, lawsuits, demands, liability, cost or expenses are the result of [FABCO's] negligence.[12]

In interpreting this provision, the Wisconsin Court of Appeals held that "the provision clearly indicates that FABCO can recover in circumstances where it is in part causally negligent; it just cannot recover for 'the extent' of its own causal negligence."[13] Therefore, FABCO was entitled to defense and indemnity at Krielkamp's expense subject to a reduction for the percentage of causal negligence ultimately attributable to FABCO.[14]

Beyond *Fabco*, another potential issue is Wisconsin Statutes § 895.447, which voids agreements in construction contracts that limit or eliminate tort liability.[15] However, "[s]ince the statute limits the common law right to freely contract, courts interpret it narrowly, placing the least possible restriction on the common law right."[16] Therefore, this statute does not necessarily extend to indemnity agreements.

The statute specifically provides:

> (1) Any provision to limit or eliminate tort liability as a part of or in connection with any contract, covenant or agreement relating to the construction, alteration, repair or maintenance of a building, structure, or other work related to construction, including any moving, demolition or excavation, is against public policy and void.
> (2) This section does not apply to any insurance contract or workers compensation plan.

8. *Id.* at 545.
9. *Id.*
10. *Id.*
11. *Id.*
12. *Id.* at 547.
13. *Id.* at 548.
14. *Id.* at 548–49.
15. Wis. Stat. § 895.447 (2014) (formerly Wis. Stat. § 895.49).
16. Gerdmann v. U.S. Fire Ins. Co., 350 N.W.2d 730, 734 (Wis. Ct. App. 1984) (citing Wis. Bankers Ass'n v. Mut. Sav & Loan Ass'n, 291 N.W.2d 869, 876–77 (Wis. 1980)).

(3) This section shall not apply to any provision of any contract, covenant or agreement entered into prior to July 1, 1978.[17]

The Wisconsin Court of Appeals explained the impact of the statute in *Gerdmann v. U.S. Fire Insurance Co.*[18] In that case, the contractor contended that an indemnity clause requiring the contractor to indemnify the owner was void pursuant to Wisconsin Statutes § 895.447.[19] The court held that the indemnification clause was not void under § 895.447 because it did not attempt to relieve the owner from liability, but merely required the contractor to indemnify the owner against loss that stemmed from liability.[20] The court explained that the statute did not void indemnity agreements, and should be narrowly construed.[21]

3. INDEMNITY AGREEMENTS AS INSURED CONTRACTS

While the Wisconsin Court of Appeals has acknowledged the "insured contract" exception to the contractual liability exclusion in the form general liability policy,[22] it has not applied the exception. In *Nu-Pak, Inc. v. Wine Specialists International, Ltd.*, the indemnitee sought coverage under the indemnitor's policy on the theory that the indemnitor had assumed tort liabilities.[23] The claim, however, was based on the indemnitor's *own* tort liabilities, as opposed to any that it had assumed under the indemnity agreement. The court held that the "insured contract" provision did not apply as the liabilities were the indemnitor's own and not those of a third party.

4. OPERATION OF AN AGREEMENT TO INDEMNIFY REFERRING TO OR REQUIRING INSURANCE

Under Wisconsin law, parties to a contract may allocate the risk of loss by agreeing that one party shall maintain insurance to save harmless the other party from liability. An insurance procurement clause will be construed to provide the extent of coverage required by the indemnity agreement.[24]

In *Michael A.P. v. Solsrud*, a subcontractor's injured employee brought suit against the general contractor.[25] In turn, the general contractor sued the subcontractor and his insurer based on an indemnity agreement. The indemnity contract required the subcontractor to procure commercial liability coverage. Since the subcontractor's obligation to indemnify the general contractor was limited to liability incurred because of the subcontractor's negligence, the court similarly limited the insurance coverage to the extent of the indemnity obligation.[26] Thus, an insurer's obligation likely will be limited to the scope of its insured's indemnity obligation.

---

17. Wis. Stat. § 895.447 (2014).
18. *Gerdmann*, 350 N.W.2d 730.
19. *Id.* at 733 (formerly Wis. Stat. § 895.49).
20. *Id.* at 734–35. *See also* Abrohams v. Wis. Tel. Co., 367 N.W.2d 242 (Wis. Ct. App. 1985) (holding an indemnity agreement between a company and a contractor was not void under Wis. Stat. § 895.49 because the agreement merely made the contractor the insurer if damages resulted and did not limit or eliminate the company's tort liability).
21. *Id.* at 734.
22. Nu-Pak, Inc. v. Wine Specialties Int'l, Ltd., 643 N.W.2d 848, 855–56 (Wis. Ct. App. 2002).
23. *Id.*
24. *See* Michael A.P. v. Solsrud, 514 N.W.2d 879 (Wis. Ct. App. 1994).
25. *Id.*
26. *Id.*

Wyoming

Gregory E. Van Houten
Haynes and Boone, LLP

1. GENERAL RULES OF CONTRACTUAL INDEMNITY

Wyoming courts consistently have recognized and enforced contracts of indemnity, except where such agreements are against public policy.[1] However, to enforce a contract of indemnity or any other contract claiming to relieve one from the consequences of his or her failure to exercise ordinary care, the parties must express their intention very clearly.[2]

As a general rule, "a contract of indemnity will not be construed to indemnify the indemnitee against losses resulting from his own negligent acts unless such intention is expressed in clear and unequivocal terms, or unless no other meaning can be ascribed to it."[3] Under this rule of strict construction, an agreement that stated only that the "Contractor shall indemnify and hold Company harmless against . . . injury or death of any person . . . resulting directly or indirectly from any and all acts or omissions of Contractor . . . in connection with the performance of any work provided for herein" would not cover the indemnitee's own negligence.[4] Further, "mere general, broad and seemingly all inclusive language in an indemnifying agreement has been said not to be sufficient to impose liability for the indemnitee's own negligence."[5]

Courts look on contracts that serve to exculpate one from consequences of his or her own negligent actions with disfavor.[6] "Therefore, an agreement for indemnity is construed strictly against the indemnitee, particularly when the indemnitee was the drafter of the instrument."[7] The test is "whether the contract language specifically focuses attention on the fact that by the agreement the indemnitor was assuming liability for indemnitee's own negligence."[8] For example, a provision in a subcontract that obligated the subcontractor to the general contractor *in the same respect that the general contractor was obligated to the owner under the prime contract* was "not a clear and unequivocal agreement to indemnify the general contractor on account of its own negligence."[9]

"In the cases where there is an express contractual provision for indemnity and the parties raise as alternative theories of indemnity, breach of contract or passive negligence, the courts usually hold that the express contractual provision for indemnity governs, and that the theories of breach of contract or passive negligence should not be allowed to enlarge upon or expand the express contractual provision for indemnity."[10] The rationale behind this policy is that the parties knowingly and "adequately set out their intention in the express contractual agreement with respect to indemnity."[11] It is important to enforce contractual indemnity provisions due to the fact that the parties themselves have dealt with the question of indemnity in the written contract and have intended for this specific issue

1. Northwinds of Wyo., Inc. v. Phillips Petroleum Co., 779 P.2d 753 (Wyo. 1989).
2. *See id.* at 758.
3. *Id.* (citing Wyo. Johnson, Inc. v. Stag Indus., Inc., 662 P.2d 96 (Wyo. 1983)).
4. *Id.*
5. *Wyo. Johnson, Inc.*, 662 P.2d at 99.
6. *See id.*
7. *Id.*
8. *Id.*
9. *Id.* (emphasis added).
10. *Id.* at 102.
11. *Id.*

to be resolved in a manner in which they mutually agree upon, rather than following some general common law rule to govern their rights and liabilities in a particular situation.[12]

Also, where there is concurrent negligence, the parties must be especially clear in their intent to indemnify.[13] "Where the injury was caused by concurrent negligence of the indemnitor and the indemnitee, the courts have frequently read into contracts of indemnity exceptions for injuries caused in part by the indemnitee, although there is authority to the contrary."[14] "Even the fact that the contract requires the indemnitor to hold the indemnitee harmless from damage caused by the indemnitor's 'negligent acts and omissions' has been held insufficient to make the indemnity clause applicable in a case where the indemnitee's negligence concurred with that of the indemnitor to cause the injury."[15] "If the indemnitee means to throw the loss upon the indemnitor for a fault in which he himself individually shares, he must express that purpose beyond any pre-adventure of doubt."[16]

"Although the Wyoming Worker's Compensation Act bars an employee and those claiming under him from suing the employer, the Act does not bar other third-parties sued by the employee from bringing an action against the employer for indemnity based on a contract between the employer and the third-party."[17]

2. EXCEPTIONS TO GENERAL RULES OF CONTRACTUAL INDEMNITY

Indemnity contracts that are deemed against public policy are unenforceable. Wyoming Statute Annotated § 30-1-131 voids and makes unenforceable any agreement to the extent it seeks to indemnify an indemnitee for its own negligence regarding any work pertaining to wells for oil, gas, or water, or mines for minerals.[18] The statute provides:

(a) All agreements, covenants or promises contained in, collateral to or affecting any agreement pertaining to any **well for oil, gas or water,** or mine for any mineral, which purport to indemnify the indemnitee against loss or liability for damages for:
  (i) Death or bodily injury to persons;
  (ii) Injury to property; or
  (iii) Any other loss, damage, or expense arising under either (i) or (ii) from:
    (A) The sole or concurrent negligence of the indemnitee or the agents or employees of the indemnitee or any independent contractor who is directly responsible to such indemnitee; or
    (B) From any accident which occurs in operations carried on at the direction or under the supervision of the indemnitee or an employee or representative of the indemnitee or in accordance with methods and means specified by the indemnitee or employees or representatives of the indemnitee, are against public policy and are void and unenforceable to the extent that such contract of indemnity by its terms purports to relieve the indemnitee from loss or liability for his own negligence. This provision shall not affect the validity of any insurance contract or any benefit conferred by the Worker's Compensation Law [§§ 27-14-101 through 27-14-805] of this state.[19]

12. *See id.* at 101.
13. Amoco Prod. Co. v. EM Nominee P'ship Co., 2 P.3d 534, 541 (Wyo. 2000); *Wyo. Johnson, Inc.*, 662 P.2d at 99.
14. *Wyo. Johnson, Inc.*, 662 P.2d at 99 (citing 41 Am. Jur. 2d *Indemnity* § 16, 703–04 (1968)).
15. *Id.*
16. *Id.*
17. *Northwinds of Wyo.*, 779 P.2d at 754 n.3.
18. Mountain Fuel Supply Co. v. Emerson, 578 P.2d 1351, 1357 (Wyo. 1978).
19. Wyo. Stat. Ann. § 30-1-131 (2006).

This section reflects the legislative determination that such indemnification provisions are against public policy.[20]

3. INDEMNITY AGREEMENTS AS INSURED CONTRACTS

An insured's contractual agreement to indemnify another constitutes an "insured contract" within the meaning of an insurance policy covering an insured's agreement to assume the tort liability of another where this intent is clearly expressed.[21] Courts will still look to the policy to determine the scope of the coverage for an insured contract, but if the policy is ambiguous as to what types of indemnity agreements are covered by the policy, coverage likely will be afforded.[22]

4. OPERATION OF AN AGREEMENT TO INDEMNIFY REFERRING TO OR REQUIRING INSURANCE

Wyoming has analyzed issues where an indemnity agreement or typical construction contract has required the parties to look to insurance for the allocation of the risks and not to each other for purposes of indemnity.[23]

In *Berger v. Teton Shadows, Inc.*, the parties specifically provided in their contract that the owner was required to purchase the necessary insurance to cover losses from fire, tornado, or other like catastrophes that may occur and damage the project.[24] During the construction of the project, a fire occurred as a result of the subcontractor's negligence.[25] The owner sued the subcontractor, and the subcontractor filed a crossclaim against the owner.[26]

The Wyoming Supreme Court found that where a contract was unambiguous and intended for the owner to carry fire insurance, thus shifting the risk of loss to the owner's insurance carrier, it was enforceable and limited the owner's recovery to the proceeds of its insurance policy.[27] As a result, the parties in *Berger* were forced to look to the insurance company for recovery and could not hold each other responsible notwithstanding an indemnification agreement between them.

---

20. *Northwinds of Wyo., Inc.*, 779 P.2d at 757 n.5; Cities Serv. Co. v. N. Prod. Co., 705 P.2d 321, 326 (Wyo. 1985).

21. Gainsco Ins. Co. v. Amoco Prod. Co., 53 P.3d 1051 (Wyo. 2002); *see also* Progressive Cas. Ins. Co. v. Brown's Crew Car of Wyo., Inc., 27 F. Supp. 2d 1288, 1293 (D. Wyo. 1998) (inferring that an indemnification and hold harmless provision could be considered an insured contract within the terms of the policy).

22. *Gainsco Ins. Co.*, 53 P.3d at 1066 (policy excluded insured contract covering the "indemnitee's sole tort liability" as it could not be determined if "sole" meant 100% liability or "sole" vis-à-vis the insured).

23. Berger v. Teton Shadows Inc., 820 P.2d 176 (Wyo. 1991).

24. *Id.* at 177.

25. *Id.* at 176.

26. *Id.*

27. *Id.* at 177–78.

ABOUT THE AUTHORS

Editors
John B. Mumford, Jr.
Hancock, Daniel & Johnson, P.C.
Richmond, VA

John Bonnie
Weinberg, Wheeler, Hudgins, Gunn & Dial, LLC
Atlanta, GA

Alabama
Christopher Frost
Maynard, Cooper & Gale, P.C.
Birmingham, AL

Alaska
Jennifer Wasson
Potter Anderson & Corroon LLP
Wilmington, DE

Arizona
E. Tanner Warnick
Polsinelli, P.C.
Phoenix, AZ

Arkansas
Jason A. Frye
Neal, Gerber & Eisenberg, LLP
Chicago, IL

California
Terrance Evans
Duane Morris, LLP
San Francisco, CA

Colorado
E. Tanner Warnick
Polsinelli, P.C.
Phoenix, AZ

Connecticut
John Malloy
LeClair Ryan
Hartford, CT

Delaware
Jennifer Wasson
Potter Anderson & Corroon LLP
Wilmington, DE

District of Columbia
James P. Bobotek
Pillsbury Winthrop Shaw Pittman LLP
McLean, VA

Florida
Steve Rapp
Weinberg, Wheeler, Hudgins, Gunn & Dial, LLC
Atlanta, GA

Georgia
John Bonnie
Weinberg, Wheeler, Hudgins, Gunn & Dial, LLC
Atlanta, GA

Hawaii
Tred Eyerly
Damon Key Leong Kupchak Hastert
Honolulu, HI

Idaho
Kathryn Kasper
Hancock, Daniel & Johnson, P.C.
Glen Allen, VA

Illinois
Jason A. Frye
Neal, Gerber & Eisenberg, LLP
Chicago, IL

Indiana
Brent W. Huber
Ice Miller, LLC
Indianapolis, IN

Iowa
Kathryn Kasper
Hancock, Daniel & Johnson, P.C.
Glen Allen, VA

Kansas
Christina Arnone
Stinson Leonard Street LLP
Kansas City, MO

Katherine Bechina
Stinson Leonard Street LLP
Kansas City, MO

Kentucky
Jason A. Frye
Neal, Gerber & Eisenberg, LLP
Chicago, IL

Louisiana
Kristen Hayes
Baker, Donelson, Bearman, Caldwell & Berkowitz, P.C.
New Orleans, LA

Matt Woolf
Baker, Donelson, Bearman, Caldwell & Berkowitz, P.C.
New Orleans, LA

Maine
Julianna Malogolowkin
Hinckley, Allen, & Snyder LLP
Boston, MA

Kurt Mullen
Nixon Peabody, LLP
Boston, MA

Sydney Pritchett
Nixon Peabody, LLP
Los Angeles, CA

Maryland
Kathryn Kasper
Hancock, Daniel & Johnson, P.C.
Glen Allen, VA

Massachusetts
Julianna Malogolowkin
Hinckley, Allen, & Snyder LLP
Boston, MA

Kurt Mullen
Nixon Peabody, LLP
Boston, MA

Sydney Pritchett
Nixon Peabody, LLP
Los Angeles, CA

Michigan
Charles M. Denton
Barnes & Thornburg LLP
Grand Rapids, MI

Minnesota
Matthew Lawlyes
Wilson Law Group
Minneapolis, MN

Mississippi
Michael Gwin
Watkins & Eager PLLC
Jackson, MS

Missouri
Kathryn Kasper
Hancock, Daniel & Johnson, P.C.
Glen Allen, VA

Montana
Erin D. Doran
Meagher & Geer, PLLP
Minneapolis, MN

Laura Hanson
Meagher & Geer, PLLP
Minneapolis, MN

Nebraska
Anthony Alt
Meagher & Geer, PLLP
Minneapolis, MN

Nevada
Howard Russell
Weinberg, Wheeler, Hudgins, Gunn & Dial, LLC
Las Vegas, NV

New Hampshire
Julianna Malogolowkin
Hinckley, Allen & Snyder LLP
Boston, MA

Kurt Mullen
Nixon Peabody, LLP
Boston, MA

Sydney Pritchett
Nixon Peabody, LLP
Los Angeles, CA

New Jersey
Sherilyn Pastor
McCarter & English, LLP
Newark, NJ

New Mexico
Howard Russell
Weinberg, Wheeler, Hudgins, Gunn & Dial, LLC
Las Vegas, NV

New York
Nicole B. Weinstein
Beveridge & Diamond, P.C.
New York, NY

North Carolina
Kathryn Kasper
Hancock, Daniel & Johnson, P.C.
Glen Allen, VA

North Dakota
Matthew Lawlyes
Wilson Law Group
Minneapolis, MN

Ohio
Jodi Spencer Johnson
Brouse McDowell LPA
Cleveland, OH

Oklahoma
Gregory E. Van Houten
Haynes and Boone, LLP
Washington, D.C.

Oregon
Kathryn Kasper
Hancock, Daniel & Johnson, P.C.
Glen Allen, VA

Pennsylvania
Joann Lytle
McCarter & English, LLP
Philadelphia, PA

Sherilyn Pastor
McCarter & English, LLP
Newark, NJ

Rhode Island
J. Tyler Butts
Robinson & Cole LLP
Hartford, CT

South Carolina
Brannon Arnold
Weinberg, Wheeler, Hudgins, Gunn & Dial, LLC
Atlanta, GA

South Dakota
Matthew Lawlyes
Wilson Law Group
Minneapolis, MN

Tennessee
Ryan Freeman
Baker, Donelson, Bearman, Caldwell, & Berkowitz, P.C.
Chattanooga, TN

Matt Woolf
Baker, Donelson, Bearman, Caldwell & Berkowitz, P.C.
New Orleans, LA

Texas
Gregory E. Van Houten
Haynes and Boone, LLP
Washington, D.C.

Utah
Nicholas Panayotopoulos
Weinberg, Wheeler, Hudgins, Gunn & Dial, LLC
Atlanta, GA

Vermont
Julianna Malogolowkin
Hinckley, Allen & Snyder LLP
Boston, MA

Kurt Mullen
Nixon Peabody, LLP
Boston, MA

Sydney Pritchett
Nixon Peabody, LLP
Los Angeles, CA

Virginia
Kathryn Kasper
Hancock, Daniel & Johnson, P.C.
Glen Allen, VA

Washington
Bryana L. Blessinger
Bullivant Houser Bailey, P.C.
Portland, OR

West Virginia
Al Emch
Jackson Kelly, PLLC
Charleston, WV

Grace Hurney
Jackson Kelly, PLLC
Charleston, WV

Wisconsin
Laura Hanson
Meagher & Geer PLLP
Minneapolis, MN

Wyoming
Gregory E. Van Houten
Haynes and Boone, LLP
Washington, D.C.